A REBEL CAME HOME

Floride Clemson

Women's Diaries and Letters of the Nineteenth-Century South

Carol Bleser and Elizabeth Fox-Genovese
General Editors of the Series

A REBEL CAME HOME:

THE DIARY AND LETTERS OF FLORIDE CLEMSON, 1863–1866

Revised Edition

Edited by Charles M. McGee, Jr.
and Ernest M. Lander, Jr.

Illustrated by Olivia Jackson McGee

University of South Carolina Press

Published in Columbia, South Carolina
by the University of South Carolina Press

"Floride Clemson's Northern Trip, July–October 1863"
first appeared as "A Confederate Girl Visits Pennsylvania"
in *The Western Pennsylvania Historical Magazine*, copyright
Historical Society of Western Pennsylvania

Manufactured in the United States of America
Library of Congress Cataloging-in-Publication Data

Library of Congress Cataloging-in-Publication Data

Clemson, Floride, 1842–1871.
    A rebel came home : the diary and letters of Floride Clemson,
1863–1866 / edited by Charles M. McGee, Jr. and Ernest M. Lander,
Jr. ; illustrated by Olivia Jackson McGee. — Rev. ed.
        p.   cm. — (Women's diaries and letters of the nineteenth-
century South)
    Includes bibliographical references.
    ISBN 0-87249-642-2
    1. Clemson, Floride, 1842–1871.   2. United States—History—Civil
War, 1861–1865—Personal narratives, Confederate.   3. South
Carolina—History—Civil War, 1861–1865—Personal narratives.
    4. Pendleton (S.C.)—Biography.   I. McGee, Charles M.   II. Lander,
Ernest McPherson.   III. Title.   IV. Series.
E605.C6   1989
973.7'82—dc20   89-16714
                                                                         CIP

In memory of Olivia Jackson McGee

CONTENTS

SERIES EDITORS' INTRODUCTION ix

FAMILY TREE xi

PREFACE xiii

FOOTNOTE ABBREVIATIONS xvi

PROLOGUE 1

The Diary of Floride Clemson 25
   I Bladensburg, Maryland, 1863–64 27
  II Beltsville, Maryland, 1864 53
 III Pendleton, South Carolina, 1865 71
 IV Pendleton, South Carolina, 1866 98

Floride Clemson's Northern Trip,
July–October 1863 117

EPILOGUE 161

APPENDIXES 165

INDEX 175

ILLUSTRATIONS

Floride Clemson _____ *frontispiece*

facing page

Portrait of Thomas Green Clemson _____ 2

John Calhoun, Floride, and
    Anna Calhoun Clemson _____ 2

Floride Clemson at age fifteen _____ 3

Calhoun Clemson, sixteen years old _____ 3

Typical page and prescription from the diary ____ 16

Calhoun Clemson in Confederate uniform _____ 17

"Fort Hill," Clemson, South Carolina _____ 50

Letter written by Floride Clemson in Saratoga 51

"Mi Casa," Pendleton, South Carolina _____ 66

St. Paul's Episcopal Church, Pendleton _____ 67

Floride Clemson Lee as a young woman _____ 98

The Clemson family after the war _____ 99

Floride Isabella Lee as a child _____ 114

Floride Isabella Lee as a young woman _____ 115

Children of Floride Isabella Lee and
    Andrew Pickens Calhoun, II _____ 115

MAPS

Bladensburg-Beltsville area _____ 26

The Clemsons' trip South _____ 69

Pendleton area _____ 70

Series Editors' Introduction

A REBEL CAME HOME: THE DIARY OF FLORIDE CLEMSON is the second volume in an on-going series of women's diaries and letters of the nineteenth-century South. In this series being published by the University of South Carolina Press will be a number of never before published diaries, some collections of unpublished correspondence, and a few published diaries that are being reprinted—a potpourri of nineteenth-century women's writings.

The Women's Diaries and Letters of the Nineteenth-Century South Series enable women to speak for themselves providing readers with a rarely opened window into Southern society before, during, and after the American Civil War. The significance of these letters and journals lies not only in the personal revelations and the writing talents of these women authors but also in the range and versatility of their contents. Taken together these publications will tell us much about the heyday and the fall of the Cotton Kingdom, the mature years of the "peculiar institution," the war years, and the adjustment of the South to a new social order following the defeat of the Confederacy. Through their writings the reader will also be presented with first-hand accounts of everyday life and social events, courtships and marriages, family life and travels, religion and education, and the life and death matters which made up the ordinary and extraordinary world of the nineteenth-century South.

A Rebel Came Home, first published in 1961 by Charles M. McGee, Jr., and Ernest M. Lander, Jr., and with illustrations by Olivia Jackson McGee, now has an newly updated introduction written by Professor Lander. Dr. Lander has also supplemented this edition by the inclusion of letters exchanged between Floride Clemson and her mother, Anna Maria Calhoun Clemson, written in the midst of the Civil War during Floride Clemson's trip North, July–October 1863. The letters between mother and daughter reveal their close ties, as well as their deep attachment to the Confederate cause and their fear of its impending collapse. In her diary begun in December 1862, as well as in her letters home, Floride Clemson, the grandaughter of the cold war warrior, John C. Calhoun, presents in compelling detail the life of an attractive, intelligent young woman during the dark years of the Civil War and the early months of Reconstruction.

Carol Bleser
Elizabeth Fox-Genovese

JOHN CALDWELL CALHOUN
(Mar. 18, 1782-Mar. 31, 1850)

m.

issue: *

FLORIDE BONNEAU COLHOUN
(Feb. 15, 1792-July 25, 1866)

Andrew Pickens Calhoun
(Oct. 15, 1811-Mar. 16, 1865)

m.

(1) Eugenia Chappell
(died without issue Feb. 8, 1834)

(2) Margaret Green
(Feb. 18, 1816-July 27, 1891)

issue:

a. Duff Green Calhoun
b. John C. Calhoun
c. Margaret Maria Calhoun
d. Andrew Pickens Calhoun
e. James Edward Calhoun
f. Patrick Calhoun
g. Mary Lucretia Calhoun

a. Duff Green Calhoun
(Apr. 21, 1839-Aug. 25, 1873)

m.

Elizabeth Beasley
(d. Sept. 27, 1894)

issue:

Andrew Pickens Calhoun, II
(Apr. 10, 1872-Oct. 6, 1942)

m.

Floride Isabella Lee
(May 15, 1870-June 4, 1935)

issue:

Margaret M. Calhoun (July 6, 1896-Jan. 12, 1959)
Gideon Lee Calhoun (Aug. 28, 1897-Dec. 19, 1897)
Patrick Calhoun, III (Aug. 19, 1899-Feb. 25, 1946)
Creighton Lee Calhoun (Oct. 31, 1901-Jan. 17, 1940)

Patrick Calhoun
(Feb. 9, 1821-June 1, 1858)
(died unmarried)

Anna Maria Calhoun
(Feb. 13, 1817-Sept. 22, 1875)

m.

Thomas Green Clemson
(July 1, 1807-Apr. 6, 1888)

issue:

a. A daughter that lived about three weeks (b. Aug. 13, 1839)
b. John Calhoun Clemson
   (July 17, 1841-Aug. 10, 1871)
   (died unmarried)
c. Floride Elizabeth Clemson
   (Dec. 29, 1842-July 23, 1871)
d. Cornelia Clemson
   (Oct. 3, 1855-Dec. 20, 1858)

c. Floride Elizabeth Clemson

m.

Gideon Lee
(Mar. 28, 1824-Apr. 22, 1894)

John Caldwell Calhoun
(May 17, 1823-July 31, 1855)

m.

(1) Anzie Adams
(Feb. 10, 1828-Sept. 15, 1850)
(died without issue)

(2) Kate Kirby Putnam
(Jan. 1, 1831-May 4, 1866)

issue:

a. John C. Calhoun
b. Benjamin P. Calhoun

Martha Cornelia Calhoun
(Apr. 22, 1824-May 2, 1857)
(died unmarried)

James Edward Calhoun
(Apr. 4, 1826-Nov. 29, 1861)
(died unmarried)

William Lowndes Calhoun
(Aug. 13, 1829-Sept. 19, 1858)

m.

(1) Margaret Cloud
(died without issue)

(2) Kate Putnam Calhoun

issue:

a. William Lowndes Calhoun

---

* Three children died in infancy.

PREFACE

FLORIDE CLEMSON kept her diary in a ruled journal with hard covers reinforced with leather at the corners and on the spine. It consists of one hundred twenty-two manuscript pages on which neither the black ink she used nor the handwriting vary very much. The pages measure 7¾ by 10¼ inches and usually have thirty-three lines of script per page. There are no voided pages and only one flyleaf, at the beginning. On the lining paper of the front cover Floride wrote

Floride Clemson.
Diary begun
1863
"The Home"

Neither right nor left margin is observed, pages 116 and 117 are blank, page 121 is blank except for the two prescriptions pasted thereon, page 122 is only one-fourth filled, and the lining paper of the back cover is blank.

Before Clemson College obtained possession of the diary, it was the property of Floride Clemson's granddaughter, Miss Margaret Calhoun of Atlanta, Georgia, who gave it to the late A. G. Holmes, Professor of History, Clemson College, and his wife, Lila S. Holmes.

The diary covers the period from January 1, 1863, through October 24, 1866, sporadically. Fragmentary notes and extraneous material, copied in the journal after 1866, are included in this book as Appendix I. The diary contains three sustained narratives: Floride's trip to Niagara in the summer of 1863; the journey from Beltsville, Maryland, to Pendleton, South Carolina, that she and her mother made in the last days of 1864; and the final illness of Floride's grandmother, Mrs. John C. Calhoun, in July, 1866. The fluency of the whole diary perhaps stems from Floride's habit of copious letter writing and certainly belies the fact that she had only two years of formal schooling, which ended at age fifteen. Like most diaries it has tantalizing enigmas, such as the hieroglyphics on page four of the manuscript (see Plate III) and this reference to Thomas Green Clemson: "Father has been in a bad humor ever since he came from Abbeville but I really do not wish to remember why, as it is by no means to his credit." There is also unintentional humor: "Matters are pretty quiet now except casual disturbances, thefts & murders."

The diary presents few textual problems, for Floride's hand is unusually legible and the manuscript is in an excellent state of preservation. The original spelling has been reproduced and editing kept to a minimum. In a few instances, however, we have taken liberties with the original punctuation for the sake of clarity. In our footnotes we have followed the practice of identifying, in so far as possible, persons, places, and events at first reference. A complete index will enable the reader to locate references and notes pertaining to any particular person or place.

The information in the "Prologue" was taken entirely from correspondence and papers in the Clemson Collection of the Clemson College Library. Catalogues of letters to and from Floride Clemson are included as Appendixes V and VI.

The editors are grateful to those who have assisted them. We wish to thank Dr. Robert C. Edwards, president of Clemson College, for permission to publish the diary; Dr. J. K. Williams, Dean of Clemson College, for arranging financial assistance for its publication; Mr. J. W. Gordon Gourlay, director of the Clemson College Library, for his complete cooperation in this project; Mrs. Betty Bartlett Davis, Clemson College Library, for arranging interlibrary loans of books and microfilm; Mr. B. Gaillard Hunter and Miss Louise Hunter, Pendleton, S. C., for giving us information about early Pendleton history and genealogy; the Reverend Mr. Howard O. Bingley, Brewster, N. Y., for searching church registers and graveyard records in Carmel, N. Y.; Mr. Horace E. Hillery, Putnam County Historian, Patterson, N. Y., for information on the Lee family; Miss Valeria L. Chisolm, Charleston, S. C., for information about the North family; Mrs. Mary Mills Ritchie, Clemson, and Mrs. Margaret S. Palmer, Custodian of the Calhoun Mansion, for Calhoun and Clemson genealogy; Dr. George H. Callcott, Department of History, University of Maryland, for information about Maryland Agricultural College personnel and students; Mr. J. P. Burns, Clemson, for photographic work; and Mrs. Vivian H. Lewis, Clemson, for typing the manuscript. For additional biographical information we also wish to thank Mrs. Louise McCeney Malone,

Silver Spring, Md.; Mrs. Florence Dundas Roller, Staunton, Va.; Mr. G. Glenn Clift, Kentucky Historical Society, Frankfort, Ky.; Mrs. Virginia R. Onderdonk, Baltimore, Md.; Mr. Archibald Rutledge, McClellanville, S. C.; and Miss Elaine Schaap, Clemson College Library.

C. M. M., Jr. and E. M. L., Jr.

FOOTNOTE ABBREVIATIONS

Biog. Dir. Cong.—Biographical Directory of the American Congress, 1774-1949.

DAB—Dictionary of American Biography.

MS. Census 1860—Eighth Census, 1860, Free Inhabitants (MSS. in National Archives).

MS. Census 1870—Ninth Census, 1870, Population (MSS. in National Archives).

SCHGM—South Carolina Historical and Genealogical Magazine.

WROR—The War of Rebellion: A Compilation of the Official Records of the Union and Confederate Armies.

Prologue

ON THURSDAY, DECEMBER 29, 1842, "at 4¹/₂ o'clock P. M. Anna gave birth to a fine little girl." Thus Thomas Green Clemson chronicled the arrival of their third child in a little more than four years of marriage to Anna Maria Calhoun, favorite child of Senator John C. Calhoun. Clemson added: "It appears from what the ladies say, that she [Anna] had a very easy time of it."

The child was named Elizabeth Floride for her grandmothers: Elizabeth for her father's mother and Floride for Anna's mother. She was generally called Floride, or sometimes "Floy" by a few female friends, and when she was baptised some years later, she dropped Elizabeth entirely. The Clemson's first child, a girl, had lived only three weeks. Their second, a robust boy, was born July 17, 1841, and named John Calhoun for his illustrious grandfather. He was called Calhoun by family and friends.

When Floride was born John C. Calhoun was in Washington attending senatorial duties. He had long served in public office, in this order: South Carolina General Assembly, the lower house of the United States Congress, secretary of war, and vice president of the United States. In December 1832 he resigned as vice president to take a seat in the United States Senate to defend his state in the nullification crisis. Now in late 1842 he was preparing to leave the Senate to run for president in the 1844 election. He saw Floride for the first time on his return to Fort Hill from Washington in March 1843.

Although a lawyer, Calhoun spent most of time when not in Washington attending his Fort Hill plantation. It was through his marriage to his cousin Floride Bonneau Colhoun that he had come into possession of this 1400-acre estate, maintained by some 50 to 75 slaves. Fort Hill was his chief source of income, for a senator's pay of $8 per diem plus limited travel money could not sustain his large family.

Thomas Green Clemson, a Pennsylvanian with four years of study in Paris, had become a successful mining engineer before he married Anna, who was almost ten years younger, on November 13, 1838. Clemson was a man of many talents: a linguist, a musician, an artist, and a scientist. He also possessed a mercurial temperament. At the

1

time of marriage he was temporarily at loose ends; hence, he tried his hand at plantation management in Abbeville District for James Edward Colhoun, Mrs. Calhoun's brother. After one planting season he moved with his bride back to Fort Hill and managed his father-in-law's estate for a few months while the latter was in Washington. He then worked briefly on a mining venture in Cuba, and from June until mid-fall 1842 he managed Calhoun's gold mine at Dahlonega, Georgia. He, Anna, and little Calhoun, returned to Fort Hill several weeks before Floride was born.[1]

The year 1843 did not begin auspiciously for the Clemsons. Their joy over the safe arrival of another baby was chilled four days later when Anna suddenly developed a high fever and rapid pulse beat. The family was almost frantic because all Pendleton physicians were out of station. For a few hours both Clemson and Mrs. Calhoun feared for Anna's life. To add to the family's fright an earthquake rattled the house at Fort Hill during Anna's crisis. In desperation, Clemson himself began to prescribe, and Anna weathered the storm. Later in the month, before Anna had recuperated, she suffered another fright when a smoldering fire downstairs filled the house with smoke before her husband awakened, sounded the alarm, and put out the fire.

While still periodically attending his father-in-law's gold mine, Clemson decided to become a planter himself, and in the winter of 1843 he made arrangements to purchase "Cane Brake" plantation on the Little Saluda River in Edgefield District, near present-day Saluda. He needed money to pay for the 1050-acre estate and hands to work it. For both he called on his brother-in-law Andrew, John C.'s oldest son. Shortly after his marriage Clemson had advanced $18,000 of hard-to-come-by money for Andrew to purchase Alabama cotton lands. John C. had also invested a small sum in the venture.

---

[1]For details of the Clemsons' and Calhouns' personal lives, see Ernest M. Lander, Jr., *The Calhoun Family and Thomas Green Clemson: The Decline of a Southern Patriarchy* (Columbia: University of South Carolina Press, 1983). For Thomas G. Clemson's public and scientific career, see Alester G. Holmes and George R. Sherrill, *Thomas Green Clemson: His Life and His Work* (Richmond: Garrett and Massie, 1937). For Clemson's service as chargé d'affaires in Brussels, see John W. Rooney, Jr., *Belgian-American Diplomatic and Consular Relations, 1830–1850* ...(Louvain: Publications Universitaires de Louvain, 1969).

Portrait of
Thomas Green Clemson
as a young man

John Calhoun Clemson
and Floride Clemson
with their mother,
Anna Calhoun Clemson

I

Floride Clemson
at age fifteen

Calhoun Clemson, sixteen years old

The Alabama deal seems to have been a loose, verbal arrangement, and Andrew had paid no interest on Clemson's loan in four years. Relations between the two, already strained, reached the breaking point when Clemson was unable to get either money or hands for his Cane Brake plantation. He regarded Andrew as "odious," and the two became permanently estranged. Only with great difficulty was Calhoun able to maintain a modicum of civility between Andrew and Clemson.

For financial reasons and the lack of field hands the Clemsons' move to Cane Brake was postponed until January 1844. Thus baby Floride spent her first year at Fort Hill, where her grandfather was engrossed in writing, planting, and politicking. The entire family seemed excited by his prospects for the Democratic presidential nomination. But by late fall Calhoun, recognizing that his star had dimmed, withdrew his name from consideration at the Baltimore convention.

Upon leaving Fort Hill for Cane Brake, the Clemsons were accompanied by two Calhoun slaves to help them settle in. Anna described their new home as a dilapidated barn—it was a rundown, windy old building. But the children remained in remarkably good health, considering their exposure in a sparsely populated cotton country where no milk cows and few supplies were for sale. In his efforts to erect a new house Clemson found building materials also difficult to procure. (The house was eventually completed by his slave carpenter after many delays.)

The Clemsons had been at Cane Brake only a few weeks when an explosion aboard the warship *Princeton* on February 28, 1844, killed Secretary of State Abel Upshur, among others, and John C. Calhoun was drawn back into the political maelstorm as his successor.[2]

One of Calhoun's first acts was to persuade President Tyler to appoint Clemson chargé d'affaires to Belgium. Clemson was anxious for a foreign assignment, and the post at Brussels was the best available at the moment. There was an annual stipend of $4,500 and an "outfit" of like amount. Clemson's appointment was placed before the Senate on June 17 and confirmed the same day, to be effective August 1.

[2]Lieutenant Patrick Calhoun was aboard the *Princeton* when the explosion occurred. He narrowly escaped injury or death himself, and he wrote his father that evening details of the tragedy.

Going to Brussels presented some problems, but they were not unsolvable. Cane Brake was left under the care of Robert Humphreys, as overseer, while John Mobley, an elderly neighbor, and Colonel Francis Pickens, a Calhoun kinsman who lives in Edgefield, agreed to look in on Humphreys and advise him. For the journey to Brussels the Clemsons took along Negro slave Basil and hired a nurse to look after the children. The party had brief sojourns in Washington, Philadelphia, and New York attending business and saying goodbyes before boarding ship on August 8. They arrived in Brussels, by way of Paris, on October 4, 1844.

In Brussels Clemson took a furnished house for $70 a month, hired two servants, rented a coach, and outfitted himself with an official court uniform which Anna found quite laughable. Clemson felt a little embarrassed by it. On the other hand, he was complimented everywhere on his command of the French language, which he considered a *sine qua non* for diplomatic service.

Clemson's chief complaint with his position was the low pay of a chargé d'affaires. On several occasions he pressed his father-in-law to get the post upgraded to that of minister, but Calhoun advised that it could not be done. Besides, if the post was upgraded Clemson might lose it. As a matter of fact, after Calhoun's break with President Polk over the conduct of the Mexican War, he had no influence with the administration.[3]

Meanwhile, Anna studied French so that she could aid her husband in official duties and teach the language to her children. She also acted as her husband's secretary. Anna considered royal etiquette ridiculous nonsense. Belgian society, she observed, though better educated than American, was more stupid and twice as ugly.

After John C. Calhoun left the State Department in March 1845—he returned to the Senate in December—Clemson remained in Belgium under the sponsorship of James Buchanan, Calhoun's successor. His services in Brussels must have been satisfactory for the Polk administration kept him on. His chief success was concluding a treaty of navigation and commerce with the Belgians which the Senate approved in March 1846.

[3]For Calhoun's opposition to Polk's war policy, see Ernest M. Lander, Jr., *Reluctant Imperialists: Calhoun, the South Carolinians, and the Mexican War* (Baton Rouge: Louisiana State University Press, 1980).

4

By the summer of 1848 the Clemsons were anxious to return to America on a visit, Thomas to see about disposing of Cane Brake plantation and Anna to be near her father whose health was obviously deteriorating. Granted official leave, Clemson, his family, and Belgian nurse Mimi sailed from Antwerp on October 4. After a stormy passage they arrived safely in New York on November 5, journeyed to Philadelphia for a brief visit with Clemson relatives, and then set out for Cane Brake.

Toward the end of November the Clemson ménage was comfortably installed in their new home, with Mrs. Calhoun and other relatives soon in attendance. Senator Calhoun stopped by briefly en route to Washington, and at Christmas the house was full. Little Calhoun and Floride enjoyed the rural existence after being cooped up in a Brussels house with no garden. At Cane Brake young Calhoun learned to ride horseback.

Meanwhile, in March 1849, President Zachary Taylor's Whig administration took charge in Washington. Clemson, nevertheless, retained his post as chargé and prepared to return to Belgium. Anna was reluctant to leave her father, whom she had always loved dearly. His declining health greatly worried her, and she feared she would never see him again.

After some delay in leaving America, the Clemson party embarked from New York and arrived in Brussels on July 9. This time the Clemsons retrenched by renting a smaller, unfurnished house and dispensing with the carriage.

The autumn of 1849 was a happy time for the family. The children were healthy and growing. Floride was almost as tall as her brother. Both were taking lessons in dancing and gymnastics in addition to regular schooling their parents conducted at home. Both were losing baby teeth, which Anna regarded as disfiguring. About Floride she wrote her father in these unqualified terms: "For Floride, she is one of the smartest & most practical little bodies you ever saw. No danger of her. She will always be able to take care of herself I assure you."

Anna classified the Americans she met abroad as either contemptible renegades who completely disavowed their homeland or brash protagonists who derided the stagnation of Europe. She confided to her father that she was unable to understand European politics, though she was wise enough to keep her opinions to herself. For his

5

part, her husband continued to grumble about his low rank and about the general incompetence of certain other American diplomats he met. He called one "a national disgrace" and another "about as unfit for the place as a bear."

As the winter of 1850 set in, the gloom was heightened by Clemson's inability to dispose of Cane Brake plantation. It was a constant worry and had not yielded him $1,000 profit in four years. It was difficult to keep an overseer on the place—four in the first three years. Moreover, Francis Pickens and his father-in-law had not the time to look after it properly. Frustrated because a prospective sale fell through, Clemson, in a lengthy letter to Calhoun, lashed out: "If there ever was a person that should be sick of a country I am the person that should be sick of the south, and if it pleases the Almighty to grant me a safe deliverance I promise never again to place my foot on its soil."

For her part, Anna was increasingly disturbed over news from home regarding her father's health. She wrote him tender entreaties to leave Washington and take care of himself, but he would neither act on her advice nor that of others. He preferred to remain at his post as long as possible. Tuberculosis, complicated with bronchitis, took his life on March 31, 1850. His son John, who was at his bedside, later said that his father realized for about a week that death was imminent, but he was a philosopher and "had no fear of the king of terrors."

With her father's death Anna knew that henceforth her husband's preferment would depend entirely on merit. President Taylor's death in July brought another change in the Washington administration, and Clemson was recalled the following December. Fortunately for him, Colonel Pickens sold Cane Brake plantation, stock, and slaves just before his recall. The sale brought more than $38,000, or about $3,000 above Clemson's minimum asking price.

The Clemson family, with nurse Mimi, left Brussels on April 9 and arrived in Philadelphia on May 5. After a brief visit with their Clemson kin they set out for Fort Hill, where they whiled away the summer. For the next two years they lived at various places in the North, and Clemson spent most of his time working on the publication of the Calhoun speeches, which with Richard K. Crallé as editor and D. Appleton as publisher were successfully concluded in January 1853.

Clemson decided to take up permanent residence in Maryland, and on June 8, 1853, he purchased 100³/₄ acres about a mile from Bladensburg, Prince Georges County, for $6,725. The Clemsons called their new place "The Home." Clemson hoped his residence near Washington would enable him to obtain government employment suited to his talents and proper schooling for Floride and Calhoun.

In the meantime, Clemson became a gentleman farmer and supplemented his income by importing Belgian furniture, guns, and articles of *virtu* for friends and relatives. It was during the Bladensburg years that Clemson performed his most significant work in scientific study and publication. He attended scientific meetings, addressed the Smithsonian Institution, wrote articles for leading scientific and agricultural journals, and carried on agricultural experiments on his farm. His studies attracted attention and comment from other scholars. His biographers note that Clemson was one of about half a dozen reputable agricultural chemists at that time. In the late 1850s he also played an active role in the organization of Maryland Agricultural College, now the University of Maryland. All the while, the Clemsons entertained frequently and developed ties of friendship with several diplomats in Washington and prominent families in the Bladensburg area.

Back in South Carolina Floride's Grandmother Calhoun remained at Fort Hill until 1854, when she decided to sell the estate to her son Andrew because it was difficult for her to manage with no white males except the overseer. She arranged with Andrew for quarters at Fort Hill for herself and her crippled daughter Cornelia. But within a few months Mrs. Calhoun and Andrew quarreled—both were hot-tempered—and she and Cornelia moved to nearby Pendleton. Mrs. Calhoun took all her possessions with her, including slaves reserved for herself in the settlement of Fort Hill with Andrew. Slave Nelly and her child, "Little Andy," she willed to Floride, and Andy was later taken to Bladensburg after his mother died in childbirth. The grandmother often inquired about the Clemson children and seemed glad to hear of the arrival of Leopold Reis, a Belgian who tutored Floride and Calhoun and helped their father on the farm after school hours.

In April 1855, when Floride was twelve, she paid her first visit away from her parents. Her father took her to Philadelphia for a

7

three- or four-week stay with his sister, Mrs. Elizabeth Barton, whose daughter Kate was several years older than Floride. Before Floride left The Home her mother gave her some money and much advice on behavior. In Philadelphia Floride visited about with the Bartons and her numerous cousins North, children of Clemson's sister Catharine North. She enjoyed herself so immensely that she wished to prolong her visit.

During Floride's absence Anna, however, became alarmed to learn that her daughter was not eating properly, was looking "delicate," and suffering from sick headaches. The mother exhorted the daughter to avoid extremes in her diet, to restrain her spirits, and to take Lady Webster's pills for headaches. She added: "Papa says you had better bring a $1 worth when you come . . . they are his standby." Floride was also told to stop by Uncle John Baker Clemson's on her way home, if only for a few days and if the household wanted her. Uncle Baker, an Episcopal clergyman at Claymont, Delaware, had a large family and ran a school to supplement the stipend from his benefice.

Back at The Home life went on in a more serious vein. Mimi, who had been with the family since early days in Brussels, had to be discharged for quarreling with the other servants. Calhoun was sick, and his father had a case of the blues, not uncommon for him. Moreover, Anna must have told her husband about this time that she was pregnant.

In late April sad news arrived from Pendleton of the death of Margaret, wife of John C. Calhoun's youngest son William Lowndes ("Willy"). Anna had hardly recovered from this bereavement when another tragedy occurred. Her brother Dr. John C. Calhoun died from tuberculosis on July 31 at age thirty-two. His was the first death among the seven Calhoun children who reached maturity. However, within the next seven years four more died.

Soon after John's death Mrs. Calhoun and Cornelia journeyed north to be with Anna during her confinement. Cornelia ("Nina") Clemson was born on October 3, 1855. Mrs. Calhoun did not tarry long thereafter, for she dreaded winters "at the North." Calhoun and schoolmaster Reis accompanied her and Cornelia back to South Carolina, where they spent most of the winter of 1856 at Millwood, James Edward Calhoun's plantation on the Savannah River, and at

Willy's home nearby. Calhoun found winter life in rural Abbeville District boring and became "ankseous" to return to Bladensburg. Meanwhile, Floride was developing into a prolific correspondent. Her Aunt Cornelia remarked on the fact that her first letter from Floride arrived on December 29, 1855, the girl's thirteenth birthday. In reply the aunt prophesied: "I suppose [you] begin to feel quite like a woman, now that you have entered your teens, & it wont be very long before you are one."

During the summer of 1856 the Clemsons decided to send Floride to boarding school. For that purpose they chose Elizabeth Barton's school, just opened on Chestnut Street in Philadelphia. The school term began in September and ran until late June 1857. The time away from home did much to give Floride maturity, but more important, it increased the bond of love and understanding between mother and daughter.

Anna and Floride agreed to exchange letters at least once a week, and Anna kept faithfully to the bargain, writing of family, friends, and the farm. She apprised Floride of little Nina's antics and intelligence, the behavior of stupid Augusta and diligent Babette, servants acquired since Mimi left. Clemson was busy building a new house on the place, which he first offered to Mrs. Barton and his mother and later to Mrs. Calhoun. All refused it.

In her letters to Floride Anna's main concern seemed to be her daughter's health and behavior. She was frank and specific with her advice: "Persevere steadily," "behave like a lady, on every occasion," "don't be a mere giggling school girl," "never give in; even for a moment, to little school girls deceptions," "do not expose yourself to the night air, or get your feet wet," "your father again urges on you attention to your bowels—you know how important I also consider it," and so on. At times these letters were those of an entreating, admonishing mother, but more often the tenor was on of woman-to-woman equality.

Anna also reported on Calhoun's health. It was particularly troublesome that summer. He seemed to be suffering from some sort of spinal ailment. As a consequence, his father took him to Northhampton, Massachusetts, where he underwent the "water cure" ("water torture," Calhoun called it) at the establishment of Dr. Charles Mundé, whom Clemson had known in Belgium. Clemson remained several days to take the treatment also and to observe the technique.

When Calhoun returned from Northhampton in October his father required him to continue the therapy for several hours each morning. Anna, who felt her son's malady was only a nervous "affection," was much annoyed at the daily mess in two rooms. It was enough "to run one crazy," she wrote, especially since she had Nina to care for and only "the same stupid lazy German woman" Augusta to clean house. Within a few days, when Calhoun contracted a cold, she persuaded her husband to discontinue the treatment until springtime.

Anna was quite anxious for Floride to develop a good relationship with her brother. As youngsters they had engaged in their share of quarreling. Now, Anna admonished Floride to write to Calhoun, to be kind and affectionate, and never to ridicule his poor spelling. Any criticism or correction should be done privately. She harped on this theme more than once. "He feels his deficiencies, much more than you think, and it mortifies him," she wrote. All the while Anna likewise urged Floride to write her father. She assured the girl that her father loved her and that his love was more evident now that she was no longer at home to irritate him.

The worst news for Floride that fall was that she could not come for Christmas because there was no one to come to escort her. As a consolation her father sent her $5 in addition to the usual gifts. The money was indeed a concession from tight-fisted Clemson, who because of the extra expense had earlier vetoed Floride's taking calisthenics and purchasing a coat. Unable to come home, Floride, on her own initiative, arranged to spend the holidays at her Uncle Baker Clemson's, where the atmosphere was less austere and dominical. She reported to her mother of her happy good time at Claymont.

At age fourteen Floride, somewhat too slim for her mother's taste in the female figure, was making progress in her education. She was reading *Harper's Weekly*, exchanging letters in German with Babette, the Clemson's servant, sending home some of her drawings to the gratitude of her artist father and adoring mother, and becoming more prudent in expenditures.

Her progress, however, was not without exception, and her mother readily scolded her "a little" for her peccadilloes and solecisms reported by Aunt Barton. Anna deprecated her sitting and standing crooked, picking her face, biting her nails, and refusing to speak French. She told her daughter of the pain she was causing and concluded with the platitude "there is no higher pleasure than the feeling of having conquered ourselves."

In March 1857 James Buchanan was inaugurated president, and a month later Clemson thought he might return to government service, for he learned that King Leopold had requested his return to Brussels. In addition, it seems that Secretary of State Lewis Cass had given approval. Anna called the mission "a god send" but counseled Floride to remain silent for there was "many a slip twixt the cup and the lip." Clemson, although a native of the President's state, had long since departed from Pennsylvania and had no influence among the politicians there, and since his father-in-law's death he had none in South Carolina. By mid-May a "slip" was apparent. Yielding to pressure to send someone else, Buchanan left Clemson in a miserable frame of mind.

Anna, unhappy over the unfortunate turn of events, was no more pleased that spring about the hasty and "indecent" behavior of her brother Willy in marrying Kate Putnam Calhoun, the widow of his brother John. Since John's death Kate and her two children had spent considerable time in Pendleton with Mrs. Calhoun. It was there that Willy began to court her. Both, having recently lost their spouses, seemed naturally inclined to each other. But as both were in wretched health, it is difficult to understand how they could agree on marriage at that time.

Why Anna disliked Kate is not clear. She had come from a prominent Florida family; her father was a well-known judge. But Anna apparently suspected her character and would have little to do with her. Mrs. Calhoun defended Kate and berated Anna for coolness to Kate. She considered one of Anna's letters about Kate so offensive that she immediately burned it.

That same spring Floride spent part of her Easter vacation in Lancaster, Pennsylvania, and the remainder with her Aunt North in Philadelphia. She had returned to school when her Grandmother Clemson died on April 17 at age eighty-three. A few days later she learned of her Aunt Cornelia's sudden death on May 2 at Willy's home in Abbeville District, where Cornelia and Mrs. Calhoun had spend most of the winter. In direct contrast to this somber news,

11

Anna wrote Floride of her father's pulling six of Babette's teeth at one time. Clemson's talents were varied; earlier that year he sewed up the wound on Calhoun's badly cut knee.

Floride completed her first year at Aunt Barton's school in late June, and Babette stopped off for her on her way home from a visit to Newark. She brought back a number of items her mother had requested, including some hoops, though Anna thought them disfiguring and bestowing equality on good and bad figures alike. Floride thus spent the summer at The Home.

Mrs. Barton came to Bladensburg in early September to accompany Floride back to Philadelphia for a second year at her school. Anna decided to permit her to return even though she had misgivings about her health and even though Clemson said he could not afford the expense. Anna planned, if necessary, to borrow the tuition money from her bachelor brother Patrick, an army captain then on leave in Washington. On the day that Floride departed there was a "thunderstorm" at The Home, apparently over money. A few days later Anna wrote Floride: "Since you left, we have had uninterrupted *quiet*, which is a great gain. . . . I keep as much as possible to myself."

Clemson was so tight-fisted that Anna secretly sent Floride pocket money with the admonition not to let her father know. "Say when you receive a letter with money, 'Your letter came safe,' " she instructed her daughter. Anna also suggested that Mrs. Barton render accounts quarterly so that the school expenses would not seem large to Floride's father. Unusual family expenses always excited and irritated Clemson, who was convinced he would be sold out and die in a poorhouse, though he had a cash balance on deposit with C. M. Leupp and Company of New York of more than $19,000 on February 1, 1858. He also had investments with Henry Gourdin in Charleston.

Meanwhile, Floride's second year at Aunt Barton's school was one of progress for her and consequent pride for her mother. She showed improvement in spelling and composition, singing, piano playing, and sewing. At first her conduct was exemplary, but in early December she broke over. Her aunt commented on her stubbornness and shouting while the teacher was out of the room. When scolded, Floride told her aunt; "I don't care, there must always be a black sheep in every school, & I will be that here." On another occasion she brought censure from her parents by withdrawing twenty dollars

12

from her aunt instead of the customary five dollars. Clemson was so irate that he refused to repay the money but Anna did.

During the winter of 1858 Anna was disturbed when she discovered that Floride was having health problems. She reproved her daughter when she became ill at a party in late February for being "dressed too tight." She urged her to wear her clothes loosely henceforth. But worse still was the report from Floride's uncles, William and Baker Clemson, that she had had pneumonia and that her lungs were inflamed. All the while, Floride had reported herself well. Hurt by this deception, Anna wrote: "I am losing your confidence and the greatest charm of your character, beautiful truthfulness."

In spite of her mother's animadversions Floride loved her very much and wrote just before she returned from school that she would not exchange Anna for any other mother in the world. Anna replied that her vanity was gratified, but she, as a mother, had not gone far wrong in doing her duty.

During the school year Floride received news of the Calhouns in South Carolina, either relayed through Anna or directly from her grandmother in Pendleton. She learned that Mrs. Calhoun had bought a home that she named "Mi Casa" and in November had left Pendleton with Kate Calhoun, her daughter-in-law, for St. Augustine, Florida. During the rail trip to Charleston some mishap occurred (Mrs. Calhoun did not explain) and Kate went into labor a few hours after arriving at the Charleston Hotel. Mrs. Calhoun was proud of herself when summoned hastily to act the part of midwife in the premature birth of William Lowndes Calhoun, Jr. After a delay of several weeks the party took the steamer in Charleston for Florida and arrived at Judge Benjamin Putnam's St. Augustine residence in early January 1858.

Although charmed with St. Augustine's winter climate and abundance of citrus, Mrs. Calhoun became anxious to return to South Carolina with the arrival of spring. Her son Patrick had joined the party in Florida with the intention of escorting his mother home, but he became bedridden with the ravages of tuberculosis. Thus, instead of aiding his mother, Patrick himself needed aid to return to Charleston to consult an eminent specialist, Dr. Eli Geddings. After an examination Dr. Geddings warned the family of Patrick's impending death. However, he believed the patient might live somewhat longer if removed from Charleston's sultry weather. Mrs. Calhoun came on from St. Augustine, and she, Willy, and servants took Patrick by rail to Pendleton, where he died on June 1, 1858, three days after arriving at Mi Casa.[4]

When Floride heard of her uncle's death she was already preparing her homecoming from Aunt Barton's school. Anna instructed her to bring all her things because she could not bear parting with her another year. And again she begged Floride to do her best to maintain peace with her father and brother.

While joyously greeting her daughter, Anna was distressed at her physical appearance. Years later, after Floride's death, she bitterly complained that she had been overpersuaded to let Floride spend a second year at Mrs. Bartons and upon her return home was "so shocked" that she cried. For Floride's distressing condition she blamed Mrs. Barton's failure to provide proper medical attention for Floride during a prolonged illness. Finally, Anna averred that she and her husband never doubted that their daughter owed her "confirmed ill health and early death to the shock her system received during two years spent at Mrs. Bartons."

Some of this severe criticism was an afterthought. At the moment Floride was well enough to be about. To further her education her mother planned a judicious course of reading at home and voice and piano lessons in Washington. Her relations with her father improved to such an extent that in late July he took her on an extended trip to New York to visit the C. M. Leupp family and on to Newport.

Back in South Carolina Mrs. Calhoun reported that Willy was not well. On September 19 he died after a year of poor health. His widow Kate collapsed at the funeral, but his mother bore up well, though she said: "It was too much almost, for me to see so soon, two sons placed side by side in the silent grave."

Suffering from loneliness at Mi Casa, Mrs. Calhoun importuned Anna and Floride to visit Pendleton, and in late fall they began planning a trip south. Before their plans were completed tragedy struck at The Home. Nina, their little darling, died on December 20, after a

[4]For details of Patrick's death, see Ernest M. Lander, Jr., "Mrs. John C. Calhoun and the Death of Patrick," *South Carolina Review*. IX (November 1976), 52–59.

few days illness, apparently from scarlet fever. The parents were dev-
astated, the moody father more so than Anna. Nina had been his favorite. He had played with her and heaped much affection on her.
She had returned his love and sometimes cried when he was absent.

Mrs. Calhoun sent letters of consolation to the heartbroken parents
and in time feared for Clemson's sanity. In her worry about his men-
tal health she agreed to journey to Bladensburg in late April 1859
with Pendleton friends on their way north. Still, she did not relish the
thought of a five-day trip by rail, inconvenienced by predawn board-
ings and a Sunday layover in Raleigh because there was no Sabbath
passenger service in North Carolina. She spent a month at The
Home—an unconscionably short stay for those times—and returned
to South Carolina by boat.

How well Floride bore up under these tragedies is not known, only
that she had a lingering cough during the winter. She seemed well
enough while Mrs. Calhoun was visiting. About August 1 Floride and
her Cousin Mattie Clemson, Uncle Baker's daughter, left to visit their
Aunt Louisa Washington in Harewood, [West] Virginia.[5] They had a
pleasant stay, as evidenced by their amusing letters, but toward the
end of the visit Floride had a return of a boil on the end of her spine
which had bothered her some weeks earlier. When her mother heard
of it she urged her daughter to put aside all modesty and see a physician. Fortunately for the girl, the boil broke and she and her cousin
were able to return to Bladensburg on schedule at the end of the
month.

Before Floride returned from Harewood her father agreed without
demur for her to visit her Grandmother Calhoun. While she was getting her things ready to leave with Pendleton friends, the Clemson
family was shocked by the suicide of Charles Leupp on October 5,
1859. Leupp had become engaged in an unprofitable partnership
with the unscrupulous Jay Gould and believed financial ruin awaited
him.[6]

Leupp's death threw Clemson into a state of despondency because

---

[5]By this time Clemson's three sisters, Elizabeth, Catharine, and Louisa were
widows.

[6]The account of Leupp's suicide appeared in the *New York Times*, October 7,
1859.

of his personal relationship and also because his investments were soon entangled with the settlement of the dead man's estate. A few days later Clemson wrote Uncle Elias Baker, his mother's younger brother, that he thought it would be "most fortunate . . . if the Grave would close over me and relieve me from a life that is becoming a heavy burthen to carry." Uncle Elias was astonished. He counseled: "You must not *always* look on the 'Black Side' of things."

Floride, properly escorted by the Van Wycks, Pendleton friends, arrived at Mi Casa on or about November 2. Uncle Andrew Calhoun and his family called immediately, all smiles and sweetness, although Andrew and his mother had feuded ever since she moved away from Fort Hill. Andrew and his wife Margaret were impressed with Floride's height and coloring, and they persuaded Mrs. Calhoun to permit her to accompany them "on the cars" to the Columbia Fair the next morning at 3 A.M. Since Clemson read Floride's letters to her mother, Anna asked her henceforth never to mention Uncle Andrew because Clemson despised him. (Clemson apparently never recovered his $18,000 loan to Andrew in 1839.)

Floride's first visit alone to her grandmother was indeed a success for herself and Mrs. Calhoun. The grandmother was delighted to show off her pretty, talented granddaughter. Floride became the object of much attention. She visited with her grandmother, rode horseback regularly with Augustus ("Gussy") Van Wyck, and attended a Christmas dance. She reported that she danced three times with young William Van Wyck, home for the holidays from Chapel Hill. But when she also told her mother that she had declined a dance with another young gentleman, Anna admonished her, warning that such behavior often fomented duels among young gentlemen, that once a young lady had refused a young gentleman, she danced no more that evening. Moreover, three dances with the same partner would cause gossip.

During Floride's six months in Pendleton, her health was unusually good. Her grandmother guarded her against imprudences and was always ready with the physic bottle whenever she thought Floride needed it. Her color was so high that on one occasion Mrs. Calhoun feared she might be developing erysipelas. Floride completely captivated her grandmother. She practiced the piano several hours each

This page (above) is typical of Floride Clemson's diary. The prescription (right) is one of several items pasted in the journal.

Calhoun Clemson served as a lieutenant in the Confederate Army.

day, sang for her grandmother, and kept her room tidy. Nor did she neglect her correspondence.

While Floride was enjoying herself in Pendleton, her brother Calhoun remained at The Home because of poor health. He had been in and out of school for the past three years. On one occasion he narrowly escaped wounding or death when his friend William ("Billy") Dundas accidentally discharged a gun as the two young men horsed around in Calhoun's room. His father let out a burst of profanity; Billy dropped the gun, fled, and remained away from The Home for weeks.

Events took a happy turn, however, and Calhoun left with G. H. Dunscomb, an English friend, on November 19 for Enterprise, Florida, on the St. John's River "far south" of Jacksonville, for four months of hunting, fishing, and camping out. While away he kept in touch with his family, and in one letter to Floride he reported: "I was stung by a scorpion last week he got up my draws a stung me twise before I could get him out; it was dread full." Also his finger was "very soar I cut it and it has not healed up." Conscious of his poor spelling, Calhoun admonished Floride never to show his letters "or I will never write you again."

The Christmas season arrived with Anna and her husband alone at The Home, except for Babette and other servants. Two days before Christmas they entertained Baron Blondell of the diplomatic corps and the Jacob Thompsons at a lavish dinner. Thompson was secretary of the interior. Anna, who cared little for such entertainment ("too much trouble and dont pay"), sent Floride details of the occasion. Thus the year ended peacefully for the Clemsons. All was tranquil at The Home.

In the meantime, events were occurring that would soon greatly alter the lives of the Clemson family. They were already peripherally touched by John Brown's raid on Harper's Ferry, near Louisa Washington's Harewood estate. Uncle William Clemson, writing to Floride in mid-November, said: "I suppose you were both surprised and shocked to hear of the death of your old beau Mr George Turner—in the insurrection at Harper's Ferry. He shouldered his gun and went down to help. He was killed while sitting on a porch.... [Cousin] Dick Washington killed the man who shot him....Poor

17

men! I pity them for their delusion—but they will get their just reward in being hung."[7]

In the first week of January 1860 Thomas Green Clemson was informed by Jacob Thompson that the Buchanan administration planned to enlarge the Agricultural Bureau of the Patent Office and make it a separate division within the Patent Office. As Thompson desired a scientific person to be in charge, he offered Clemson the position of Superintendent of Agricultural Affairs. Clemson readily accepted. In passing the news on to Floride, Anna commented: "The occupation will be a great thing for him." The salary would put them more at ease, she said. The new position, officially starting on February 3, proved to be an exhilarating challenge to Clemson. He soon got along "famously," Anna reported.

During Floride's absence Anna became pregnant. At age forty-three she encountered difficulty, and on March 8 she wrote her daughter of a miscarriage. She had felt bad for some time, she said, and supposed the miscarriage was destined to occur. As for her husband, she wrote: "Your father is as kind as he knows how. He was terribly frightened and stranger still very much *disappointed*." Anna gave no indication of her own feelings about the loss.

With the coming of spring Calhoun left Dunscomb in Florida and made his way to Pendleton, where he, Floride, Mrs. Calhoun, and slave boy Andy departed for Maryland on April 24. Mrs. Calhoun visited for six months and Andy, who belonged to Floride, remained at Bladensburg.

During the spring and summer 1860 The Home bustled with visitors, including Aunt Barton, her daughter Kate, and Laura Leupp, the witty and attractive daughter of the late Charles Leupp. Laura had become a close friend of Floride, and the two girls visited back and forth. In the midst of all this activity Clemson spruced up his farm and left in July for Europe on a mission for the Agricultural Bureau.

Before departing, Clemson had his tranquility sorely taxed by two quarrels with family and an in-law. The first involved his sister Louisa Washington's son George L. It was the result of tangled finan-

---

[7]Turner was probably one of the locals who squired Floride around while she visited Aunt Louisa. There is no mention of him in other family letters.

cial relations going back to Clemson's early days in Paris, when, by his account, his brother John Baker Clemson drew some $1,800 from his trust for Louisa's benefit. In later years Clemson furnished Louisa additional money and at auction bought some of her dead husband's property. This included a valuable medal that had once belonged to President George Washington. Clemson had left the medal in Louisa's hands. Just how the dispute arose is not clear, but at Louisa's impassioned request Clemson dropped the matter. Nevertheless, he continued to harbor a grudge against her son.[8]

At the same time a serious dispute came to a head with his brother-in-law James Calhoun, a lawyer and entrepreneur in California. In 1855–1856 Clemson had entrusted over $11,000 of his funds to James to invest in highly valued San Francisco real estate at $1^{1/2}$ to 2 percent per month. With passing time Clemson received no interest, and James became increasingly evasive of his queries, in fact, almost ceased to correspond. In early 1860 Clemson demanded a strict accounting from James. It was not forthcoming, hence by early June Clemson was convinced that James had defrauded him by wasting his money on a Sonora surveying venture that had failed.[9]

While her father was in Europe, Floride was busy with social functions in Washington, some at the White House. Somewhere along the way Floride formed a lasting friendship with Harriet Lane, attractive niece of President Buchanan and official White House hostess for her bachelor uncle. In August, while the *Great Eastern*, the world's largest steamship, was on her maiden voyage to America, she paid a call at Annapolis. On August 9 President Buchanan, Miss Lane, and "a distinguished party" went aboard for a tour and a luncheon. Floride was among the guests.[10]

Shortly thereafter, the Prince of Wales (later Edward VII) began his American tour. His party arrived in Washington on October 3.

---

[8]After the Civil War, John Baker Clemson sold the Washington medal to the city of Boston for $5,000 and pocketed the money. By threatening a lawsuit, Louisa's daughters forced their uncle to share the proceeds. Thomas G. Clemson received nothing. The medal is now in the Boston Public Library.

[9]Clemson's suspicions were correct, for James died a pauper of tuberculosis in November 1861.

[10]For the *Great Eastern*'s trip, see the *New York Times*, July 31, August 11, 1860.

The next day the President held a public reception at noon and a small state dinner in early evening in the Prince's honor. The dinner was followed by another reception and a fireworks display to which Miss Lane's friends were also invited.[11] Floride was present "beautifully dressed and looking very handsome," Miss Lane reported. Five days later Floride, accompanied by Billy Dundas, back in the Clemsons' good graces, left for New York to visit the Leupps.

On October 31, 1860, Clemson arrived home from Europe in "a wonderfully good humor" and bearing gifts for his family. His doctor had advised him to remain tranquil, he told his wife. When she passed the good news on to Floride she jubilantly added: "All glory and honour to *that* doctor say I. If he effects a cure, I think we should erect a monument to him." At the same time she strongly urged Floride upon her return from New York to do her "utmost" to avoid worrying her father. Meanwhile, as soon as Mrs. Calhoun had paid her respects to Clemson, she hurried back to South Carolina, escorted by her grandson.

Political storm clouds appeared on the horizon in November with the election of Abraham Lincoln as president. With South Carolina preparing to secede from the Union both Clemson and Anna became greatly worried about the "very dark" future. Clemson immediately got in touch with his investment brokers, D. W. Lee of C. M. Leupp and Company and Henry Gourdin in Charleston. Lee offered Clemson $5,000 on his account with fifteen days notice, while Gourdin sent him a statement of his account (more than $19,000), which consisted mainly of railroad and bank stocks. He offered to forward Clemson his small cash balance, if so requested.

With the secession of seven states, led by South Carolina, and the establishment of the Confederate States of America, tension between the two sections rapidly increased, although Mrs. Calhoun at first did not believe war was likely, for as she said: "The South has already been dreaded by the North, when she is in earnest, which they now see she is." Within a few days her optimism began to fade.[12]

---

[11]For the Prince's visit, see the *New York Times*, October 4–6, 1860.

[12]See also Ernest M. Lander, Jr., "Mrs. John C. Calhoun and the Coming of the Civil War," *Civil War History*, XXII (December 1976), 308–317.

With political excitement running high the Clemsons had no special Christmas celebration at The Home that year. Calhoun was in Pendleton and Floride was spending the week with neighborhood friends. The only news of note at The Home was Irish maid Rosanna's slovenly ways and Andy's misbehavior. The slave boy was pleased with his Christmas gifts but "could not pass the day without a whipping for stealing."

Thomas Green Clemson resigned his position in the Interior Department shortly after Lincoln's inaugural and in view of the threat of war ordered Calhoun home from Pendleton. A few days later Clemson and Anna literally sneaked out of Washington for a hasty trip south, she to see her mother and he to attend business in Charleston. Floride and Calhoun were left in the care of Aunt Elizabeth Barton and Lisette Daub, Anna's cook and companion. With the Confederate attack on Fort Sumter on April 12, the Clemsons hurried back to Bladensburg.

The spring of 1861 at The Home was filled with arrival and departure of friends and relatives, but Clemson felt no urgency to desert his residence, and he spent the time planting crops and tending his garden. However, a warlike atmosphere descended on the tranquil community soon after General Winfield Scott, on April 27, suspended the writ of habeas corpus in parts of Maryland. The Blandensburg area was the home of Confederate sympathizers, and shortly thereafter federal officials began to arrest suspects. Believing himself to be under suspicion, Clemson departed with his son for the South on June 9, leaving Anna and Floride surrounded by soldiers. He had been assured by his Pennsylvania relatives and New York friends that they would aid his wife and daughter, if need be. Years later Clemson was to declare that he had been driven from his home.

Calhoun Clemson enlisted in the Confederate army on July 20, 1861, and his father engaged in unknown activities, but most of his time was apparently spent in Pendleton with his mother-in-law. At The Home D. W. Lee, bachelor brother-in-law of the late Charles Leupp, played friend to the Clemson women's needs on several occasions during the summer and fall of 1861. They later referred to Lee as the "Gallant Defender." He advised Anna to stay on her property as long as possible and to demand evaluation and payment in case the house was demolished for military fortifications. Demolition might have occurred for Washington was in great turmoil after the Union defeat at Bull Run in late July. Lee later advised Anna not to transfer title to her property to him to prevent confiscation and not to apply to General George McClellan for a safeguard since the one she held issued by General Scott was valid unless specifically revoked by General McClellan. Such acts, Lee thought, would arouse suspicion.

Little is known of the matriarchy at The Home in 1862. The Bartons, who had been visiting for some months, departed in early summer for Pennsylvania. Apparently, Anna stayed close to home. The Gallant Defender looked in from time to time. The summer quiet was interrupted in late July by the appearance of Lisette Daub's husband, now a Union soldier. He quarreled with his wife and threatened to kill her and Anna. Departing in a dark mood, Daub warned he would return in August. Anna, though frightened, was not cowed. She learned that Daub was stationed at a nearby camp and decided, if possible, to have him arrested. She failed in that; nevertheless, he did not return to torment them further. D. W. Lee expressed the hope that Daub would die of a Confederate bullet but doubted that he would have such luck. Fortunately for Floride, she was absent from The Home during the Daub incident.

During the war Anna and Floride kept in touch with the "travelers" via Nassau, New Providence, using pseudonyms in their correspondence. Calhoun, who had been at Castle Pinckney in the Charleston harbor since his enlistment, was promoted to second lieutenant in January 1862, retroactive to December 16, 1861. At Charleston Calhoun acted as official purveyor and provisioner of food and clothing for his grandmother, his great Uncle James Edward Calhoun, and his father, whom he evidently saw frequently.

After the Daub fright a peaceful routine returned to The Home. Of course, there were comings and goings of military personnel and strangers in the area, and Anna found it increasingly difficult to obtain hired hands to attend to the farm chores. With the approach of Christmas 1862 Floride accepted an invitation by the John H. B. Latrobe family to spend the Yuletide season with them in Baltimore. During her visit she began the commendable practice of keeping a diary. On October 1, 1838, Anna had had a similar urge but failed to carry through.

PROLOGUE

In diary keeping the daughter proved superior to her mother, for
Floride persisted until she filled a whole notebook of 122 pages. Her
diary presents, in graphic detail, events—and reactions they
provoked—in the life of an attractive, aristocratic young woman during the Confederacy's dark Civil War years and the early months of
Reconstruction.

The Diary
of
Floride Clemson

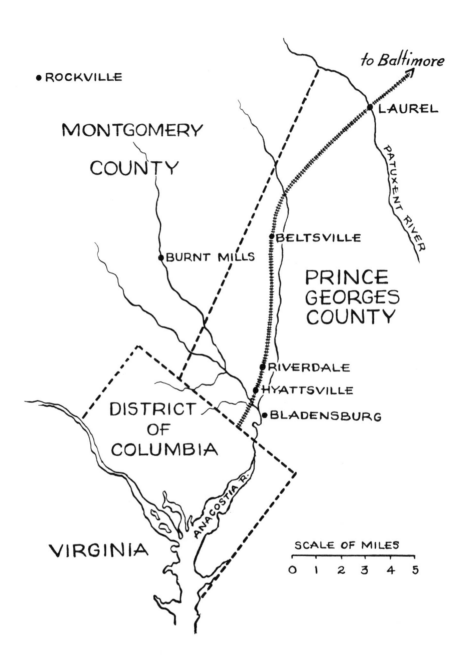

ROCKVILLE

MONTGOMERY

COUNTY

to Baltimore

LAUREL

PATUXENT RIVER

BELTSVILLE

BURNT MILLS

PRINCE
GEORGES
COUNTY

RIVERDALE
HYATTSVILLE
BLADENSBURG

DISTRICT
OF
COLUMBIA

ANACOSTIA R.

VIRGINIA

SCALE OF MILES

0   1   2   3   4   5

I

Bladensburg, Maryland

1863=1864

Jan. 1st 1863. I am now in Baltimore, where I have been ever since the Tuesday before Xmas. I am staying with John H. B. Latrobe's[1] family. The city is not very gay, but we have seen plenty of maskaraders. I have been invited out often & have made many friends. I have visited the cotton mills twice, & also an iron foundery. I injoyed these vastly, as I am very fond of machinery. I have also been driven through the park, and to all the reservoirs. I am perfectly delighted with this city, its cleanliness, elegance, and Southernness, the beauty of its ladies, & its hospitality. Mrs. Latrobe[2] has been kindness personified. I bought a braid at last today, which is a bad beginning for the new year, but I could not help it as, though my hair is quite thick, I can not make large enough plaits in front without taking too much of back hair, & no one thinks head dresses becoming to me. I was delighted to meet Maggie Bright (Sen B.'s[3] daughter) here, also Lewis Washington[4] daughters whom I used

---

[1] John Hazlehurst Boneval Latrobe (May 4, 1803-Sept. 11, 1891), a lawyer, inventor, public servant, and author. He was the son of Benjamin H. Latrobe, the famous architect. *DAB*, XI, 27-28.

[2] Charlotte Virginia Claiborne Latrobe, second wife of John H. B. Latrobe (married Dec. 6, 1832), and daughter of Gen. Ferdinand L. Claiborne of Mississippi. The Latrobes were Confederate sympathizers, and their son Osmun was General Longstreet's chief of staff. John E. Semmes, *John H. B. Latrobe and His Times, 1803-1891* (Baltimore: The Norman, Remington Co., 1917), pp. 260, 397-98, 577.

[3] Jesse David Bright (Dec. 18, 1812-May 20, 1875), U. S. Senator from Indiana from 1845 to Feb. 5, 1862. He was expelled for his Confederate sympathies and moved to Kentucky in 1863. His daughter Margaret was 21 years old in 1860. *Biog. Dir. Cong.* p. 890; MS. Census 1860, First Ward, D. C.

[4] Thomas G. Clemson's sister Louisa married Samuel Washington, of Virginia. Alester G. Holmes and George R. Sherrill, *Thomas Green Clemson, His Life and His Work* (Richmond, Va.: Garrett and Massie, Inc., 1937), p. 3. Undoubtedly, the Lewis Washingtons were relatives.

to know in Jefferson Co. Va. I was 20 last Monday, but do not feel quite so old. I do not think I look any worse for wear *yet*. My year old cough is better, & I look as well as I ever did. Last Xmas. was quiet. My only present was a pair of sleeve buttons from mother. My singing is much liked, especially in Southern songs. All are Southern here almost.

Jan. 8th. I got home to day after a delightful visit to Baltimore. The Hon. Henry May[5] was my escort home. He is the most Southern of the members of Congress, & a nice man. I spent a few days with Mrs. John S. Gittings and was so pressed to stay longer I could hardly get away. The *Ben Latrobes*[6] also wanted me to make them a visit but I could not. I found on my return that mother had had a slight attac of inflamation of the lungs, she is still not at all well. I am so worried about her. While I was away the battle of Merfreesboro[7] in Tenn. took place—Bragg versus Rosencranz. I think it may be called a drawn battle with the advantages on our side. We took 8000 prisoners & about 40 cannon, although inferior in force. The Monitor[8] went down off the cost of North Carolina with all on board. She was going to Charleston S. C. I believe. We hear constantly from the South. All are well, everything dear, but little misery, considering. I am having all the music I bought & got last year bound.

Jan. 20th. Mr. Lee[9] has been here just a week & I do not know how long he will remain. He is no longer in the army. Mother is

[5] Henry May (Feb. 16, 1816-Sept. 25, 1866), Democratic Congressman from Maryland, 1853-1855, 1861-1863. *Biog. Dir. Cong.*, p. 1516. Floride wrote "Sen. May of Md's autograph with speech" across the top of page three of the diary and affixed a brown paper clipping which reads "Free

H. May

MC"

[6] Benjamin H. Latrobe, Jr. (1806-1878), brother of John H. B. Latrobe. Semmes, *Latrobe and His Times*, pp. 578-79.

[7] On December 31, 1862, General Braxton Bragg's Confederate forces met General William S. Rosecrans' Union army at Murfreesboro. It was a drawn battle with casualties about equal on both sides. For Bragg and Rosecrans see *DAB*, II, 585-87, XVI, 163-64.

[8] During the night of December 30-31, 1862, while bound for Beaufort, N. C., the "Monitor" sank in a gale off Cape Hatteras. Some of the crew were saved.

[9] D. Williamson Lee, brother of W. Creighton and Gideon Lee, and son of the late Gideon Lee, onetime mayor of New York City and U. S. Congressman.

little if any better, scarce able to get out of bed. Dr. Hall is to come out to day. (He *did not*) Last New Years Day Gen. McGruder presented Galveston Texas with six hundred prisoners, &c. to the Confederate government. He also took the Harriet Lane which I was on board of once, [when] I returned from my visit to the Great Eastern three years ago, in company with the Presidents party.[10] She looked very little, by contrast I suppose. A new privateer, the "Retribution"[11] has made its appearance. May she rival the world renowned, & glorious Alabama!

Feb. 1st. I am just recovering from an attack of *laryngetus* or very bad sore throat. I have been the best part of this last week confined to my room & bed, & pretty sick. Dangerously so, they tell me.

Feb. 20th. I have still a dreadful cough & pain in my side. It seems to me I get little or no better. We have just received a letter from *forign parts.* Calhoun[12] is now first lieutenant, & in command of Ft. Ripley[13] in the Charleston harbor. F[ather]. writes, & says he is doing wonders, & is very steady. Weighs 185 lbs, is over 6 feet 3 in, gets $90 a month which keeps him, & has many children named after him; one girl, and one boy "Stonewall Jackson John Calhoun

---

Letter from Mr. Horace E. Hillary, Patterson, N. Y., Dec. 22, 1959. T. G. Clemson had business dealings with the Lees, and in 1869 Floride married Gideon Lee. However, in 1863 and 1864 family letters reveal that Floride was infatuated with D. W. Lee, who obviously did not share her feeling.

[10] Confederate General John Bankhead Magruder (Aug. 15, 1810-Feb. 18, 1871) on January 1, 1863, captured Galveston and the revenue cutter "Harriet Lane" and drove off the Federal blockading fleet. *DAB*, XII, 204-05. The "Harriet Lane," named for President Buchanan's niece and White House hostess, was apparently used as a presidential yacht. The "Great Eastern," launched in 1857 as the largest ship afloat, visited New York and Baltimore in 1860. President Buchanan, his cabinet, and friends, lunched aboard the ship on August 9. James Dugan, *The Great Iron Ship* (New York: Harper & Brothers, 1953), pp. 80-83.

[11] The "Retribution," a privateer of 120 tons and five guns, ran the blockade in late 1862. In January and February, 1863, it destroyed three Union vessels, but the following September it was seized in New York as it attempted to enter the harbor disguised under another name. *Baltimore Sun*, Sept. 5, 1863; J. Thomas Scharf, *History of the Confederate Navy* . . . (Atlanta, Ga.: W. H. Shepard & Co., 1887), p. 818.

[12] John Calhoun Clemson (b. July 17, 1841), Floride's brother.

[13] A relatively small fort in Charleston harbor, closer to land than Ft. Sumter.

C. (something) Hughes"! Grandma[14] & father are both well; so is Calhoun. F's last letter is most encouraging. He says that all are heros & none descouraged. Mother is well.

April 10th. I had a long ride with Henry McCeney[15] to day (who is home for the Easter holidays) to Beltsville, in order to see Mrs. Sanders[16] who has just moved there. I rode Mr. Onderdonk's[17] horse which he had lent me while he was away, & came near breaking my leg. She fell with me three times, but did not throw me, for Henry managed to get me off. I have never yet been thrown, & am considered the best rider in the county, I hear on all sides. We have just rented our place out on shares to Mr. Harvey, & son in law of Yost's.[18] I hope he will do well & give us no more trouble about the place. Mr. Lee is still here. I am *very* well. F wrote us a short time since that Calhoun had been promoted to first Lieutenant, & was in command of Ft. Ripley in Charleston harbor, which is a great compliment. He is very energetic, & attentive to his business, & quite steady. We have had an attrocious winter. Rain, snow, & sleet consecutively nearly all the time, but very little cold weather. We

[14] Mrs. John C. Calhoun, then residing at "Mi Casa" in Pendleton, S. C.

[15] In 1860 the well-to-do farm family of George and Harriet Patterson McCeney included five children, two of whom were Edgar Patterson and Henry Cole. MS. Census 1860, County of Wash., D. C. (Unless otherwise noted, all ages hereinafter taken from census returns are for the year 1860). Edgar (Oct. 25, 1844-Jan. 22, 1912) married Eliza Bowie. Henry (June 15, 1846-1891) never married. Both became holders of much farm property. Letter from Mrs. Louise McCeney Malone, Silver Spring, Md., Dec. 2, 1959. In 1862 Henry McCeney was a student at Maryland Military Institute at Bellview, Md. Henry McCeney to Floride Clemson, Nov. 1, 1862, Clemson Papers.

[16] Caroline C. Sanders (age 50) lived in District of Columbia with the family of Dr. John C. Fairfax. Her property was valued at $60,000. In 1870 the family's address was Buena Vista P.O., Prince Georges County, Md. MS. Census 1860, County of Wash., D. C.; MS. Census 1870, Prince Georges County, Md.

[17] Henry Onderdonk was president of Maryland Agricultural College at Beltsville until his ousting in 1864 because of pronounced Confederate sympathies. Thereafter, he briefly operated a private school. In 1867 he reopened the St. James School, near Hagerstown, Md., and acted as headmaster until his death in 1896. Letter from Mrs. Virginia R. Onderdonk, Baltimore, Md., Aug. 25, 1959. See also *Circular of the Maryland Agricultural College (1864-1865)* (Baltimore: John Murphy & Co., 1864).

[18] Charles Harvey (age 27) married Emma (age 22), daughter of Benedict and Elizabeth Yost of the Bladensburg District. Yost was a blacksmith. MS. Census 1860, Prince Georges County, Md.; *Ibid.*, 1870.

have not been able to get the ice house more than half full of poor ice. Every thing is beginning to bud out now, though spring plowing has not been started, on account of the wet weather. The roads have been all but impassable almost ever since Xmas. I had my teeth fixed last week. They needed but little, & are in good order. Though I have many plugs in my mouth, still I have never lost a tooth, & will probably loose none for some time, as they are quite good, & reckoned my best feature. I went for the first time to Dr. Gibbs. My teeth have heretofore been attended to by Drs. Maynard, & Cockerille.[19] I went over to Dr. Dare's this week and much against my will over heard a most complimentary conversation between two young men about my self. My voice never was better than now, & I am almost quite well even of my throat.

April 20th. Mr. Lee took mother, & me to the opera, twice last week. We saw "Il Trovatore," & "Don Jiovani." The stars were: Signoras Lorini, Morensi, & Mlle. Cordier. Brignoli, Susini, Amodio, Maccafer[r]i, besides others of minor importance. The house was wretched, (Carousi's Hall)[20] & the scenery worse. The singing very good. The roads were dreadful, & the nights dark. I enjoyed it exceedingly.

April 23rd. Last night I went to hear Norma with M. Lee & mother. It was well rendered by Siga. Lorini. Mlle Morensi, Maccaferi, & Susini. I have heard this opera twice before, but enjoyed it all the more this time. I have just received an invitation to Mme. Lisboa's.[21] Her daughter has been married lately. Yesterday I took

[19] Samuel T. Cockerille (age 28), Edward Maynard (age 47), James B. Gibbs (age 48) were all listed as dentists in 1860. MS. Census 1860, First Ward and County of Wash., D. C. However, Clemson paid a bill of $35, Feb. 7, 1861, to J. J. Cockerille for professional services to his daughter. Clemson Papers. Dr. Gibbs was a South Carolinian by birth.

[20] Carusi's Hall, northeast corner of 11th and C streets and famous for several presidential inaugural balls between 1822 and 1857, was converted into a theatre during Buchanan's administration. It was named for Louis Carusi, who remodeled it from a partially burned theatre in 1822. WPA Federal Writers' Project, *Washington: City and Capital* (American Guide Series; Washington: U. S. Government Printing Office, 1937), p. 636.

[21] Mme. Isabel Lisboa, wife of Miguel M. Lisboa, who was the Brazilian Minister to the United States. His eldest daughter (Eufraria?) married Mariano del Prado, First Secretary of the Spanish Legation on April 8, 1863. *Washington Evening Star,* April 9, 1863; MS. Census 1860, First and Second Wards, D. C.

a long walk, and gathered many wild flowers. Every thing begins to look most spring-like. But still rain! rain! & bad roads.

May 1st. Last week we went to the opera again, & heard the same troupe in Lucritzia Borgia & Lucia de Lamermoor. This latter was a failure as Mme. Lorini was sick, & it had to be cobbled up. A moon being being cut into the middle of a mountain in the senery thus: [drawing.] This is Friday; the monday & tuesday of this week I went with Mr. Lee to a concert given by Gotschalk,[22] assisted by Mlle. Vivier (not much) & the brothers Bretto, 7 & 11 old. The oldest played the violin excuisitely, & the younger played quite well on the cornet a piston. I stayed these two days with Mrs. Dr. Stone,[23] a most pleasant woman. The Friday & Saturday of last week we (Mother Mr. Lee & myself) spent at Brown Metropolitan hotel for the benefit of the opera. I am still very well. Poor Dr. Magruder[24] died last night. I'm so sorry. We called up[on] Dr. Morants family this morning. I think they are pretty common; they have just bought Dr. Penns' (or McGills) place. *Mr. Lee started on a visit to the Va. U. S. army today* [Editors' italics. This sentence was marked out by Floride Clemson] *(Didn't)*[25]

May 12th. Yesterday the thermometer stood at 92. And it bids fair to be as high today. We received a letter from F[ather]. today, dated 19th April. He is not well. C[alhoun]. has recruited near 400 men. Was in Castle Pinckney[26] during the late engagement there,

[22] Louis Moreau Gottschalk (May 8, 1829-Dec. 18, 1869) was a world-renowned pianist and composer, born in New Orleans. He once turned down a P. T. Barnum offer of $20,000 a year. *DAB,* VII, 441-42. He appeared in two concerts at Willard's Hall, April 27-28, with Louise Vivier, vocalist, and Bernard and Richard Bretto. Floride's appraisal agreed with that of a Washington music critic, who called the concert "a brilliant affair" while giving Mlle. Vivier only moderate praise. *Washington Evening Star,* April 28, 1863.

[23] Robert King Stone (1822-April 23, 1872), M.D. from University of Pennsylvania, and personal physician to Abraham Lincoln. In 1849 he married Margaret, daughter of Thomas Ritchie, a prominent Richmond newspaper editor. *History of the Medical Society of the District of Columbia, 1817-1909* (Washington: The Medical Society of D. C., 1909), pp. 238-39.

[24] Dr. Archibald S. Magruder (age 46) of Bladensburg. *Washington Evening Star,* May 1, 1863.

[25] D. W. Lee did not go, but on April 30, 1863, he had written Anna C. Clemson giving instructions to be executed by her in case he did not return from his trip, which he asked to be kept a secret from his family. Clemson Papers.

[26] In Charleston Harbor, on the south side.

& says no one was killed on our side, & the only woulds [wounds] were from the dismounting of a gun. Gen. Van Dorn[27] has just been shot by a private enemy.

[Accounts of death of Stonewall Jackson taken from *Philadelphia Press*, May 13; *Philadelphia Inquirer*, May 13; *Charleston Courier*, May 11, were pasted in the diary here.][28] This is perhaps our greatest political misfortune. The victory was not worth it. Alas! I suppose these extracts are mainly true. Great, good man!

May 30th. Lizzie Robinson[29] has just spent a couple of days with me. Next to Laura Leupp[30] I love her best of all my friends. We hear pretty often & most encourageingly from the absentees. All are well & doing well. The letters breathe the most determined endurance, & heroism. We are just now much excited about Vicksburg. We believe all is going on well, but the Yankees are trying every thing against that devoted city. Every day or two we hear it is taken, which news is always contradicted before night fall. "Hope on, hope ever!"

June 1st. A day or two ago there was an order passed in Washington forbidding any groceries, or any thing of the sort, from being carried out of the city, unless the owners had a pass, which they can only obtain by proving themselves *union*! I don't know what we are to do. This is to prevent the contraband trade that is alledged to be carried on between this state & the South. Confiscation &c. is going on fast. Roses are just in bloom here, but we are late this year.

2nd. Eliza Bowie[31] has just spent a night here, with her brother.

[27] Confederate General Earl Van Dorn (Sept. 17, 1820-May 8, 1863) was assassinated at his headquarters desk by a personal enemy. *DAB*, XIX, 185-86.

[28] These extracts from three newspapers were obviously reprints from Washington or Baltimore papers that Floride read.

[29] Conway Robinson (age 55) was a prosperous Virginia-born lawyer living near Bladensburg. Besides his wife Mary (age 43), his family included seven children, four of whom were Leigh (age 19), Elizabeth (18), Cary (16), and William (15). MS. Census 1860, County of Wash., D. C.

[30] Daughter of Charles M. Leupp, a New York businessman who was a friend of Thomas G. Clemson. Leupp committed suicide on Oct. 5, 1859. Laura Leupp to Mrs. A. C. Clemson, Oct. 6, 1859, Clemson Papers.

[31] Eliza Coombs Bowie (died Jan. 22, 1912) of Thorpland Farm, Prince Georges County, later married Edgar P. McCeney. Letter from Mrs. Louise McCeney Malone, Silver Spring, Md., Dec. 2, 1959.

June 3rd. I went today to Carrie Hickey's[32] wedding with Will. Dougherty of Harrisburg Penn. Another neighbor gone! Mrs. [Robert K.] Stone Mrs. & Miss [Lizzie] Giles, & father's first cousin, Wash. Baker (who is attentive to Miss Giles I believe) spent the evening here.

June 5th. Received two letters, dated May 6th & 3rd. C. & F. in Rd. [Richmond] on their way to Texas. The former has been transferred to a higher grade. They say all well at Mi Casa. The spirit of the news high, and hopeful, as ever. This date is to be remembered as an era on which a *change* has taken place. *Ertin Bu.*[33] *Trans. Miss.* How long will this last. Will it be fraught with danger to any one? Hope on, & trust; that's all!

June 10th. The whole country is parched with drought. I think it has not raind more than once, & that slightly for over a month. After the incessant rains of last winter & spring this is dreadful, for everything was planted late. Grant has *not* taken Vickburg yet, but has met innumerable repulses. May this continue. The Yankees were also severely repulsed from Port Hudson [La.] I have planted many flowers, & made four flower beds this spring.

June 19th. Yesterday we had the first *rain* (not *sprinkle*) we have had for over six weeks. Everything looked parched & dry, & there seemed no hope for crops. I hope the [rain] will save us from famine. There seems to be great activity among the armies of this state & Virginia. There have been rumors & statements for some days that the Southern army entire has passed the line of this state for Penn. It may be true, but it seems more than probable that it all arises from a cavalry raid of some two or three regiments to Chambersburg Penn. However there is great commotion, & anxiety. All (or many of) the horses have been siezed in Baltimore, for cavalry service. So many rumors in short, are afloat, that I do not know what to think. Mary Latrobe[34] has been with us over a week. I like her. She is about 5 or 6 years my senior. Father's first cousin Wash.

---

[32] Caroline T. Hickey (age 20) one of six children of William and Cecilia A. Hickey. William Hickey (age 57) was a clerk and farmer, whose property was valued at $44,000. MS. Census 1860, County of Wash., D. C.

[33] "Ertin" is "Nitre" spelled backwards. Clemson was attached to the Confederate Nitre and Mining Bureau.

[34] Mary Elizabeth Latrobe (Aug. 1836-1916), daughter of Benjamin H. Latrobe, Jr. Semmes, *Latrobe and His Times*, pp. 578-79.

Baker, & Miss Giles whom he seems to be engaged to, spent a day or too with us. He is a fine man, & suits *us* in feeling.

Guv. Morris, Laura's friend, spent a night here. Grandma well, on the 19th of May. All with her yet, will soon go, however.

June 28th. Sund. The night before last, I went to the Commencement ball, & to the commencement in the morning. I was dressed in a white spotted muslin, & danced every set. We got to bed at 5 o'clock in broad day-light! There were more than a hundred, at least. Mary Latrobe went with me, & we stayed all night at the Wharton's.[35] Mary returned home yesterday, with her father who spent the day here. Miss Giles goes South tomorrow, she & cousin W. Baker, were at the ball. They made me their confidant, & go-between. I am sorry for them. They are engaged.[36] We spent Thursday evening at Mrs. Calvert's, & Wednesday at Mrs. Merricks.[37] The commencement exercises were very interesting. Charlie Calvert graduated, & Eugine spoke best of all. I am just now very well, except that I am much troubled by a nervous contraction of the muscles of the throat, which is very troublesome in swallowing, & sometimes nearly starves me by preventing my doing so all together, without pain however. The Confederates are all in Penn. now. All about here are in a terrible state of fear, & excitement. Baltimore is barricaded with wagons & tobaco hogsheads. We are pretty uneasy. Well time will show. Uncle Elias[38] is to come for me

[35] Dr. G. O. Wharton (age 55) and his children Elizabeth (21), Sarah (20), and William (16) lived at Beltsville in 1860. MS. Census 1860, Prince Georges County, Md.

[36] Lizzie Giles soon jilted Washington Baker for a General Quarles. Anna C. Clemson to Floride Clemson, Aug. 9, 1863, Clemson Papers. Thomas G. Clemson's mother was Elizabeth Baker.

[37] William Matthew Merrick (Sept. 1, 1818-Feb. 4, 1889) was Circuit Court justice in D. C., 1854-1863, and U. S. Congressman, 1871-1873. *Biog. Dir. Cong.*, p. 1557. Charles Benedict Calvert (Aug. 23, 1808-May 12, 1864) of Bladensburg was a descendant of the original founders of Maryland. His wife was the former Charlotte Augusta Norris. The Calvert children's ages in 1863 were as follows: Ella (23), George Henry (21), Charles Baltimore (20), William Norris (17), and Eugene Stier (16). John Bailey Calvert Nicklin, "The Calvert Family," *Maryland Historical Magazine*, XVI (Sept., 1921), 316. Calvert's property was listed at $240,000 in 1860. MS. Census 1860, Prince Georges County, Md.

[38] Elias Baker, a brother of Thomas G. Clemson's mother, Elizabeth Baker Clemson.

to pay a visit to him in two week. If things are not settled by that time of course I wont. Probably wont anyhow.

June 30th. The Confederate forces have reach Harrisburg, Penn., but last accounts said they had not taken it. Cavalry raids have come within 18 miles of here. No depradations have been made. All is excitement. They have come to 7 miles of Baltimore, *& have been at Laurel on this railroad.* [Editors' italics. This clause was marked out by Floride Clemson.]

July 5th. Well, the news seems bad enough. The battle of Gettysburg has taken place and all the papers say (God grant it may not be true) that the Confederates have been defeated. It is hard not to believe the fabulous accounts that are given of our losses but we have had so many lessons as to how much men *can* lie, that we ought not to be down hearted yet. The battle lasted from the 1st. inst. to the 4th. (Sat.) I do not know when I have been so anxious before. Southern raids have come very near here. They have certainly been to Rockville & some say much nearer. Picketts have been placed so thickly about here, that it was not worth the trouble to go out at night. 5 between here & Bladensburg. Mr. Lee has been away in the city over a week. Last letter from grandma was dated June 12th. C. had left for Texas. Port Hudson, & Vicksburg still seem to hold their own firmly. The Southerners have nearly all Louisiana back again. I am very well. The Southern troops behaved so well in Penn. They committed no depredations, even their enemies have to own to their Christian, civilized, & grand conduct, & contrast it with their own.

July 15th. The news is very confusing. The Yankees say Vicksburg was taken on the 4th; yet no official report from Grant has been received, & the Southern accounts of a much later date do not mention it. Some do not believe it yet although semi official accounts of its capture have been given. They also talk of the taking of Port Hudson. Two or three days ago we had one of the most terrible falls of rain I ever heard of. It was continuously as hard as I ever saw water fall, for a day & night. Bladensburg was submerged so that the inhabitants had to be taken from their houses in boats. All Mr. Crawford's[39] hay was carried off, our road nearly washed away,

[39] Samuel C. Crawford, a Bladensburg farmer who had frequent business dealings with the Clemsons. His property was valued at $24,000 in 1860. MS. Census 1860, Prince Georges County, Md.

& every one has suffered severely. Bridges were carried away every where. The Wash. & Balt. rail road has been so damaged that trains have not run for two days. There is a fearful riot in New York about the draft. Houses have been burnt, & people killed in an unprecedented manner.[40] Mr. Lee is still in the city. He brought Mr. Seymour out to see us, he belongs to the English legation, & mother knew his parents in Brussells. They say Gen. Lee has recrossed the Potomac with all his forces, stores, &c. It may be so. We have perhaps more company now than usual. I get plenty of chances to ride, & am therefor well.

July 17th. Today Calhoun is 22 years old. I wonder where he is? I will wish him here many happy returns as I can not do so in person. I went to St. Aloysious Catholic Church to hear Mozart's requium for Bishop Kendric[41] of Baltimore. The voices were fine but too few for the organ & church. The sermon by [the Rev. Charles] Stonestreet, about the poorest I ever heard. I don't think the times ever looked so dark as they do now. Vickburg, Port Hudson, & rumor says Charleston too (God grant this be not true) are gone. Lee not conquered, but weakened, & Bragg retreating. I hope it may be true that darkness comes before day. The riot in New York is abating, but has been terrible. Took a pew at Rock Creek Church[42] today. 15$ a year. To date from August 1st.

July 18th. Mrs. Dundas[43] died last night of rheumatism & heart desease. Her daughters were all with her. Mrs. Oldham lost her baby only a week before.

July 27th. Left home this morning (Monday) at 7 o'clock for Altoona with Uncle Elias. Reached Philla the same afternoon, & went to see aunt North.[44] The whole family except Walter were

[40] The "draft riots" took place on July 13-16, during which time possibly as many as 1,000 persons were killed. U. S. Army troops from Pennsylvania finally restored order.

[41] "The Most Rev. Francis Patrick Kenrick, Archbishop of Baltimore," died July 7, 1863, age 76. He was a native of Ireland, but migrated early to the United States. *Baltimore Sun*, July 9, 1863. Also see *DAB*, X, 339-40.

[42] St. Paul's Episcopal Church at Rock Creek still stands.

[43] Mary Y. Dundas (age 56), wife of William H. Dundas (age 66), Assistant Postmaster General in 1860 and a native of Virginia. Their four children included William O. (age 17), a close friend of John Calhoun Clemson. MS. Census 1860, County of Wash., D. C.

[44] Catharine Clemson, sister of Thomas G., married George W. North of Philadelphia.

37

away. Willie & Clem came home from a two months campaingn with the army, this evening.

Sep. 19th. I got home this morning from my long trip north & visit to my uncle Elias. I had a delightful visit to his family. See my letters to mother for particulars. His house is of blocks of nearly white marble, & quite palatial. Situated among the mountains. Cousin Anna [Baker] is about 27 with a magnificent suit of hair, not very good looking or smart, but good, & kind. Auntie [Hettie Baker] is about 60 & looks no more than 40 & is refined & handsome. Has a great taste for flowers. Cousin Sylvester [Baker] is 38, red haired, & with regular features. He was very kind to me, & I liked him. He took me buggy driving to all the places of interest in the vicinity, & I was perfectly charmed by the mountains. The view from the Wopsenonock where Mr. Onderdonck accompanied me while he was at Altoona on a visit *to me,* was grand. I saw ore banks & furnaces, machine shops &c., without number. Altoona has some 5000 inhab's. I saw cousin Sarah [Baker] (Woods'[45] wife) & Luly his daughter. The former is the best little woman I ever saw. The latter a sweet sma[r]t child of 11. I was baptized on the 23rd Aug. by uncle Baker.[46] Witnessed by cousins Mary & Sarah. Mary Clemson & Mattie, both paid a week's visit at uncle Elias' while I was there, with uncle Baker Clemson. Carrie McClelland[47] my distant cousin & schoolmate is consumptive. I saw her a great deal. She had Lizzie McIlvain, & Kate Russell our other cousin staying with her. Saw Miss Jennie Cammeron.

Thursday, Sep. 3d. Started from Altoona, on my great trip North. There were six of us. Uncle Elias, cousins Anna & Sarah Baker, Luly, & Sadie Sterrett, aunt Hetty's niece. Reached Pittsburgh Thursday noon, 117 miles. Saw glass blowing & pressing, cannon foundaries, & iron rolling, the semitary, &c. The town is too dirty to live in or look at. Started next day (Friday) at noon for Cleveland

---

[45] Woods Baker, deceased son of Elias Baker.

[46] John Baker Clemson, an Episcopal minister and brother of Thomas G. The two Clemson brothers were not on intimate terms at this time, and later became bitter toward each other. Clemson Papers, *passim.* Mary and Mattie were daughters of John Baker Clemson.

[47] Carrie McClelland and Lizzie McIlwain were schoolmates of Floride Clemson when she attended her Aunt Elizabeth Barton's boarding school (Sept., 1856-June, 1858) in Philadelphia. See Floride Clemson to Anna Calhoun Clemson, Aug. 2, 1863, Clemson Papers.

Ohio 150, & reached there after dark. Drove over it next morning, & thought it a the most beautiful city I ever saw. Lake Erie looked like a quiet sea. Ohio is too flat for anything, & too uninteresting. Started for Niagara at 11 o'clock, reached the Clifton house Canada, after dark Saturday 210 miles, very dusty & the country uninteresting. Saw Buffalo, a fine city, & Erie. Rested Sunday, & saw our truncks for the first time since we left Altoona. Monday did up the Canada side, whirlpool, burning spring, museum, suspension bridge, Lundies Lane, the rapids, & *I* went under the falls with a guide. [Floride elaborates thus in her letter of September 9, 1863, to her mother: "This last acheivement I did much aginst the wishes of the rest of the party, but I knew it was not dangerous, as it was not, so I took off my hoops, & all above them, and put on a suitable oil cloth dress, & with a mulatto guide went under from the Canadian side, yesterday."] Tuesday did the American side, rapids, Goat, & Lunar Islands, Terrapin Tower, Indian stores &c. Wednesday morning left. Saw plenty of Southerners & English, & found the falls above my highest expectations. Wednesday at 3 o'clock reached Syracuse, N. Y. 160 miles. Saw the salt works, Seline, & the city generally. Left about noon Thursday. Reached Saratoga Springs 145 miles after dark. Forgot to say we took the upper road by the canal, & did not pass by the lakes to Syracuse. All the ride through N. Y. was beautiful, but not striking till we reached the Mohawk, & mountains. I was sick at Saratoga, & was disgusted with the waters. We were not delighted there anyhow, & left Saturday morning, traveling down the railroad by the side of the Hudson, wich was grand passed expression. Reached N. Y. 170 miles Saturday 4 o'clock. Went to the Metropolitan [Hotel]. See my letters to mother until Sunday 13th my last. Monday saw Laura [Leupp] who is engaged to Frank Marbury 5 years younger than hersef & Zeruah Banks, & her father.[48] Bought a black silk dress & did other shopping. Left N. Y. Tuesday morning. Reached Philla at noon, 90 miles.

---

[48] Zeruah Van Wyck (age 17), daughter of William Van Wyck, of New York, and Lydia Ann Maverick Van Wyck, of Pendleton, married Charles Banks of New York. In 1860 William Van Wyck, a lawyer, was residing with his family in Pendleton. His personal and real property were valued at $225,000. MS. Census 1860, Anderson District, S. C.; R. W. Simpson, *History of Old Pendleton District* . . . (Anderson, S. C.: Oulla Printing & Binding Company, 1913); pp. 109-10. Zeruah died in late January, 1864. Laura Leupp to Floride Clemson, Feb. 1, 1864, Clemson Papers.

Cousin Anna, Sadie, & myself, traveled this alone as uncle had to return for our trunks which he had forgotten, & Luly & cousin Sarah left us at N. Y. Stayed at the Girard. Left cousin Anna here, & Sadie left for home next morning early. Went out to aunt North, where Kate Barton came by appointment, saw aunt Sue, Mattie, Walter, Clarrie, Bessie, (14) Herbert, who is a large boy of 7, Willie, & aunt & uncle North.[49] Neither of the latter were well. Next day saw cousin Tom C. Kate nearly had a fit, she was so glad to see me, indeed they all seemed to be. Wednesday evening at 4 left with uncle for Landcaster. Was sick there. The Russells where we stayed were very kind. Saw [great] aunt Kitty [Baker] Ikleberger where aunt Barton was paying a visit, whom I also saw (pshaw!) & cousin Hannah Giger who is partly paralized & blind. Spent most of the next day at Wheatlands[50] with Miss Lane, who seemed overjoyed at seeing me, & looked fat & well. Mr. Buchanan was also hearty looking. They pressed me to stay with them a long time. There was a large democratic meeting in Landcaster, & when we got into the cars they were so full that we had to go into an emigrant car with no other lady, & more drunken men than I ever saw before. They sang such songs & swore so, that I was nearly wild. We reached Harrisburg about a hundred and twenty miles from Philla after a two hours' & a half ride at 10 P. M. where we stayed all night, as the Southerners had cut the branch railroad bridge from Landcaster to York, & we could not make the connection otherwise. Next morning (Friday) we started early, & got to Baltimore about noon some 80 miles, where I payed a visit to Mary Latrobe, & started for home at 5 P. M. There had been a bad freshet, which carried the rail road bridge at Laurel off again the same night we crossed it. We reached Hyattsville after dark. Mr. Lee met us. We got entangled in a stump at the first branch & had to wait an hour in the middle of that raging stream while Mr. Lee took out the horses & got a

[49] Kate Barton was daughter of Elizabeth Clemson Barton; Aunt Sue, the wife of William, brother of Thomas G. Clemson; Mattie Clemson; the remainder were Norths. Anna Calhoun Clemson distrusted some of her husband's relatives and advised Floride: "Do be cautious what you say to the Clemson's, & Kate. Dont say anything about your aunt B[arton].—keep quiet, & be discreet. Dont make any visits, or promises to visit. Keep in the vague. . . . Dont be humbugged by professions, you have learnt the worth of them." Aug. 23, 1863, Clemson Papers.

[50] "Wheatland" was the home of President Buchanan near Lancaster, Pa.

wagon. The stream kept rising, into the carriage. With much difficulty we got across in the waggon & at the other stream which was
dreadfully swolen nearly got drowned. The horses reared when
they had to swim, & got into the bed of the stream, we nearly gave
them up as lost, but cut them loose at last, & let them to the side of
the waggon where I got on Logan, & *swam* out straddle. The waggon was carried off when uncle's weight got out of it. They say I
behaved wonderfully well. We stayed in B. [Bladensburg] all night
& next morning got home. Mr. Lee had painted all the inside of the
house during my absense, & all looked very nicely. Mother was
well. I am still quite sick from the over fatigue of my trip & the
diorea which stuck to me during the whole of it & put me to bed
several times during its continuence. If I had not been so sick, it
would scarce have had a mar for the weather was charming, being
only troubled by dust once, (between Cleveland & Niagara.) & not
at all by rain, for the only that came was after we left Harrisburg
so I did not mind. We had no accidents & the scenery was lovely
most of the way. I think the finest was the Hudson river, & between
Harrissburg & Pittsburgh, along the Susquehanna, & Juniata, never
leaving mountains untill near Pittsburgh. That was the most grand
near Altoona. No one troubled me about politics, & I spent my
time delightfully, but want *rest*. I went in all about 1639 miles as
near as I could estimate by the guide book we had.

October 4th Sunday. For the first week or ten days after I got
home, I managed to keep from going to bed though I generally laid
on the sofa but I was so weakened by having the diorea so long &
traveling that I broke down & had to go to bed regularly last Monday, where I stayed, Dr. Wells attending me till the day before
yesterday. I am now much better than I have been since my return
& in a fair way of getting well. I have been so little bed ridden in
my life, that it goes quite hard with me now. I have no cough at all.
C. is now a prisoner it appears by the papers, but we do not know
where, though we are trying hard to find out.[51] This account is from
a letter from Cairo of Sep 19th in the Philla. Inquierer of the 25th.

---

[51] First Lt. John Calhoun Clemson, assigned to duty with the Nitre and
Mining Bureau, May 7, 1863, was captured at Bolivar, Miss., Sept. 9, 1863,
and imprisoned at Johnson's Island, Sandusky, Ohio, until June 11, 1865. F. de
Sales Dundas, *The Calhoun Settlement, District of Abbeville, South Carolina*
(Staunton, Va.: F. de Sales Dundas, 1949), p. 18.

We suppose he is at Sandusky or Chicago, out west. Calhoun was captured the 9th.

"Le général [Lewis] Cass est aujourd'hui âgé de 81 ans; il date de 1782. Dans la même année sont nés John C. Calhoun, Thomas H. Benton, Daniel Webster, et l'ex-président Martin Van Buren,—tous morts." [newspaper clipping pasted perpendicular to a cut-out portion of the diary page.] Mother went to Annapolis yesterday to see Mrs. Bourne[52] who will take a trunk for her. She (Mrs. B.) is again a widow. She comes from England. She left her home near Grandma's a year ago with her husband. She is in very bad health. Poor John Singleton[53] was killed in Kentucky with Morgan, just before I left for Altoona in July. Charleston is still holding out so nobly. God protect her! All our folks well a month ago.

Octo. 7th Wednesday. Had Lizzie Ross staying with me two days & took her home yesterday. I spent the day, & night at Middleton's[54] returning this morning. I like them very much. No news yet from Calhoun, as to where he is, though every inquiery had been made. Poor fellow, I trust he is not suffering. A gentlemen told me he saw me mentioned in a New York Herald, last summer, as an active *rebel,* & *secessionist,* who ought to be watched, besides more he did not remember. So I have been in print anyhow! I wonder if they are right as to my sentiments? I am fast getting well, & strong again; & they say looking better than I ever did before, & *handsomer!*

[52] Elizabeth, daughter of Jacob and Sophia Fraser Warley of Pendleton, married C. J. Bourne, a civil engineer born in England. She did not remarry and died on Mar. 1, 1884, age 56. Simpson, *Old Pendleton District*, pp. 201-02; MS. Census 1860, Anderson Dist., S. C.; Register, St. Paul's Episcopal Church, Pendleton, S. C.

[53] First Lt. John W. Singleton, of Pickens, S. C., was with Gen. John Hunt Morgan during the latter's ill-fated raid into Kentucky and Ohio in July, 1863. All but a few hundred of Morgan's 2,500 men were killed or captured. A. S. Salley (comp.), *South Carolina Troops in Confederate Service* (3 vols., Columbia, S. C.: The R. L. Bryan Co. and The State Co., 1913-1930), II, 641. For Morgan see *DAB.*, XIII, 174-75.

[54] Probably the family of E. J. Middleton (age 56), Washington-born clerk whose property was valued at $50,000. The family included Ellen R. (age 41), Mary V(irginia?) (29), E. J. (15), and two elderly persons. These were the only Middletons living near Bladensburg that were listed in the 1860 census. MS. Census 1860. County of Wash., D. C.

Octo. 10th Saturday. We found out that Calhoun was at St. Johnson's Island Sandusky, Oo., last Thursday. Mother got Lincoln's permission to go to see him, next day but [Sec. of War] Stanton would not permit her on account he said of Northern ladies not being allowed to *go from here* South to see their husbands. This is very hard as mother has made all her arrangements to start for Sandusky the day after tomorrow, where she expected to spend a week or so. Stanton says that if any Northern ladies are allowed to visit the prisoners South, he will let her go. I was to spend my time among the neighbors during her absence. Mr. Lee is to start for home tomorrow morning, but expects to be back again this winter he says. He gave me a photograph album & left his horse [Bruno] & pistol for me to use. Mother had some excellant half length *cartes* [photographs] taken yesterday with her bonnet on. We can not get work men at all now & have the greatest trouble. Mr. Harvey who took the place on shares, turned out badly, & has left. Indeed it is great trouble. The house is all painted, but very badly. Everything is double price.

Octo. 12th. Just received at letter from Calhoun dated Sep. 25th saying he was captured two weeks before & wants to get transferred to some prison here or elsewhere. He is well. Mr. Lee left this morning, as he could not go yesterday.

Octo. 18th. Some of our chickens were stolen by a gang of some 20 run away negroes last night. Depredations are going on all through the country & we are in constant dread our horses will go. It is almost impossible to get servants, & our negro woman had to groom our horses & do all the *man* work for over a month. Calhoun writes he is well, but that Johnsons Is. is very cold. It is principally a prison for officers. He says he sleeps with 68 men in a room no larger than our dining room. We sent him a nice box of eatables &c. last week. Mother is so troubled with the place, which has to be kept up at a ruinous expense, that it almost makes her sick. I am fast getting well, I think. Lizzie Robinson spent some days last week with me. She is such a lovely girl. Billy D.s[55] is a prisoner.

[55] William O. Dundas, son of William H. Dundas, was a Confederate paymaster and also captured at Bolivar, Miss., about the same time Calhoun Clemson was taken prisoner. Dundas, *The Calhoun Settlement*, p. 18.

Tom King[56] is a companion of Calhoun's at Sandusky. The balls from the surrounding forts fall into our enclosure constantly. Two trees in the wood below the stables have been struck, & one ball fell in the orchard. These are 32 lbers. We have now six or more which have fallen on or near this place. They whistle fearfully. Charleston still holds out wonderfully. I am so proud of my old city. God protect it. There appears to have been a great battle near Manassas again lately, but as they say so little about it I suppose we whipped as usual.

Octo. 29th. I have just planted out many roses, bulbs, & shrubs, & have trimmed the hedges &c. I also attend much to the horses. I am very busy. Calhoun got his box of comforts &c. Mother went to see Stanton herself to get permission to go to see him, but he would not grant it. We are well but have much trouble in getting hands to work. Hurrah for Charleston yet! I have had two more teeth filled.

Octo. 30th. Attended a debating (public) at the Agricultural college last evening. Subject: "Was the execution of Mary Queen of Scots justifiable or not?" Wm. & Dick Goldsborough spoke wonderfully well extemporaniously. George Calvert, & Davy Hall[57] spoke badly.

Nov. 1st. Sunday. I became a communicant to day, for the first time.

Nov. 5th. Mother has sold the carved furniture to Dr. Maynard. It goes to day. The price is $3,000. I am more grieved than enough. The bro[n]ze horses went too. I could cry. Poor Willie Robinson was shot through the head, & killed on the 15th of last month. He was only 19. I liked him best of those boys. Mrs. Craig died the day before yesterday.

[56] T. M. King (age 19), born in Virginia, was son of U. S. Army surgeon Benjamin King (age 62). The family also included Virginia King (age 15). MS. Census 1860, County of Wash., D. C.

[57] William and Richard Goldsborough of Easton, Md.; S. D. Hall of Millersville, Md.; and George Calvert, of Riverdale. The latter, eldest son of Charles Benedict and Charlotte Augusta Norris Calvert, was not listed as a student at Maryland Agricultural College in 1863. *Circular of the Maryland Agricultural College* (1863-1864), pp. 5-6.

Nov. 6th. I drove mother around visiting today, we went to see Mrs. Crawford, Dare, Hyatt, Calvert, Pinckney, & Chew.[58] We got along nicely.

Nov. 8th. I stood Godmother for Willhelmina Floride Daub to day, with her mother.[59] Mother went to Baltimore yesterday on account of a letter received from a lady who said she had something of importance to tell her. She expects to return tomorrow. (She came.)

Nov. 12th. I went to the wedding of two of the Miss Keeches.[60] Kate to Barnard, Rose to a cousin Keech. Nora Latrobe[61] came home with me. She will probably leave Tuesday this is Thursday. Tuesday she left.

Nov. 18th. *Drove* mother visiting. Brought Lizzie Walker[62] home.

Nov. 22nd. Took Lizzie Walker to church, & went to stay with Jennie King who has brought Gertrude Magoffin[63] home from Ky. with her to spend the winter. We have no man again, & have lost our cows. Still no man to work.

Nov. 28. Found one cow. Stayed until Wednesday with Jennie King, brought her & Gertrude home, they went back Thursday. We

[58] Mrs. Sophia Chew (age 34), wife of John H. Chew (age 38), Episcopal minister; Mrs. S. C. Crawford; Mrs. Charles B. Calvert; Mrs. Elizabeth Pinkney (age 56), wife of William Pinkney; possibly Mrs. Frances Hyatt (age 38), wife of Christopher Hyatt (age 60), a merchant. MS. Census 1860, Prince Georges County, Md.; *Ibid.,* 1870. All were listed near Bladensburg. William Pinkney, nephew of Maryland diplomat William Pinkney, was the Protestant Episcopal Bishop of Maryland. Because of his Confederate sympathies and refusal to pray for a Union victory, he was barred from his Washington Church. *Washington: City and Capital,* pp. 617, 827.

[59] Mrs. Lisette Daub was a servant in the Clemson home. The daughter was called Mina.

[60] Kate Hope Keech married John J. Barnard of Georgetown, D. C.; Rose Keech married William S. Keech of Baltimore County, Md. The brides were daughters of Alexander Keech. Announcement in *Baltimore Sun,* Nov. 14, 1863.

[61] Maria Eleanor Latrobe, younger sister of Mary Latrobe. She married Hammond Vinton and died in 1911, leaving three children. Semmes, *Latrobe and His Times,* pp. 578-80.

[62] Elizabeth Walker (age 30), daughter of (widow?) Mary Walker (age 52), who farmed near Bladensburg. MS. Census 1860, County of Wash., D. C.

[63] Gertrude Magoffin, daughter of Kentucky Governor Beriah and Anna Nelson Shelby Magoffin, was born Mar. 4, 1845. Letter from G. Glenn Clift, Kentucky Historical Society, Aug. 15, 1959.

have a great deal of company for us lately, & I get many rides. We can not hear often from the south. Father is well, & at Shreveport. Complains of the people being lawless, but says the crops are good. Calhoun can not receive anything from us any more, as the war department has stopped everything of the kind. I am sorry, for the poor fellow is quite downhearted. I pray there may be an exchange of prisoners soon in spite of what they say. Sallie Harwood[64] was married to a Babcock in the navy the day before yesterday. I could not go to the wedding. I think of beginning a Sunday school at the little school house near here tomorrow. We have no man yet. This country is heteful.

Dec. 1st. John Morgan[65] reached Toronto Canada Nov. 30th. I dont believe we were defeated so much at Chattanoga Tenn.[66] Heard of Su Nott's sister Mrs. Pennington today, in Baltimore. [Newspaper clipping recounting the escape of John Morgan from the Ohio Penitentiary was pasted in the diary here.]

Dec. 3rd. There was fiering, & saluting all day yesterday in honor of the erection of the statue of Freedom[67] on the dome of the Capitol at W. I suppose they make such a fuss over the semblance, because they have not the reality. There seems to be heavy fighting between Mead & Lee in Va.

Dec. 7th. Began my Sunday School yesterday. I think there will not be more than 15 schollars.

Dec. 28th. Monday. Returned yesterday from a visit to Lizzie Robinson. Went last Tuesday, & helped to dress the church with winter greens for Xmas, also practiced for that day, as I am just now, & indeed have been almost ever since the Woods left, the only *passable* voice in the choir. I had a very pleasent time, though there was not much gaiety. I received a brush & comb from mother, for

[64] Sarah A. (age 17), daughter of H. H. Harwood (age 56), Captain, U. S. Navy. MS. Census 1860, Prince Georges County, Md.

[65] General John Morgan escaped from prison near Columbus, Ohio, on Nov. 26, 1863. He was subsequently killed in action at Greeneville, Tenn., Sept. 4, 1864. See note 53.

[66] This was the battle of Lookout Mountain and Missionary Ridge, Nov. 23-25, in which Grant's army shattered Bragg's forces.

[67] A nineteen-foot bronze statue of "Armed Freedom" was raised to the dome of the capitol amid much ceremony on Dec. 2. *Baltimore Sun*, Dec. 3, 1863; Margaret Leech, *Reveille in Washington, 1860-1865* (New York: Harper & Bros., 1941), p. 279.

a Xmas present, a bonbonière from Mr. Seymour, a little fancy wax match box from Lizzie R., Spencers "Fairie Queen" from Mr. Onderdonk, & a book from Miss Lizzie Walker. Mr. Seymour, Mr. Henedge (both of the English legation) & Edgar & Henry McCeney dined here yesterday. I can not imagine why I receive so much more attention than I ever did before, but certain it is that I do. Ever since Mr. Lee left it seems to me I have been almost a belle! Among my more constant visitors I may recon Edgar & Henry McCeney, Mr. Onderdonk, George & Charlie Calvert, Mr. Seymour, Jerry Berry, Johny Bowie (!), Dr. Eversfield,[68] Mr. Lee (!) & some *accidentals*. Tomorrow is my 21st birthday. I have had a bad cold nearly a month now. Calhoun is well.

Dec. 29th. This is my 21st birth day, & I am of age. No great occasion in a womans life! I do not think I feel over joyed at being so old. Mr. Onderdonk & the two McCeneys dined here. Mother gave me a pair of home knit red mits, & a collar. I have been drawing likenesses again, which are said to be quite good sketches.

Jan 1st 1864. Mayst thou have a happy New Year oh Floride! May thy shadow never be less. Mayst have many returns. Mayst always be better, more fortunate (if possible) & in short I wish thee all good wishes, & all bliss now & evermore! This morning was dark & lowering, but about ten it cleared & the rest of the day has been fine though windy. I was sick yesterday from a too long ride on a wretched horse of Mr. Crawford's with Mr. Onderdonk, but am pretty well to day, & not much troubled with my old cough. Mother is well & full of her intended trip to Johnsons Island next month. Mr. Dunscomb,[69] Calhouns Water cure & Florida friend, is in W. We expect him out. On the whole I am a happy fortunate girl. I suppose from what I hear pretty much at my best in looks, but I hope not in everything else. If this year ended in peace to this land, I should have little to wish for. "Thy will oh Lord, not mine be done."

[68] Jerry Berry (age 20), son of Eliza (age 45) and William Berry (50), a planter whose property was valued at $173,000; probably John T. Eversfield (age 37), a physician whose property was valued at $50,000. MS. Census 1860, Prince Georges County, Md.

[69] G. H. Dunscomb, a close family friend, accompanied young Calhoun Clemson to Enterprise, Fla., in November, 1859, to help him regain his health. He frequently signed his letters with "A. S. F." (A Southern Friend?) Anna Calhoun Clemson to Floride, Nov. 13, Nov. 27, 1859, Clemson Papers.

Jan. 4th. Mr. Dunscomb, Calhoun's friend has been here a day or two. It is snowing hard, & very cold. I took a walk to Hyattsville, then back by Dr. Dare, over the bridge home near 5 miles. The longest walk I ever took I think.

["Chronological Record of Engagements For The Year 1863. (From The Army and Navy Journal.)"—newspaper clippings. Also account from *New York Times,* Jan. 9, 1863, of death of William Makepeace Thackeray.]

1864.

Jan. 8th. We have gathered our ice. It was about 4 in. thick. I think there will be a little more put in today, which will make the house fuller than it ever was before. Yesterday I returned from a visit to the Whartons'. The day before Dr. Eversfield drove the Wharton girls [Lizzie and Sarah], over to take me my first *sleigh ride!* We upset before we got out of the gate, but were not hurt. We had a break down also just before the Wharton's gate, the runners running off & leaving us comfortably seated in the body of the sleigh. Yesterday I came home in a buggy. We did not have very good sleighing as the snow was too dry & shallow, but last night there fell two inches more, which will make it better. I had a right merry time at the W's. They will leave in a week or so, & intend giving up the house. When they return some time in the spring they intend trying to get board with the people who hire the house.

Jan. 18th. Monday. Last Friday morning uncle Elias Baker came down here with a Mr. Bartholomew, who has rented the place for one or five years. Uncle bought it this morning (the place) for 10,000. *All* agreements made on this subject, Mr. Stephens, Mr. Crawford, & I witnessed. Mother & I will probably leave the place in the spring. I really feel badly about it, for who knows how it may all end? Mother has given up going to Sandusky as the prisoners may soon be moved & the uncertainty too great.

Sat. Jan 23rd. Started for Baltimore on a visit to Mary Latrobe. Will probably be away a week. Was vaccinated yesterday. Am not very well but have no cold. Sick headaches again.

Sat. Feb. 6th. Returned from Baltimore to day after an exactly two weeks visit. I spent all my time with Mary Latrobe. Sally Ingham was there & I liked her very much. I went to two concerts (amateur) at one of which I sang in a chorus. Also to two of Vandenhoff's[70] readings (delightful) & to two parties, one at Mrs. Templeton's, & an other given to Sallie, & I by the family. My visit was delightful. I also heard some most excellent sermons from Drs. Hawks, & Schenck.[71] I had a great many visitors. Among others Mrs. Thomas (the French lady—Zarvona's Mother.) Mary Washington, Jennie Smith, & I dont remember who all. The weather was delightful. I had my black silk made. I had an invitation to a large party at the Riggs[72] in Washington but could not go. I was to stay with them. I saw Judge Merrick's brother Dick, & his bride Miss Maguire[73] (that was.) Dined at Mrs. John Latrobe's. Had my share of *admiration & attention,* & "sang with unbounded applause." Spent $35 somehow *partly on the making of a black silk dress.* My measurements are now: Waist $2^3{}_4$ [meaning 23 or 24 inches?] inches; Weight 166 lbs; Skirt 52 behind/in front 46. Around breast 35. Shoulders 42. Neck 16. Arm hole 15. Wrist 7. Sleeve 18 in front, 24 behind. Length of body: Front 13½; back 16. Shoulder 10 long. This is for dress making.

Feb. 17th. To day is by far the coldest of the year. The thermometer has steadily lowered from 18° this morning to 9° now (near sundown). This is the first day since last Wednesday I have been well enough to write. I had a return of my last summer's sickness, & was confined to the bed & sofa several days. I am not well yet. The prisoners have been moved from Johnsons Island (at least some of them) & we are most anxious to know where they are. Poor Calhoun where is he? We have heard from Shreiveport. *He* [Clemson] is well but broke his left arm some time since during a wagon ride over the country. The vehicle was upset, & he had to

---

[70] George Vandenhoff (b. Feb. 18, 1820), son of an English actor, migrated to America and obtained a reputation in New York as an actor and a teacher of elocution and as a writer of a volume of theatrical anecdotes. He gave three "dramatic entertainments" at the Odd Fellows' Hall on Feb. 1, 2, and 4. *Baltimore Sun,* Jan. 28, 1864. Also see *Dictionary of National Biography,* XX, 99.

[71] Francis L. Hawkes, pastor of Christ Church, and Noah H. Schenck. *Baltimore Sun,* Nov. 12, 1863, Oct. 24, 1864.

[72] The prominent banking family of George W. (age 46) and Janet Riggs (age 42). Riggs' personal and real property was valued at $500,000 in 1860. Floride was a friend of the Riggs daughters: Alice (age 18), Katherine (17), and Cecilia (16). MS. Census 1860, First Ward, D. C.

[73] Dick Merrick married Nannie Maguire of Washington. Floride to Anna Calhoun Clemson, Jan. 26, 1864, Clemson Papers.

ride more than 20 miles before reaching medical aid. Grandma also writes she is well. Mr. Dunscomb has been here. He taught me the new [card] game of Bezique. I'm nearly frozen. Pshaw!

Feb. 24th. Mr. Dunscomb has been here ever since Saturday (today is Wednesday) On the 22nd I tried rifle shooting for the first time. Mr. D's rifle has a tellescope sight & we (Mr. Onderdonk, Edgar McCeney, Mr. D & myself) shot at a mark of 3 inches at 104 yds. Edgar & I were the only ones hit the mark. I did the best shooting. Yesterday we shot without a rest, only leaning on one knees, Mr. D & I, & without the tellescope, at 75 yds. with a 6 inch mark we fired 40 times. Only 14 (7 a peice) went outside of 2 in. out. 10 in the mark, 5 a peice. My shooting was best again. I have walked about 4 miles each day now. Last Sunday Miss Lizzie W[alker] Edith W[iltberger],[74] & myself (nearly) fainted. Lovely weather. Mrs. McCeney sick.

Sat. March 12th. Went into the city to day to stay with the Riggs'. Walked 7 miles in a day. Mr. Dunscomb went into the city too.

Sat. March 19th. Came back from the city sick. I have not been able to read for two months without pain. The Dr. Stone said I was threatened with amarosis[75] & forbids all use of my eyes, on pain of blindness. I have constant fainting fits & nervous chills & spasms. I am not at all strong or well. I had a photo taken. Mr. Dunscomb came back with me. He is very kind, & pleasent. I like him. He took me walking almost every day. The Riggs are a delightful family & I am much pleased with them. They have much company, principally among the foreigners. I saw many of these while there.

March 30th. Nina Burks[76] is staying with me. I dont know for how long. She is not well. I have spent a week in bed ever since

[74] Edith Wiltberger (age 13), most likely the daughter of John B. (age 38) and Mary E. Wiltberger (36) in the family of Charles H. (age 64) and Verlinda M. Wiltberger (59). Beside Edith, there were Emma (15) and three other children (ages 2½ to 12). MS. Census 1860, County of Wash., D. C.

[75] Amaurosis—a darkening, a total loss of vision without discoverable lesion in the eye structure or optic nerve. Steadman's *Medical Dictionary*, p. 55.

[76] Nina Burks (age 17) and Emily Burks (age 38) lived with the neighboring family of Elizabeth Wood in 1860. MS. Census 1860, County of Wash., D. C. Later Nina Burks lived at 710 Lansom St., Philadelphia. Nina Burks to Floride Clemson, Mar. 30, 1863, Clemson Papers.

"Fort Hill"
Clemson, South Carolina

CONGRESS HALL [Sept. 12 1863]

H. H. HATHORN, B. McMICHAEL, PROPRIETORS.   Saratoga Springs, N.Y.

of this. The place itself is quite
a pretty one, but from what I can
hear, there is little of interest in
the vicinity. The surrounding
country is not uncommonly
beautiful, as far as I can see.
There was a hop here last night,
which we looked at, till eleven.
The ladies wear scarcely any hoops.
"small quakers" are all the fashion,
some had none on, others still
wore ordinary ones. The hair is
worn over rats, high in front & hanging far down behind thus:
in loops or curls, with fancy combs.

*Floride wrote this letter to her family from
Saratoga Springs.*

VI

my return, or rather on the sofa, with diorea, which I got last fall travelling.

Sund. April 3rd. Mary Latrobe & Mr. Onderdonck have been here since Friday, & left this morning. We had a merry time. I have been sick again.

April 12th. Nina Burks left today after a little more than a fortnight's visit. She is staying at the Middleton's. I can not use my eyes yet.

April 18th. Mother, & Mr. Dunscomb started this morning for Sandusky to see Calhoun. I am to stay with my friends. I am not very well.

April 26th. Mother & Mr. Dunscomb returned today from their trip to Sandusky having been away a week & a day. They saw Calhoun twice. He looks well & handsome they say. Mother got a pass from Gen. [H. D.] Terry who commands Johnson's Is. without any difficulty & says she was treated with the greatest consideration by him & all his officers that she saw. Calhoun says he has nothing to complain of now & that he is well treated in any way. Mother was detained twice on the road by accidents. They stopped a day at uncle Elias Baker's at Altoona. Calhoun gave her some rings he made & Mr. D. a stick of his cutting. I spent my time between Mrs. Calvert & Lizzie Robinson. Had my teeth fixed (three). My eyes are better, but I am still unable to read.

May 9th. Mr. Dunscomb left us today, after a visit of over two months. He was very kind & pleasent & took me walking &c. a great deal. I miss him a good deal. Lizzie Robinson has been staying with us. We are making every preparation to leave this place for Beltsville by the end of this month. It nearly breaks my heart for I do not want to go *away* or *there* either. The house begins already to look denuded. It is very hard! The place looks so lovely, all the lilacs in full bloom, for the weather has been exceedingly hot during the past few days. I am pretty well again, & eyes much better.

May 15th. Mr. Charles B. Calvert of Riversdale near here, died yesterday at about four o'clock, from a stroke of paralysis which took him Tuesday last. He never either spoke or rallied, & seemed unconcious. This neighborhood is completely broken up. Mr. John

C. Reives[77] having died less than a month ago. We have all been in a state of anxiety, & excitement for the past week about the movements of the armies. There has been more terrible fighting in the Wilderness near the old Chancellorsville, & Fredrickburg battle fields. Thank God so far we seem to be successful, may we remain so! Banks[78] expedition towards Shreveport La. has proved a complete failiure, & he is reported to have capitulated. The ram Albamarle[79] of N. C. has been fighting successfully. Charleston has been released from its unsuccessful seige. Everything looks bright & cheering. Uncle Elias Baker left this morning after a visit of two or three days. The dear old gentleman does not look well. Summer is nearly full.

May 17th. Leave home to day for Mrs. Middleton's.

May 21st. Leave Mrs. Middletons for Lizzie Robinsons. Had a very pleasent visit. Got bording for Mr. Seymour at the Magruders' near there. We had a serenade from the soldiers of the forts, which was beautiful. Went to Mrs. Hickeys' funeral. She died, the day Mr. Calvert was burried, of paralysis after 2 days illness.

[77] A former partner of Francis Preston Blair on *The Globe,* John C. Rives was once a member of President Jackson's "kitchen cabinet." In 1860 the property of Rives (age 62) was valued at $340,000. MS. Census 1860, Prince Georges County, Md.; *Washington: City and Capital,* p. 824.

[78] Gen. Nathaniel P. Banks (Jan. 30, 1816-Sept. 1, 1894), defeated by Confederate forces on April 9, was forced to give up his attack on Shreveport. *DAB,* I, 577-80.

[79] The ram "Albemarle," built in North Carolina, began operations in May, despite desperate Union attempts to destroy it. Finally, on Oct. 27 the U. S. Navy torpedoed and sank it. Edgar S. Maclay, *A History of the United States Navy from 1775 to 1901* (2 vols., New York: D. Appleton & Co., 1893-98), II, 475-90.

II

Beltsville, Maryland

1864

May 26th. Went home again & stayed till Tuesday, May 31st. When I went back to Lizzie's. During this visit home saw many of our friends, & was almost broken hearted at seeing all the furniture &c. go to be stored & sold. Oh dear! Returned home again Friday, June 3rd & stayed till Tuesday June 7th, when I went back to Lizzie Robinsons' & stayed till Tuesday, June 14th. When we all drove up to our new place near Betsville. Lizzie R., Jennie King, & myself in a buggy. Mr. & Mrs. King, Mrs. Robinson & a driver in the carriage. Mother joined us & we all spent the day at Mrs. Sander's about half a mile off. Mr. Seymour rode as far as Hyattsville with us. (I forgot to say mother moved here June 7th, Tuesday with all our goods & chattels, & the same day, Mr. Ed. Towers[1] took possession of The Home on consideration of $40 a month for the house & lot. Our horses sold for $68 a peice, only).

June [1]9th. This house has but four rooms & a kitchen, low ceilings but of a good size, very common. The place is very pretty surrounded by trees, & a wood close by. One very fine oak tree before the door makes an out door parlour, where we have chairs & a hammock. We are about a mile from Beltsville & nearly a half one from Mrs. Sanders. Mr. Ed. Herbert lives about the same distance off; all are very kind. I took a ride with Dr. Eversfield yesterday, & Henry McCeney has been here sleeping on the sofa ever since we came. Miss Curley Mrs. [J. C.] Fairfax sister is staying there [at the Fairfaxes'].

June 30th. Thursday. A week ago last Saturday I went with Mr. Onderdonk to the college to hear a Mr. Taverner read, & liked

---

[1] Edward Towers (age 47), warehouseman whose property was valued at $13,000 in 1860. MS. Census 1860, Fifth Ward, D. C.

him better than Vandenhoff whom I heard last winter in Baltimore. He read several of the Ingoldsby Legends, & Poe's "Bells," &c. most beautifully. It was a lovely moon light cool night, & I enjoyed it amazingly. Last Tuesday week we spent at Mrs. Contee's,[2] Mrs. Sanders' sister, & met the two Miss Jenkens. The eldest Lizzie is very handsome & seems lovely; the other is a regular romp. Mrs. Herbert took me, & Mrs. Sanders mother. I spent the evening before with Mrs. Herbert whom I like very much. To day week I went to Mrs. John's at the college, & the same evening heard Dr. Johns[3] deliver a lecture on "Literary Culture["] or something of the sort, awfully dull, & long, especialy as the evening was very hot. Next day Friday was the commencement, which I enjoyed wonderfully. S. D. Hall, W. T. P. Turpin, & C. M. Newman graduated. There were nine original speaches. The best were; Wm. Goldsborough's poetical *dream* on the Development of the Present; Dick Goldsborough on the Sighning of the Magna Carter; L. Roberts on The Farmer; & best of all Richard Owens on the Heroes of the World, or *Liberty* as he made it. I should think this latter would make his mark in the world. After the exercises the band serenaded *me,* and I payed a visit to Sarah Wharton who now boards at her old house. Next day Mr. Onderdonk drove me to see Lizzie Robinson, & the Woods[4] who have just returned from Paris, & were staying with the Middletons. They seemed delighted to see me, & I was to meet them again. They are much prettier and pleasenter than they were. Gertrude [Wood] is nearly & tall as I am & much larger, but not as pretty as I thought she would be. They had a delightful time in Paris, London, & the world in general, & come home determined to sell their place & return. They left Jefferson [Wood] in England. I returned with Dr. Eversfield Sunday, after a very hot, & pleasent visit, except that Mrs. & Dr. Johns raised a report that I was engaged to Mr. Onderdonk which was *not* pleasant. Dr. Eversfield

[2] Probably Mrs. Ann L. Contee (age 60). Her property was valued at $65,000, and her family included Charles (age 28) and Elizabeth Contee (19). MS. Census 1860, Prince Georges County, Md.

[3] Montgomery Johns, A.M., M.D., Professor of the Science of Agriculture, Chemistry, Geology and Mineralogy. *Circular of the Maryland Agricultural College* (1863-1866). (Baltimore: John Murphy & Co., 1863-65).

[4] The family of Elizabeth D. Wood (age 42), a farmer whose property was valued at $70,000 in 1860, had the following children: Emily (age 18), Virginia (16), Gertrude (12), and Jefferson (10).

took me a nice long ride last evening & an other last week. Mr. Seymour was here the day before yesterday & Mr. Onderdonk *constantly*. I go up to see Mrs. Fairfax every day almost, & hear her sister read. I can not read yet. The day before yesterday Mr. Onderdonk took me to the city where we met Mr. Glover who showed, & explained us over the Patent Office, & Smithsonian. He is so well informed on most sientific subjects. I saw the librarian of the Smithsonian, Dr. Gill,[5] who explained me somethings most learnedly & unintelligibly. What I was most interested in was a fine collection of paintings &c. from Pompiien frescoes. I have just received a letter from Miss [Harriet] Lane saying she is not going to sea shore where I wished to accompany her, so I expect to go with Mrs. Herbert. We have heard from Grandma, & father; both well.

July 10th. I have at last found a party bound to the sea shore. Mr. & Mrs. Herbert, Mr. Onderdonk, myself & perhaps some others, will start for Squam Beach,[6] N. J. on the 18th probably, for a two weeks tour. I am making my bathing dress which I got in Baltimore last week, of dark blue flannel trimmed with solfarino [fuchsia colored] braid. Miss Lane wrote me she did not intend to go to the sea shore this year, but wants me to join her at Bedford, but my eyes are no better & I must try what promises to do them most good. We have had some letters from Jefferson Co. Va. All are well, & cousin Annie W.[7] has gone to Claymont Del. to spend the summer with her father. The Confederates are again in Maryland, in Hagerstown & near Frederick, but no one seems to have any idea of their numbers. I wish JEB Stuart was still alive, to head this raid, if raid it is, though some seem to think there are not far from 40,000. Grant is not even spoken of in the papers with his grand "on to Richmond.["] I suppose he is stuck in a swamp down there. Gold is about 275 per cent, & every thing in proportion. We have constant company here, & are having a very pleasent time. Indeed I sometimes think I am too happy, I have so much to be thankful for. I get plenty of rides on *mule* & horse back, & have so many

[5] Theodore Nicholas Gill (Mar. 21, 1837-Sept. 25, 1914), zoologist, lawyer, and "master of taxonomy," who became a member of the Smithsonian staff in 1861. *DAB*, VII, 285-86.

[6] The northern part of Island Beach was formerly called Squan Beach.

[7] Anna, daughter of the Rev. John Baker Clemson, married her first cousin George L. Washington. F. W. Brown to T. G. Clemson, Aug. 8, 1885, Clemson Papers.

kind friends. It has always been so with me, I am so fortunate; every one is kind to me, & all turns out for the best. Then I enjoy *everything* so much. Singing & riding, my two passions however, & almost everyone seems to like my voice. I am most of the choir at the Beltsville church. If I could only read. The Allabama[8] was sunk by the Kersage lately near Cherbourg.

July 12th. We are in a tremendous excitement about here now.[9] One army of Confederates within sight of Baltimore & only 3 miles from the Relay House on his road, the other knocking at the gates of Washington. We heard the fiering of musketry & cannonading all day yesterday & the rumor is that the fighting is at Ft. Slocum. They have taken Ft. Massachusetts, burnt Blair's & Bradford's places, & got possession of the Chain Bridge. Lincoln they say, has gotten possession of his Scotch cap, & departed. The cars still run, but we expect them to stop daily, or rather secondly. Five bridges were burnt between Baltimore & Pila. The Gunpowder & others.[10] The last news last night was that the *Rebels* were 2½ miles from the Capitol. I saw the smoke from the battle field last evening during a ride I took to the college with Dr. Eversfield. I suppose this puts an end to our sea shore excursion at least for the present. We seem to have left *home* [Bladensburg] in time.

1 o'clock. The Confederates over a thousand strong are at Beltsville not a mile from here. There has been some fiering there & just now 4 yankee soldiers ran through the place & told us the news. Running away!

7 o'clock. We spent all day at the Sanders, where there were hundreds of Cavalry. Gen. Bradly Johnson[11] was there & I had a

[8] The U. S. S. "Kearsarge" sank the famous Confederate raider "Alabama" on June 19, 1864.

[9] At this point Floride pasted in her diary: "*Deo Vindico* (Confederate motto)." She became an eye witness to Confederate General Jubal A. Early's raid to the outskirts of Washington.

[10] The residence of Francis Preston Blair, Sr., and the county residence of Maryland Governor Andrew W. Bradford were burned. The "Chain Bridge" was over the Potomac. The five bridges reported destroyed were over smaller streams. *Baltimore Sun*, July 12, 1864.

[11] Brig. Gen. Bradley T. Johnson, a Maryland lawyer who joined the Confederates and became a brigade commander for Early. Douglas Southall Freeman, *Lee's Lieutenants, A Study in Command* (3 vols., New York: Charles Scribner's Sons, 1942-1944), III, 548-49.

long talk with him, also Capt. Emack[12] & many others. Heard from some freinds. They are very strong, well clothed & expect to sweep the state. Still before W. & all around. The rail road has been cut & burnt. They were *so* handsome, so noble looking, Oh!

July 14th. Yesterday morning the Confederates left this part of the country, & directed their steps toward the Soldiers' Home near which the infantry under Gen. Early are said to be encamped. There are so many hundred reports that one has no idea what to believe. By some this is said to be a mere raiding party, by others an organized movement to take Wash. Some say the Soldiers Home is burnt, others say not. Ft. Totten *is* and is *not* taken. Blair's house *is* & is *not* burnt. All is uncertain. Here we are nearly on the battle field & know nothing. The troops here, under Bradly Johnson, numbered 1600 cavalry, with near 200 prisoners. They said they has destroyed this rail road, perhaps they did, but the cars commenced running by here yesterday evening & still do, perhaps not far. Some 3,000 Union troops are near Laurel they say (?), The [Confederate] cavalry was mounted on Maryland horses, taken since their arrival but they complain of their inefficiency, being too fat. Bradly Johnson passed by the college yesterday, & mounted the next hill from where he saw 400 Yankees drawn up near Hyattsville, the same that one company of Confed's routed the day before. He threw one, or two shells toward them, & they scattered—skedaddled! They [Confederates] took about one hundred mules near here, but I believe let them go as they could not be driven. They burnt some stationary working cars near here & took all they wanted from the Beltsville store,[13] but commited no wanton destruction. They say they only burnt Gov. Bradford's house in retaliation for Gov. Letcher's in Va.[14] burnt wantonly by Yankees.

[12] Captain George (?) Emack (age 17), whose father, A. G. Emack (age 56) was a Beltsville farmer. MS. Census 1860, Prince Georges County, Md. *Baltimore Sun,* July 16, 1864, carried a brief account of a Union soldier's dying in the Emack home during the battle.

[13] *Baltimore Sun,* July 16, 1864, reported the Confederates, by order of Gen. Johnson, entered the Beltsville store of John Simms and took about $2,000 worth of goods, and compelled private citizens to give them money, whiskey, oats, nearly all the horses in the neighborhood, and about 200 to 300 mules.

[14] On June 12, 1864, U. S. General David Hunter burned the Lexington home of ex-Governor John Letcher of Virginia for "inciting the population of the country to rise and wage a guerrilla warfare" on Federal troops. *WROR* (Series I), XXXVII, Part I, p. 97.

July 23rd. The Confederates have all gotten safe over the river, & the force appears to have been ridiculously small, not 10,000. They seemed to have committed no acts of wanton violence, & took nothing they did not need. There is some account of a fight with them at Sni[c]ker's Gap, but nothing certain. Bradly Johnson during a skirmish near Rockville Md. was captured by the Yankees, but recaptured by his men. Young McKnew[15] from near here was separated from his regiment & met over 50 Yankee cavalry alone. He charged into them screaming "Come on boys," to no one & fiering his pistols & routed them all. He afterwards turned back, & the Yankee's rallied & pursued. He however escaped by lying along his horses' side, & though hundreds of shots were fired at him, escaped unharmed. This was told me by some eyewitnesses. Mr. Onderdonk has left, on account of having been arrested & fear of further trouble, to get lodgings for our party at the sea side, where we expect to go August 1st now. Mr. Dunscomb who writes constantly, talks of joining us—*me.* We are in the midst of a frightful drought. We have had no rain since we have been here, save three showers, which did not wet the ground more than half an inch collectively. The weather is alternately *very* hot, & *very* cold. They say no crops will be made. Mr. Seymour comes every holliday here, & Dr. Eversfield rides constantly with me. Mr. Onderdonks pet horse Sally was taken by the Unioners lately.

July 25th. It is *raining* for the first time since we came here June 1st but I fear it is too late to save some of the crops. Such a drought!

July 31st. The Confederates have gotten back in to Maryland, much stronger than they were they say. They whipped the Yankees near Winchester & drove them back to Harper's Ferry. Now quite a large body has penetrated Penn. & burnt part if not the whole of Chambersburg. I am sorry for those made homeless by this, but so much worse has been done at the South that retaliation is necessary. 500 factory girls from Georgia have been taken to the North,[16]

[15] "Captain Morris McKnew, who formerly resided in that vicinity [Beltsville] is known to have been among the rebel visitors there on Tuesday." *Baltimore Sun,* July 14, 1864.

[16] When Gen. W. T. Sherman's cavalry captured the cotton-mill town of Roswell, Georgia, several hundred female operatives were loaded aboard wagons and sent to Marietta (Ga.) "to be sent north of the Ohio [via rail?] and set at liberty." *Baltimore Sun,* July 23, 1864. What eventually became of the girls is still a mystery.

then sent out of the boundaries of the United States, to starve, I suppose. Gen. [David] Hunter has issued an order that such people as are *suspected* of being Southern in Fredrick Md. shall be arrested, confiscated, banished (the women & children) to the South, & the men sent to prison. Some ladies I know of have been sent to Mass. to work in the prisons for corresponding with their friends South! Our trip to the sea shore is again postponed on account of the Confederates. It is now our intention (will it ever be more?) to go to Long Beach [N.J.] Wednesday instead of tomorrow, if the Southerners retreat; & matters look less threatening. I am making some beautiful night gowns, tucked yokes.

Aug. 1st. I am busy making preparations to start Wednesday if nothing happens, for the sea shore. They say this morning that Grant has mined & blown up some of the fortifications before Petersburg.[17]

Aug. 3rd. We left for Long Beach to day, but only got as far as Philadelphia, where we intend spending the night. I went out to aunt [Catharine Clemson] No[r]th's but found every one away except George, w[h]o had gotten home for a day or two on leave. I bid good bye to Tom Franklin[18] on the cars, he was on his way to South America. (Reached L. B. next day)

Aug 18th Philadel. I returned from Long Beach yesterday. It was no place for ladies, being a sporting resort for gentlemen where they appear at meals, & all times in their flanel over shirt sleeves. The hotel we said [stayed] at was almost the only house on the Island which is 20 miles long & very narrow, not more than ¾ of a mile near the house, sandy & without one tree on it. It is devided from the main shore of N. J. by Egg Harbor bay [Little Egg Harbor] which is delightful to sail on & very safe. It is reached by a sail boat from Atlantic City, a distance of of about 20 miles. We had a nice sail last Thursday week going, nearly all being sea sick, except myself, but coming home, the tide was low in the bay passage & too rough out side so we had to stop half way & stage 10 miles to Absecom, & never got to Phila, over the dreadfully N. J. railroad, till nine o'clock. There is hardly a full grown tree all the way, no

[17] Followed by the bloody "Battle of the Crater," July 30.

[18] An acquaintance Floride met while visiting the Latrobes in Baltimore. He escorted her to several social functions there. Floride to Anna Calhoun Clemson, Jan. 26, 1864, Clemson Papers.

fields, nothing but scrub oak, on a flat country, sand, & a few shanties. Half bur[n]t by car cinders! Mr. Seymour, Dr. Eversfield & Mr. Onderdonk joined me at Long Beach. After I left, Mr. Dunscomb, & Mr. Lee also started to go there. I learned to float like a cork, better than any man or woman there, & could swim, but not make much head way in the breakers which are very strong there, though the bathing is considered the best on the coast. We went out fishing six times but caught very little. Sheapshead, black, wheat, king, & dog, were all that are found there pretty much, I had average luck. We went sailing in the bay often, it was spended [splendid], especially moon light nights. The weather was hot. I met Mrs. O'Brian, her husband, his brother, his sister Mrs. Talliaferro, Mrs. Slack, but very few other ladies. My room was scarce more than six feet by 7, & right over the bar, so that I heard all the rowdy goings on, & singing. I played ten pins, & billiards with moderate success. The gentlemen were only there during the last half of the time & left when I did. I had a falling out with Mr. Onderdonk, & dont think I enjoyed having three men to entertain a bit, but was kept in constant hot water. We had nothing but fish to eat, & I had diarrhoea all the time, & felt very weak, but my eyes got well while there. Mr. and Mrs. Herbert were very kind, & I had not much to do with the doleful Mrs. Stephen. I part here with all the party except Dr. Eversfield who stays till Tuesday next. All that are at home here are aunt & uncle North, Walter, Clarence, & Herbert.

Sep. 7th. Reached Lancaster this morning where I was met with open arms by Miss Lane, also very cordially by Mr. Buchanan. I came up in the cars most of the way with uncle Baker Clemson, & lost a common shawl. I spent three weeks in Philadel. with aunt North who was very kind to me. Kate Barton, Mary & Sally Clemson[19] spent most of the time with me. All got home after I got there save George, who is aid to Averil [?] & Clem who is in partnership with cousin Fisher Hazzard[20] at Mauck Chunck [Mauch Chunk]. Bessie [North] is fifteen now, but very childish & stupid &

[19] Kate, daughter of Elizabeth Clemson Barton; Mary and Sally, daughters of the Rev. John Baker Clemson.

[20] Lizzie, daughter of the Rev. John Baker Clemson, married Fisher Hazzard of Mauch Chunk, Pa. T. C. North to T. G. Clemson, Oct. 29, 1883, Clemson Papers.

not pretty. Willie [North] is a handsome fellow nearly as old as I am, & full of genious & enthusiasm for music. He plays delightfully on the organ, & has a very fine parlor organ at home. Walter [North] is eighteen, homely, & quiet, but I like him best of any. He is tall, & very kind & good. He is to study for the ministry. I gave him singing lessons, & found he had a nice voice with much ear for music as they all had. Clarence [North] is very small for twelve. Herbert [North] nearly as tall as he is & eight. They are a lovely family, & live most harmoniously together. I learned to play four handed chess while there, & enjoyed it mightily. I spent one day, the Monday week after I got there, at Claymont [Del.]. I saw Mary & Mattie, aunt Pheby [Clemson],[21] uncle Baker [Clemson], Sally, & Kate Barton, Tom Clemson, aunt & uncle Elias Baker, & the Browns of Claymont. Mary stayed with me in West Phila a few days, & looks just as she did. Sally, Kate, Mary & I, had ourselves ferrotyped (a new art) in a group to commemorate my visit. Uncle Elias Baker is much broken, & looks badly. I am so sorry. I went to consult Dr. Hays[22] the most eminent occulist in Phila. about my eyes. He says they are severely strained, & I must continue not to use them for nearly a year certainly, & perhaps more. I will not go blind but may never be able to use them again if I read or strain them again. My nervous system was put so much out of order by my illness (diarrhoea) last fall, & winter, that it has attacked my eyes. I am pretty fat for all, & look pretty well now however. I payed Dr. H. $20 for four visits. He gave me an irritant linament of red pepper &c for my forhead, iron pills, & a preparation of syrup of iron, & ordered bathing my eyes in salt water. I also use London smoke glasses in a bright light. My eyes got much better at the sea shore, but pained me as much as ever after I left. Aunt North seemed very fond of me, & Kate, & Sallie nearly eat me up with love, & petting. Sallie looks & is very delicate now, she has lost most of her beauty. She is two months younger than Kate who is two years & a half older than me. Mary is two months older than I am. Kate looks very well. Aunt Pheby is getting more weak, & sickly

[21] Pheby, third (?) wife of the Rev. John Baker Clemson.

[22] Isaac Hays (July 5, 1796-April 13, 1879), M.D. from University of Pennsylvania, an outstanding medical editor, a pioneer in ophthalmology, and a surgeon at Wills Eye Hospital. He was one of the first doctors to detect astigmatism and to study color blindness. *DAB*, VIII, 462-63.

than she was. Uncle Baker looks very well. Mattie is the same old 76 she was though improved. I went out to Fairmount park, a new thing since I went to school, also visited the State house, Mint, & Philadelphia library where I saw very many interesting books. I went over the Academy of fine arts also. They are building the Chesnut St. Bridge over the Schuykill now.

Sep. 23rd. I left Lancaster the day before yesterday after a very pleasent visit of just two weeks. It is strange all my *starts* during this trip were made on Wednesdays. Aug 3rd (Wednesday) left home for Long Beach, stayed nearly two weeks & left for Phila Wednesday 17th. Stayed there three weeks, & left for Lancaster Wednesday Sep 7th. Left there for home Wednesday, Sep 21st. I was away in all, just 7 weeks, during which I managed to spend $160. The mere travelling, & boarding at the sea shore expenses, were some $70. Dr. Hays & medicines took $25 more, & the rest went, dear knows how, I dont. At Lancaster I had a most delightful visit with Miss Lane. We passed our time very quietly for there is very little company there. I suppose I scarce saw twenty persons in all. The family of a Dutch reform minister, Mr. Nevin, was the only one I saw at all on a sociable footing, or often. I went to see old aunt Kitty [Baker] Ickleburger. She has been very ill, & looks much older than when I saw her last, & more decrepid. She says she does not expect to live much longer as she is already 82, the age at which her two sisters (grandma & Mrs. Free) died. It seems probable. She is much softened by age, & was most affectionate to me. They say she is fond of me. I also saw Miss Hetty Barton; Kate's aunt, & her uncle Graff Barton. None of the Russells were at home except Louise, & Mrs. R. towards the last. Kate R. is engaged. She & Margery were away at Detroit Migan, with an uncle. Mr. Buchanan's horses were lame so we did not have many rides. One to Liti[t]z the day before I left was most pleasent. This is a Moravian settlement some ten miles from Lancaster, noted for its fine spring of pure water, which flows from under a rock, in sufficient quantity almost to turn a mill. It is near the mountains, & is said to have very fine pure air also. I went to the two schools, which are quite celebrated, one for boys, & one for girls. I also visited the church, & grave yard attached to it. This latter is laid out in stiff rows of square mounds in which the dead are lain, not in families but in the order in which they die, the men on one side, & the women on the other. The place is small,

& there is but one hotel, quite a large one, which has been lately built, as none were allowed during the stricter days of the sect. Miss Lane is now about thirty two or three I suppose & still very handsome, large, but not too much so for a fine figure. She looks much younger than she is. I love her very dearly, & she seems equally attached to me. We have always corresponded since she left the White House, where I stayed with her some time once. We spent the mornings in taking long walks, generally to Lancaster for the mail; the afternoons with a pleasent game of croquet which I saw here for the first time; & the evenings in reading aloud, & talking, with an occasional game of Bezique. Mr. Buchanan had a fall from walking out after night while I was there, which laid him up for a week or more. He was otherwise quite hail & robust for so old a man. He was also very kind to me, & kissed me good bye, with which I could have dispensed, when I left. He is a crooked old fellow however, & seems little grateful for the sacrifices Miss Lane makes for him. She is very devoted to him. He is writing a history of the times, & a kind of a biography of himself I believe, so we rarely saw him even when he was well, except at meals, & for an hour or so in the evening. There is a crabed old housekeeper there, Miss Hetty Parker, who has been with Mr. B. for near 30 years, & is as cranky to Miss Lane as possible. I called Miss Lane "Lady Constance", a name which she has adopted in our intercourse. I think it suits her. Mr. B. calls her *Miss Lane*!! I came home all by myself through a mistake. Mother wrote me to meet Dr. Eversfield in Harrisburg last Wednesday in time for the one o'clock train for Baltimore. Miss Lane had offered to take me home herself but I liked this better than troubling her. I left Lancaster in the eleven o'clock train which ordinarily joins that one, but was unfortunately an hour late, so Dr. E. had started before me. I could not leave before next morning so I waited comfortably at the house of Mrs. Dougherty, Carrie Hickey that was, whom I fortunately thought of, in my delima. She took me a lovely drive along the banks of the Susquehanna towards sun set, & next morning at 7 o'clock I left for Baltimore, which I reached a twelve o'clock. I spent the intervening time until half past three with the Ben Latrobes, & got home salfely. Finding a neighbor's carriage at the depôt I rode home & surprised mother. There was a lar[g]e Democratic McClellan meeting in Lancaster while I was there which we attended, & Valandingham[23] was expected to speak but did not arrive. The procession was quite amusing with its mottos &c. We dined at a Mr. Shank's [?] that day. [The following unidentified news clipping appeared at this point.]

Espionage of the Express on Ex-President Buchanan.

The Express of last evening informs its readers that a "distinguished visitor, Miss CLEMSON, the grand-daughter of the late JOHN C. CALHOUN, of South Carolina, is at present a guest of Ex-President BUCHANAN, at Wheatland.

This young lady is not at Wheatland. With her mother, the daughter of the long since deceased Mr. CALHOUN, she has been living in seclusion in the vicinity of Washington ever since the commencement of our national troubles, both universally respected. Being now on a visit to her relatives in this State—most of whom, we may observe, are strong Republicans—she expects on her return home to visit Wheatland, where she will be a most welcome guest.

This young lady's name has thus been brought before the public in a political newspaper, for the first time in her life, without regard to her feelings, for the malignant purpose of injuring Mr. BUCHANAN—and this, although the record of the country, as well as every act of his life, proves that he has ever been the active and consistent opponent of nullification and secession, in opposition to the views of her justly and highly distinguished grandfather.

The Express is too much in the habit of reproachfully introducing the names of ladies into its columns. This it has done on a recent occasion without a shadow of truth. In this practice it stands alone among respectable journals of both parties. We warn it that the manly and gallant spirit of our people will not suffer it to pursue this course with impunity.

Octo. 5th. Mr. D. W. Lee has been here ever since last Friday. Mother wrote for him to come on business, that is to settle matters before she left. He is in one of his pleasent moods, & looks better. He sleeps down at Bells, a farm house only a few hundred yards from here. Mother wants me to stay behind when she goes South, & I suppose I will have to if she insists but I dont see sufficient cause. More of this hereafter. I have seen most of my friends, since my return, & have been very busy sewing for mother, & myself. I

[23] Clement L. Vallandigham (July 29, 1820-June 17, 1871), famous "Copperhead" and ex-Senator from Ohio. He had attended the Democratic convention which nominated General George B. McClellan for president in 1864. *Biog. Dir. Cong.*, p. 1946.

am very well just now, though I had the diarrhoea all the time I was away. My eyes are better also.

Octo 9th. Sunday Poor Lizzie Walker died last Wednesday, & I attended her funeral on Friday. She had a long illness of Typhoid fever, & was given up some time before her death. I went with Mrs. Sanders. She was buried at Rock Creek. How much we shall miss her at church! She was the organist, & one of the most active members of the congregation. Every one seemed fond of her, & the attendence at the funeral was very large. We hear very distressing accounts from Va. Aunt Louisa[24] writes that she does not know from one day to an other where the food is to come from, as everything is taken, even the cattle. She reclaimed her cows the other day, & drove them home herself. Cousin Christine has gone farther into the interior of the state to Augustine Washington's place. The cloths even of cousin Lucy's children were torn up or stolen. It is too too bad.

Octo. 16 Sunday Mrs. Keich died last Thursday, & was burried yesterday. Her husband died this year also. The Robinson's & Kings spent last Thursday here, & left Lizzie R. at the Sander's to spend some days. She is as lovely as ever, & I see her constantly of course. Mrs. Stark of this neighborhood also died last week. The mortality has been fearful this year. Mother speaks of letting me go South with her now, so I am very busy. Dr. Eversfield took me to ride last Tuesday, to the Bur[n]t Mills, & coming home, very unexpectedly offered himself to me. I am so sorry, for I like him.

Nov. 9th. Yesterday was the election for President; in a day or two we shall know what the fate of the nation is to be. Aunt Louisa Washington arrived here last Wednesday evening. She came down from Jefferson, to see if she could do anything towards the release of Cousin Christine's son Johny who was captured near his home on the charge that he was one of Mosby's[25] riders! Poor deformed boy, he is only 16 years old. Aunt Louisa looks very well, but gives a most deplorable account of the state of things in the valley of Va.

[24] Louisa Clemson, sister of Thomas G. Clemson, married Samuel Washington, of Virginia. Christine and Lucy are undoubtedly two of her three daughters. Holmes and Sherrill, *Thomas Green Clemson*, p. 3; Forrest W(ashington) Brown to T. G. Clemson, Aug. 8, Sept. 29, 1885, Clemson Papers.

[25] John Singleton Mosby (Dec. 6, 1833-May 30, 1916), famous Confederate ranger. *DAB*, XIII, 272-73.

Among other shifts they have to make is that of knitting stockings
of the ravelings of old tents. The dear old lady will probably stay
with us until she can do something for Johny, though she has met
with nothing but disappointment yet, & can not even send anything
to the boy. Yesterday week I went to Baltimore to shop, & spent
over a hundred dollars in a very short time, not getting what in old
times would have been considered one third of the worth of my
money. I got a grey mid-season cloak, a brown merino dress, & a
bright plaid for every day besides other things. Mr. Lee is still here
& pleasant. Mr. Onderdonk has taken a place near Baltimore for a
school on his own hook. Mr. Dunscomb is to come tomorrow. Dr.
Eversfield left for California on the 22nd of last month, in the
steamer North Star. Poor fellow, he wrote such a nice letter to
mother, bidding us good bye. The Robinson's are in trouble. Mr. R
was arrested on the charge of making signal lights,—all nonsense,—
but they threaten the whole family with banishment South. I am
very well now, but have been quite ailing again.

Nov 10th Mr. Dunscomb came.

Nov 23rd. I have just returned from a six days' visit to the
Woods, in the old neighborhood, I went down to attend a confirmation held by Bishop Southgate at Rock Creek Church. I was confirmed yesterday (Tuesday) morning with 17 others, among whom
were Jennie Wood, Jennie King, Emma, & Edith Wiltberger, &
Mary Ross. Bishop Southgate has been a missionary bishop to Con-
stantinople, & has a church in N. Y. now. He has no diosese. He is
a short, fine looking man, of about fifty, & delivered a very good
address. I pray I may prove a consistant christian. I have been a
pretty regular communicant every since my baptism over a year
ago, & have always intended being confirmed on the first opportunity. The poor Robinsons have met with an other severe affliction.
Cary their second son was killed about the 13th of this month while
carrying the colors at the head of Mahon's[26] Brigade. It was just
a year & 13 days after poor Willie's death. They were such fine
boys. The Robinsons expect they may be sent South any time now.
Mary Latrobe spent a few days here about one week ago. We slept
in a most crowded way for dear aunt Louisa was here at the same
time. Johny is released. She [Mary] carried on a great flirtation with

[26] William Mahone (Dec. 1, 1826-Oct. 8, 1895), Confederate major general
from Virginia and hero of the "Battle of the Crater." *DAB*, XII, 211-12.

"Mi Casa"
Pendleton, South Carolina

St. Paul's Episcopal Church
Pendleton, South Carolina

Messers Lee, Dunscomb, & Onderdonk, who were all here. The
Woods made a great deal of me during my visit there, & showed me
all the things they got abroad. I do wish I could have such a trip
as they had, all over Italy, France, England &c. I am just recovering from the first cold I have had since a year. I got well of my
cough during my trip to Niagara &c. & have had no returns of it
since, though I do not seem to be otherwise stronger. The Robinsons have sold their place, & will leave any how in the Spring for
England or Canada if they are not sent South. Jennie Middleton
expects to be married soon to a Federal surgeon. Mother is still
trying to get a pass but with no success as none are granted now.
It is horrid staying in this little hole on an uncertainty waiting for
events. Calhoun writes he is very well poor fellow.

Nov. 29th Yesterday one of Mr. Creighton Lee's clerks came
after Mr. D. W. L. [his brother] here. He brought me a letter
from Laura [Leupp] saying she "wishes me to use my influence to
send him home as it is necessary he should be there." He is getting
disagreeable again though heretofor he has been unusually pleasent.
He & Mr. Dunscomb are here from before breakfast till bed time,
which is rather too much of a bad thing, as they do not like each
other. I feel quite certain all I do or say is misunderstood, & I am
always afraid some fuss may arise between them. Then it is so very
hard to be equally pleasant to both! The constant worry makes me
almost sick. The neighbors dont understand the case, & think I am
a great flirt because there are so many gentlemen about, & dear
knows there is nothing I try harder to avoid, or have less temptation for. I do get so tired of men, that I almost hate them sometimes, though one at a time, or even more for an evening is pleasent.
I do wish we could get a pass a get away! After all however it is
rather flattering to one's vanity to be admired. Mr. Seymour still
spends his holiday Sundays here (once a fortnight.) Mr. White, a
man man we have had a year, left us yesterday. He was really a
very worthy man, & just suited us except that he would sometimes
get on sprees. I scarce know how the war is getting on. Atlanta Ga.
is burnt by Gen Sherman, who is marching dear knows where;
Hood is working up into Tenessee; Grant & Lee face each other
with occasional spurts or skirmises, or battles before Richmond, &

Petersberg. Price[27] is driven away out west. There is a great fuss made about the taking of the Florida.[28] There was an unsuccessful attempt to burn down N. Y. by setting fire to the hotels, &c.

Dec. 7th. This morning we received a Tellegraph from cousin Sylvester [Baker] telling us of the death of dear old uncle Elias Baker. He died the day before yesterday. We have lost a kind friend in this good old man, whom we loved very dearly. He has been failing quite a long time, but was better when we last heard of him, so that we had no idea the end was so near. I have just made myself a set of night gowns & chimeses, both the prettiest I ever had. I have also just gotten 6 pair of shoes from Phila. This winter I only bought two dresses, a brown merino trimed with black velvet which came to near $40! & a bright plaid for every day.

Dec 11th Sunday We have just received our pass today. Mr. Taswell Taylor[29] was in Norfolk last week, & happened to be at Gen. Shepley's[30] office (the military governer of that city) when two ladies were about being sent South, asked if we might not go. Gen. S. said that as mother was the intimate friend of his dearly loved cousin Mrs. Barstow, he would send her if she came there, & gave us a pass to that city, to prevent our taking the oath. We will get ready as soon as possible. Generals [Benjamin F.] Butler & Grant, Stanton, & Lincoln all have refused us passes when applied to by our friends. I will send my pet setter Leo, to Miss Lane. Mrs. Daub can not go with us on account of her old mother. Andy,[31] who is of course free with all Md. negroes, will go to Dr. Cooks'[32] near here.

[27] Confederate General Sterling Price (Sept. 20, 1809-Sept. 29, 1867). *DAB,* XV, 216-17.

[28] The "Florida," built in Liverpool, was captured in the harbor of Bahia, Brazil, by U. S. sloop of war "Wachusett," Oct. 7, 1864. *Baltimore Sun,* Nov. 10, 1864.

[29] Tazewell Taylor was a business friend of Thomas G. Clemson.

[30] George Foster Shepley (Jan. 1, 1819-July 20, 1878), brigadier general assigned to the command of the District of Eastern Virginia in May, 1864. *DAB,* XVII, 78-79. General Benjamin F. Butler had been in charge of the district since early 1863. *Ibid.,* III, 357-59.

[31] Andy, young son of the deceased slave Nelly, came to Maryland with the Clemsons in 1860. He belonged to Mrs. John C. Calhoun, who had earlier provided in her will that he should go to Floride. Mrs. Calhoun and the Clemsons took great interest in him, and he was frequently mentioned in family correspondence as "little Andy."

[32] Dr. Septimus Cook (age 53), a Virginia-born physician living with his family near Bladensburg. MS. Census 1860, Prince Georges County, Md.

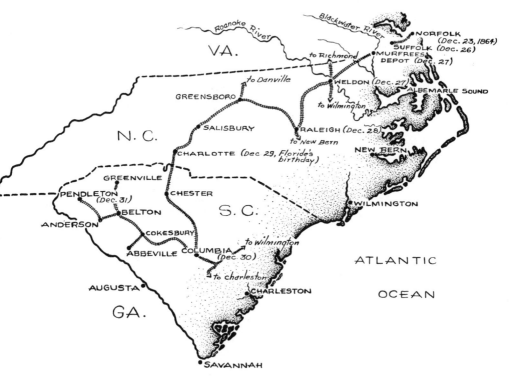

Route of the Clemsons' trip South

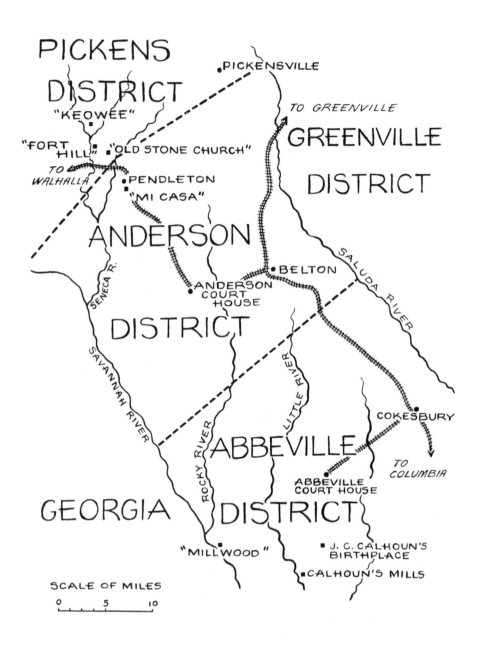

PICKENS
DISTRICT

"KEOWEE"

• PICKENSVILLE

TO GREENVILLE

GREENVILLE

"FORT HILL" • "OLD STONE CHURCH"

TO WALHALLA

• PENDLETON

"MI CASA"

DISTRICT

ANDERSON

SENECA R.

BELTON

SALUDA RIVER

ANDERSON
COURT
HOUSE

DISTRICT

SAVANNAH RIVER

LITTLE RIVER

COKESBURY

ABBEVILLE

ROCKY RIVER

TO COLUMBIA

ABBEVILLE
COURT HOUSE

GEORGIA

DISTRICT

"MILLWOOD"

■ J. C. CALHOUN'S
BIRTHPLACE

■ CALHOUN'S MILLS

SCALE OF MILES

0   5   10

III

Pendleton, South Carolina

1865

Jan. 1st Pendleton S. C. 1865.

We reached here last evening at nine o'clock, & found grandmother quite ailing, though able to be about. Aunt Kate Calhoun,[1] & her two boys Putman, & Willie, is & has been here a year I believe. She [Mrs. Calhoun] is pretty much confined to her bed all the time. Now for my travels &c. We got our pass on Sunday the 11th of last month, after having lost all hope that we would succeed. We made all haste to get things in readiness to start as soon as possible. On Friday I went to Washington & had 6 teeth plugged, besides doing much shopping. Went out in the carriage with the McCeney's after dark, to the Robinson's. Found them all at home except Mrs. King. Next morning left there, & grieved much to part with dear Lizzie, my dearest friend. Went to the Woods on my way back to Wash., but saw only Emily, the others being away. Drove into the city with Dr. King, saw Cecelia Riggs, (Kate, & Alice are in England), Mrs. Dr. Stone, & did some more shopping. Left in the 3 o'clock train. Edgar McCeney spent Sunday with us as did Mr. Seymour, who gave a beautiful & well stocked bonbonière. Henry McC. came Tuesday as did the Sanders, Fairfaxes, Herberts, Dr. Cook, Mrs. Contee & others to bid us good bye. We left Beltsville Tuesday evening the 20th, with five trunks, a large carpet bag for shawls &c. two baskets of provisions, & two hand bags, to which we added a huge umbrella in Norfolk. Our friends tried their best to dissuade us, especially Mr. Lee, but mother would come & of course I would not be left behind alone. Mr. Lee left Wednesday night. We stayed in Baltimore till Thursday after noon, shopping

---

[1] Kate Kirby Putnam of St. Augustine, Fla., married John C. Calhoun, Jr. (May 17, 1823-July 31, 1855), and after his death, his brother William Lowndes Calhoun (Aug. 13, 1829-Sept. 19, 1858). A. S. Salley, Jr., *The Calhoun Family of South Carolina* (Columbia, S. C.: 1906), pp. 28-29.

& making arrangements. I was with Mary Latrobe most of the time, & saw the John Latrobe's, Mrs. Merrick, with whom we spent the night, & Mrs. Marcoe.[2] Thursday at four o'clock P. M. we left in a wretched little boat for Norfolk. It blew abominably & was so cold we could scarce lie in bed. We got to Fortress Monroe early in the morning, & Mr. Dunscomb, & I walked all around it for near an hour till ordered back by a sentnel. We got to Norfolk about nine o'clock, & walked up to Gen. Shepley's office. Found him a nice looking man. He was polite, but not more, to us, made little objection to the baggage. We stayed at the Atlantic hotel, & were most politely treated by the people of the place, who flocked to see us in a perfect levee after the manner of those in Martin Chuzzlewit when that unfortunate was going to Eden. The Miss Tasubes were particularly polite, & we spent an evening there. We went to Church on Xmas., when I went to communion for the first time since I was confirmed. We left Monday morning in a special flag of truce train to Suffolk[3] which we reached about twelve o'clock; here we left Mr. Dunscomb. We had a letter to a Mr. Riddle there who got us some Confederate money at 10 to one for greenbacks, which were 2.30 [compared with gold] when we left. The place looked very forlorn & deserted. We left there at two o'clock in the only carriage in the place, with the only horse! Our baggage following in two mule carts. We had only gone ten miles before dark, as we had to walk all the way on account of the rain which had, & was falling. We went ten more after dark through the terrible debatable ground to a man's by the name of Jones, where we stayed all night. The next morning we got up before day light, & did the remaining eight miles to Murphrys depôt about 40 miles from Weldon. Here we bid good bye to Mr. Jones our driver. We had to pay $55 in green backs to the carriage, & carts. We had to cross the Black Water in a ferry boat which the first Confederate picket we had seen brought across for us. At Murphry's depot we waited in a log hut with the soldiers &c. till one o'clock, the station houses having been burnt by a raid[4] a short time since. We reached Weldon about

[2] Mrs. Mary Markoe (age 47), was wife of Francis Markoe (age 58), a State Department official from Pennsylvania. His property was valued at $72,000 in 1860. MS. Census 1860, First Ward, D. C.

[3] See map on page 69 for route traveled.

[4] On Oct. 16, 1864, a Federal cavalry raid, under the command of Lt. Col. D. M. Evans, crossed the Blackwater River and attacked Murfree's Station.

five, our baggage having been slightly searched on the road, as it was on the other side going to Suffolk; this was to prevent contraband trade. At Weldon our room had no fire, & the windows were broken so we laid on the dirtiest bed in the dirtiest room I ever saw, till three in the morning when we left for Raliegh, which we should have reached at two in the day, & made the connection but the train in front of us broke down, & detained us a couple of hours, so we had to stay till one at night. A Mr. Baine, & his sister Mrs. McCree helped us along so far, & introduced us to a Lt. Brown[5] of the "Florida" who saw us far as Charlotte. We reached this last named place at about 5 o'clock Thursday evening, but our train broke down when 25 miles off, & we came near being run into by a train behind us, & had to do the rest of the distance crowded into a baggage car, at a dangerous speed, to make the connection. (My 22nd birth day was spent on the road between Raliegh, & Charlotte. A weary way, safely gotten through.) We expected to get to Columbia at 3 o'clock A. M. but did not until after nine, as our engine had given out & could not make steam, whereby we missed the train up here, & had to stay till next morning at eight. Here we met Gen Wigfall,[6] his wife, & daughter Louise, who is very pretty. They were just from the trans Miss. department, & gave us late news of father who was very well. A Capt. Conell who took some little charge of us the last days' journey, was just going there, & took a letter to him for us. The Harrisses[7] called upon us. Sallie died over a year ago. We saw Gen. Joe Johnson [Joseph E. Johnston], & Gen D. H. Hill[8] there. We spent the evening most pleasantly with music. Here we also met Mrs. Sam Van Wyck,[9] who told

---

"They thoroughly destroyed the depot buildings and the warehouses in the vicinity." *WROR*, XLII, Part I, Series I, pp. 958-59.

[5] When the "Florida" put to sea in January, 1863, one of its officers was assistant engineer E. H. Brown. Scharf, *The Confederate States Navy*, p. 791.

[6] Louis T. Wigfall (Apr. 21, 1816-Feb. 17, 1874), Congressman and Confederate general from Texas, but formerly from South Carolina. *Biog. Dir. Cong.*, p. 2010.

[7] Mrs. Harris, née Sarah Jeter, had long been a close friend of Mrs. Clemson. Sarah Jeter Harris to Anna Calhoun Clemson, July 25, 1859, Clemson Papers.

[8] For Generals Hill and Johnston see *DAB*, IX, 27-28, X, 144-46.

[9] Margaret C. Broyles married Dr. Samuel M. Van Wyck, son of Lydia Ann Maverick of Pendleton and William Van Wyck of New York. Other children of the William Van Wycks were William, Zeruah, Benjamin, Lydia ("Lilly"), Augustus, and Robert. Simpson, *Old Pendleton District*, pp. 109-10.

us that her mother in law, Lilly [Lydia], & Bennie, had run the blockade in Octo. by the way of Norfolk, to go to see William who is dying of consumption in Hallifax. Poor fellow I am too sorry. Gussy [Augustus] is staying here, but is in dreadful health. He injured his back while in the army & can not walk without assistance, being threatened with paralysis. Lilly is delicate too. Fanny Adams[10] came up in the same train with us, & got us home in her carriage. Grandma had been expecting us so long that she was not much surprised at our coming, but was overjoyed. We brought her a trunk full of tea & things. The cars travel very slowly, & the rolling stock is much out of order. The trains were crowded with soldiers going home on furlough, & but very few ladies. We met with no rudeness, & lost only one handkerchief. Everyone seemed well shod, & comfortably clothed in homespun. Hats are almost altogether worn, high crowns & wide brims. We still have bad colds contracted on the road. Col. Orr, Mr. Trescot,[11] & everyone speaks so well of Calhoun. He must have done nobly.

Jan. 8th. We have been here just a week yesterday.

Our friends have flocked fast to see us. The ladies look a little shabbyly & old fashioned but there seems little real want. Confederate money is twenty to one of gold, but when things are brought to a gold basis, they are little higher than at the North. Luxuries are almost unatainable, sugar, & meat dear. For the former sorghum syrup is almost exclusively used, & is a good substitute. Tallow candles are the only lights, but there is plenty corn, flour, salt, sorghum, & even poultry, about here, & I believe there is little suffering off of the tracks of the armies. The ingenuity of the people is wonder full in making things, & furnishing "substitutes," which is a word in every ones mouth. The greatest want, alas! is of men. Men to fight. There are scarce any out of the army now, & too few there. The people, as far as I have seen, are very dispirited now. We heard of the fall of Savannah on our way, & that of Charleston,

---

[10] Frances Adams (born Apr. 9, 1839), daughter of Dr. Jasper Adams (died Oct. 25, 1841), and Placidia Mayrant Adams. Register, St. Paul's Episcopal Church, Pendleton, S. C.; *SCHGM*, XXVII (Jan., 1926), 87.

[11] Former Congressman James L. Orr and diplomat William H. Trescot. See *DAB*, XIV, 59-60, XVIII, 639-40.

& even Columbia[12] is anticipated. I pray we may be saved from the horrors of raids here. An army would find little to tempt them to this place, but raids from the mountains are to be dreaded, if not immediately, still at no distant date, probably. Mother & I have spent much of our time writing letters for persons North, to their friends South. Today I heard for the first time, with joy, the prayers for the President, soldiers, & people of the Confederacy. By the way, they give a free dinner to the soldiers on the trains every day, on this road, of delicacies they do not allow themselves. Such a people I trust can not be conquered. "Thy will oh Lord not mine."

Jan. 20th. There was a terrible freshet here last Tuesday week, & we hear it extended all over the country, washing away all rail road bridges, & tressels, so that there will probably be no trains for a month, & even no mails. Sherman is still at Savannah they say.

Feb 12th. The rail road is not yet rebuilt, & there seems little hope that it will be finished for a month to come. We have not had a regular mail yet though letters get through occasionally. We have not seen a paper since the break. Sherman they say is at Branchville [S. C.], & there seems little opposition to be made to him. Indeed these days are dark. It seems to me that the only ray of hope comes through an unfixable report that France & England mean to recognize soon & have demanded an armistice. Every one talks of this, & that commissioners[13] are sent, but no one knows whether it is true. I am weary of this hope deferred. The spirit seems to be getting very despondent every where, & I fear half the people are at heart conquored. Everything is rediculously dear, & almost impossible to get. Common shoes from $60 to 100. Coarse home spun from $6 to 10 a yd, butter $7, beef $1½, pork 3, bacon 5 per lb. Gold is now 30 times Confederate money, & sometimes has sold at 60. Corn is at $15 a bushel, & everything in proportion. Chickens $4 apiece. I pray God will be good enough to extend his help to us soon. We have heard from Calhoun up to Jan. 11th. He is well; also have

[12] General Sherman occupied Savannah on Dec. 21, 1864, and Columbia on Feb. 17, 1865. His main army by-passed Charleston. See John G. Barrett, *Sherman's March Through the Carolinas* (Chapel Hill: University of North Carolina Press, 1956), pp. 24, 70-71.

[13] Probably a reference to the futile Duncan Kenner mission, which left for Europe in December, 1864, with the offer to free the Negroes in return for European aid.

received a personal through the papers. I am much ill of late, with my headaches &c with fainting.

[Floride inserted the following newspaper clipping at this point.]

Baltimore, Jan. 9, 1865.

To Florida, Pendleton, S. C.—Your notice, dated Greensboro, December 29, received, and communicated to your friends. We are devoutly and fervently thankful, but anxious to hear again. J. C. C. well and cheerful, 31st December; had received money and clothes.

A. S. F. [Dunscomb]

Feb. 19th. Went to church this morning, & find that our worst fears are realized. Columbia has been surrendered, & Charleston evacuated. It is dreadful, & my heart sinks at the thought of what may yet happen to this poor state. There is much consternation about here, for fear of raids either from Sherman, or over the mountains from the Tories, deserters, & Federal cavalry there. I can not but feel that there is little hope for our cause, everything shows that our resources are nearly if not quite exhausted, especially in men, & there is little hope from abroad, I might say, none. I have little fear for ourselves, at lea[s]t for the present, & feel that God will deal with us according to his mercy, & justice, & pray to be given strength to bear whatever chastenings he has in store for us with a proper spirit. Oh but my heart is very anxious, & desponding! It has been now a year at least since I have felt that our case was almost despirate. We had a beautiful sermon today, on the efficacy of prayer, from Mr. Elliot.[14] Provisions are very scarce here, & if many more refugees come as is expected, I do not know what we are to do. Still a disgraceful peace may come too soon; now all depends on the next great battle, probably in North Carolina or Va. God have mercy upon, & protect us! I suppose we will get no more mails now, except from the neighboring districts. Grandma is most of the time in bed. She has a kidney affection which causes an exterior irritation which is very painful. Aunt Kate also keeps her room with falling of the womb. They say St. Micheal's Church in Charleston in [is] blown up, & the city garizoned by negroes.

[14] The Rev. John H. Elliott, Episcopal rector at Pendleton and Anderson during the war. Albert S. Thomas, *A Historical Account of the Protestant Episcopal Church in South Carolina, 1820-1957* (Columbia, S. C.: A. S. Thomas, 1957), pp. 497, 600, 640.

Wednesday

March 15th. It has been long since I have written here. Our beautiful Columbia has been laid in ashes by the Northern Vandals, in the mean time. All the main st. & some squares on either side, have been burnt, with the old state house, the depôts, & all provisions &c. so that the inhabitants are many of them starving. The Yankees were there only from Friday 17th to Tuesday 21st [February] I believe, but committed all manner of outrages in that time. Throwing back whatever people were trying to save from their burning houses into the flames. The day before yesterday we attended a meeting for the relief of the sufferers, who are not only starving, but utterly destitute & sleeping in the sts, many of them, & heard a lecture from Dr. Adger,[15] at the Methodist church. Mother & I gave $150, & some cloths. Grandma, five bushels of corn, a ham, $50, & cloths, which is as much as we can afford these times. Immediately after the lecture, I went up to, & spoke to uncle Andrew [Calhoun],[16] whom I had not before seen. He was very pleasent to me, as he was when I was here before, when he showed me every attention. He then drove up here to see grandma, for the first time in over a year,[17] I believe, that any of them have been here. The visit was in consiquence of a note mother wrote him, telling him how sick grandma is, & that she [Mrs. Calhoun] had expressed a desire to see him. She did not know of this, & the interview proved in every way satisfactory. God grant the comparitively good feeling may last. I saw aunt Margaret[18] & some of the younger children at a fair at which I had a table, just after the great freshet. Last Friday was a Confederate day of fasting, & prayes. It was the first that I have been able to go to church, & I availed myself of the

[15] John B. Adger, D.D., the Presbyterian minister at Pendleton. Simpson, *Old Pendleton District*, p. 123; John B. Adger, D.D., *My Life and Times, 1810-1899* (Richmond, Va.: The Presbyterian Committee on Publication, 1899).

[16] Andrew Pickens Calhoun (Oct. 15, 1811-Mar. 16, 1865) and his wife Margaret had the following children living in 1860: Duff G. (age 21), John C. (16), Margaret (13), Andrew P. (8), James E. (6), and Patrick (4). His property was valued at $294,000. MS. Census 1860, Pickens Dist., S. C.

[17] Mrs. John C. Calhoun and her son Andrew had a dispute over the Fort Hill property.

[18] Margaret (Feb. 18, 1816-July 27, 1891), daughter of the famous Washington editor Duff Green, married Andrew Pickens Calhoun, May 5, 1836. Salley, *The Calhoun Family*, p. 28; marker in Clemson College Cemetery.

privilege. Mr. Elliot gave us a good sermon, & I hope that the earnest prayes offerered on that day may be heard in behaf of our prec-
ious cause. It is today two weeks since Ash Wednesday, & I trust
I shall be able to attend the Lent services often, never before having been situated so that I could. I sit in the choir here, as at Rock
Creek, & sing second, almost all together, which is what my voice
is best fitted for. They say all the prisoners are being exchanged,
so I suppose we shall see Calhoun soon. I almost hope he will be
one of the extra ones, paroled, for I am so afraid he will get killed.
Every one speaks in the highest terms of his energy here. I have
put myself, & my poor eyes under the care of Dr. Maxwell[19] here,
as I am by no means in good health. He says just what the others
do about the affection being partial paralysis, or insipiant amarosis,
& gives me no hope for reading, at least for a very long time. This
is very hard indeed. Grandma is still confined to her bed or room,
but more from nervousness than anything else, we think. Neither is
aunt Kate able to be about. We have had so wet a winter that
nothing is planted yet, & I think we have had several pretty good
attempts at a deluge. I have joined a Presbyterian society for the
soldiers which meet the first Wednesdy every month, when you
bring either one dollar or its worth in work.

Sunday

March 19th. Uncle Andrew Calhoun died last Thursday, a little
after day light, after only two hour's illness, of congestion of the
heart. Johnny sent us a note that he was dying but before mother
& I could start we heard he was dead. I drove mother through a
pelting rain there, & upon their expressing a great desire that I
should do so, I stayed until after the funeral yesterday. He was
buried at eleven, by Dr. Adger (Presbyterian). The attendence was
very large. The poor will miss him dreadfully, as he was very
charitable to them. I believe that the 18th (yesterday) was grandfather's birth day. It also was that of uncle Andrew's son Jimmie,
who was eleven. All the family were at home, except Duff, from
whom they have not heard since the great freshet, & are very
anxious about him. Johnny & Duff are both captains, the former is

[19] Dr. John H. Maxwell (age 27), son of Captain John Maxwell and Elizabeth Earle Maxwell. Simpson, *Old Pendleton District*, pp. 175-76; MS. Census
1860, Anderson Dist., S. C.

in dreadful health, as his back is injured & he has a terrible affection of the kidneys. He is about a year younger than myself. Margie has grown up very pretty. She is nearly 18 now. Andrew, who is thirteen, seems to be the most remarkable of the family, in intelligence, and character. He has glorious eyes, & looks very like grandfather they say. Pat is eight, and they say very bright. The youngest, a girl, born since I was here is three years & a month old. Her name is Mary Lucretia, but they call her Lula. She seems a dear good, bright little thing. Jonny & Duff are not very smart, but all the children are well raised, & seem remarkably good, & affectionate. It seems to me providential that uncle Andrew came to see grandma last Monday. We are so thankful for it. Aunt Margaret & all the children were coming in the day he died. They have not been here, nor had I been there during the whole of this visit. It appears that uncle Andrew has always expressed himself very fond of me, & proud of me. The day before he died he was making plans that I should have one of his horses to ride, so as to recruit my health. Aunt Margaret & all the family, indeed, have always taken the greatest pains to make me feel that they loved me. Aunt Margaret, although she is not pleasent to me, is certainly an exemplary wife, mother, & housekeeper. Her grief, & that of all the family, who are unusually devoted to each other, was really harrowing, & I was quite broken down by my visit. Aunt M. had a dreadful nervous spasm the last night from surpressed grief. Uncle Andrew was 54 years old. He was fatter than mother, whom he resembled exceedingly in appearence. Now mother is the only one left of all the seven children grandfather left when he died. We had our first letters from the North (except that dated 11th Jan. from Calhoun), last night. Two from Mr. Dunscomb, & one from Mr. Lee. The last dated Feb. 6th. We had heard from exchanged prisoners that Calhoun had been paroled, & had gone to Shrieveport two months ago, but from these letters & a note from Rob. Goldsborough who left him on the 20th last month it would seem not. All freinds well.

Friday

March 24th. We received three letters from father last evening, the last dated Feb. 6th. It appears that he has heard through a letter from Calhoun that we had come South, but does not know that we have reached here safely. He is as usual very uneasy about us, &

wishes we had staid North, at any rate thinks we had better not leave this place. He is well, & thinks of going to Mexico on a mission. We also got a ferrotype of Calhoun, by an exchanged prisoner, last night. It is excessively handsome. We still hear that he is exchanged but he was not a month ago. Last Tuesday night we had the most dreadful hail storm ever known about here. We got a bowl full of which none were smaller than hickory nuts, & many as large as hen's eggs. Some fell 8 in. in surcomference, & many as large as goose eggs, they say. There was also a tornado above here, which carried quite a large house over the tops of the trees some distance, & killed a girl 10 years old. Fortunately vegitation was not far enough advanced to be much injured, though early flowers, johnquils, &c. are nearly over. Aunt Margaret Calhoun, Margie, & Jimmie, & Lula, were here on Wednesday to see grandma. I do feel such a longing to see some of my old friends, any familiar face, any one whom I have long known, & who *knows* me. I feel so *alone*, not even to hear from Lizzie Robinson or any one I love. I do not feel this is *home*, & my heart seems withering within me.

Tuesday

April 4th. Cousin Ed. Noble[20] arrived here very unexpectedly yesterday week, on his way to Fort Hill. He stayed only a day or two, & looks much better than he used to. Aunt Margaret sent for me on Wednesday, & I stayed till next evening. Duff was wounded some little time since in the finger, & came home last night. My eyes are no better. Grandma about the same, seldom out of her room. Aunt Kate not able to walk out of the house. Just to think that sugar is about $20 a lb! Salt is at *least* 300$ a bushel of 50 lbs. I have become a great carpenter & cobler of old & broken things, & do the tinckering & mending of the house. We have just gotten a new girl Mary, & hope she will do, as we needed an other servant much. I dont know how people get along here as well as they do; everything is so high, & hard to get at any price. The suffering in the lower part of the state is very great they say, negroes unmanageable, & the Yankees barbarous.

[20] Edward Noble, an Abbeville, S. C., lawyer, and son of Gov. Patrick and Elizabeth Bonneau Pickens Noble. Gov. Patrick Noble's mother was Catherine Calhoun, a first cousin of John C. Calhoun. Monroe Pickens (comp.), *Cousin Monroe's History of the Pickens Family* (Easley, S. C.: Kate Pickens Day, 1951), p. 50; Salley, *The Calhoun Family*, pp. 18, 22.

April 9th Sunday. All last week rumors of fighting around Richmond reached us, & the day before yesterday we heard the sad tidings of its evacuation by our troops [April 2]. Although we had long expected this, still it came like a thunder bolt upon us. It shows so much weakness, that we can not keep one place against the foe. As this movement has been contemplated some time, I hope very much has been saved from our noble capital, of course not all. It makes my very heart bleed to think what is in store for that city. Charleston & Savannah are garisoned by negro troops now, & ground to the dust.

Easter Sunday, April 16th. All today we have been in a great commotion. A courier brough[t] the news last evening that a large force of Yankees, Tories, & deserters had come down from the mountains & were marching either on this place or Greenville, being within twenty miles of us. The numbers varying from 1500, to 25000! This afternoon however we hear that the report arose from a raid of a couple of hundreds of deserters, &c who went back to the mountains after having taken some cattle &c. So we had a bad scare & that's all. Have some dread of these raids though.

April 21st. Well the game's up I fear. The rumor reached here yesterday morning & the news last night, that Lee our noble hero had surrendered with all his army, on the 10th [April 9]. It is dreadful. They say Grant returned him his sword, & there was little or no exultation. There were but 10,000 efficient fighting men left, though somewhere near thirty thousand surrendered. The Yankee forces were some two hundred thousand strong & Grant is *said* to have said that he was not conquored, but overwhelmed. Gen Johnson has still some 30,000 left, & they say is making his way toward Georgia. I pray he may get off. President Davis & his cabinet are making their way towards Georgia, on horseback, also. Of [course] I wish we were all in the trans Mississippi department, & the army too. I pray God may have mercy on us, for they have none. I hear so much that is dreadful, that I am trembling at their idea of their coming. Oh these are dreadful times to live in. I suppose we may expect raids now any day, & God only knows how we are to bear it, for the country is starving now. Confederate money of course is worth little or nothing, & we have little else. I suppose we will die of starvation, I suppose the next news will be Johnson's capture.

We spent yesterday at Major Simpson's,[21] & the day before at cousin Tom Picken's,[22] both sending for us. As all the captured men were paroled & sent home, I suppose they will soon know what has become of Sam & Miles. We have lately received several letters, one from father dated March 6th. He was well, & wanted for no *essentials* except chocolat, & fresh fish. One from Mary Latrobe, & an other from Mr. Dunscomb, dated March 15th, when Calhoun was still in prison. All freinds were well. Mary's was the first letter I have received from across the lines. I was just beginning to feel bright & cheerful again, for the first time since I have been here, about two weeks before this terrible news came, & now it seems almost wicked to laugh, for I consider that we are already subjugated, & subjugation means ruin, or worse.

Sunday 22nd. They are getting up all kind of reports now to keep up the currency, which of course is worth little, or nothing now. There is an armistice now, & hostilities are not to be resumed without 48 hour's notice, but they say this will do more harm than good. Fra[n]ce they say has recognized us. Miles Pickens is home. Duff & Hall Calhoun[23] have been here.

Monday.

1st of May. We are just getting over a terrible scare. We heard this morning about twelve or one o'clock that the Yankees were near here. We immediately made preparations, about an hour afterwards we heard on all sides that they were not more than a mile off, & still nearer, some said 3000, & some 30 strong!! but I suppose about 60. Finding so large a force here to oppose them, they left, & now about [left blank] o'clock I am writing quietly about this second big scare. However we need not feel too safely, for some

[21] Richard F. Simpson (age 62), a farmer and lawyer whose property was worth $92,300 in 1860. A former U. S. Congressman and signer of the Ordinance of Secession, he was the father of Richard W. Simpson, who later became a close friend of Thomas G. Clemson and chairman of the first board of trustees of Clemson College. Simpson, *Old Pendleton District*, pp. 5-8; MS. Census 1860, Anderson Dist., S. C.

[22] Col. Thomas J. Pickens (Apr. 26, 1808-July 2, 1894). He married Keziah A. Miles (July 30, 1810-Nov. 1, 1889). Two of their children were Col. Samuel B. Pickens and John Miles Pickens. Pickens, *The Pickens Family*, pp. 50-52.

[23] Henry Davis ("Hall") Colhoun (born Sept. 2, 1838), son of Col. John Ewing and Martha Davis Colhoun. Register, St. Paul's. John Ewing Colhoun was a brother of Mrs. John C. Calhoun.

say these are but Stoneman's vanguard, & some that they are a set of Wheelers[24] cavalry on a marauding expedition under Yankee disguise. They have stolen horses, & one watch, as far as I have heard. Well we hear all kinds of reports. I had a good cry Saturday night on hearing that peace had been declared, we having gone back, negroes permanent, & assuming one quarter of the Northern debt, they the rest, & repudiating our. And then we have heard of recognition from many powers which may or may not be so. And last but not least I suppose it is pretty certain Lincoln & Seward[25] have been assassinated. The former in Ford's theatre Wton. Where he was witnessing "Our American cousin." The man who killed him saying " 'Sic sempre tyrannis' Virginia is avenged," & escaping in the confusion. Seward was killed in bed. Now they say Andy Johnson is killed, & two of his cabinet, & that Grant will be dictator, then that Lee is to be president, & Grant vice president; then there is to be a general vote for president. In short when thou lookest at this record in thine old age, my future self, know that history judgeing events by consiquences *may* be true, but report is only so once in more times than I can set down here, & is not to be ascertained until the fact has lost almost all interest, & novelty. We scarcely ever see a news paper, & are bewildered groping in impenetrable darkness, & mystery. I returned yesterday from Fort Hill where I spent two days. Johny came for me, to be with Margie on her 18th birthday. I had three rides the first since that one on which Dr. Eversfield offered himself to me.

7th of May. I had hardly done writing what precedes, when the allarm was again given, that the Yankees surrounded the village, sure enough at least a hundred strong; what at first caused the confusion & uncertainty was that a body of Wheelers men arrived near the place when they did, but finding them before them made a detour & came in on an other side. Well the Yankees got to within

---

[24] Confederate General Joseph Wheeler (Sept. 10, 1836-Jan. 25, 1906) and Union General George Stoneman (Aug. 8, 1822-Sept. 5, 1894). The latter raided Western North Carolina, but did not get near Pendleton. *DAB*, XVIII, 92-93, XX, 50-52.

[25] Another conspirator wounded Secretary of State William H. Seward, but the one assigned to dispatch Vice-President Andrew Johnson withheld his blow.

a mile of here, as far as McBride's, Holmes, & Warleys,[26] but did not enter the village as they took it into their head that we had a large force here from hearing & seeing Jone's[27] men wherever they went. In truth there were not more than 75 or 50 fighting men mostly boys of between 16 & 17, but they rushed about so wildly, scouting & making a fuss that the impression got abroad that there were over a thousand; but I will not laugh for under heaven, they saved us from the horrors of a sack such a[s] fell to the lot of poor Anderson where over a thousand of Stoneman's raiders made their head quarters three or four days. Mr. Henry Gourdin[28] who is here now, had 300 dozen of wine there which they drank. They were principally in scearch of Jeff Davis, the treasury, horses & jewelry. Some had knapsacks full of watches, trinkets & rings. They came as far a[s] Seabourn's[29] & the Picken's, but they did not enter the latter place. They went to Major Simpson's however. Three nights in succession we went to bed & before twelve were roused by allarms. Mr. Kenuff, cousin Duff, Mr. Seabourne, Capt. Jones, Ham Warley, & Mr. Duke,[30] all came in the different nights with allarms. We expected the Yankees in every minute almost during Monday Tuesday & Wednesday. Once a flag of truce was stationed near our gate thinking the enemy would be in, in a few minutes. Once the

[26] T. L. McBryde (age 43), D.D., was a Presbyterian minister at Pendleton at the time of his death on April 15, 1863. Jacob and Sophia Fraser Warley (age 60) had nine children, including Anna, who married John H. Holmes. MS. Census 1860, Anderson Dist., S. C.; Simpson, *Old Pendleton District*, pp. 201-02; F. D. Jones and W. H. Mills (eds.), *History of the Presbyterian Church in South Carolina Since 1850* (Columbia, S. C.: The R. L. Bryan Co., 1926), p. 955.

[27] Probably W. R. Jones (age 32), a Pendleton druggist. MS. Census 1860, Anderson Dist., S. C. There was a local militia company in Pendleton called "Jones' Rifles."

[28] Henry Gourdin (age 55), Charleston merchant whose property was valued at $114,000 in 1860, acted as a factor for the Clemsons and Calhouns. MS. Census 1860, Ward 1, Charleston Dist., S. C.; Clemson Papers, *passim*.

[29] Major George Seaborn (Aug. 1, 1797-Mar. 13, 1877) married Sarah Anne Earle (Mar. 6, 1806-Apr. 22, 1879). His property was worth $92,000 in 1860. MS. Census 1860, Anderson Dist., S. C.; Register, St. Paul's.

[30] William James Knauff (Apr. 8, 1801-Feb. 27, 1867), a cabinetmaker. *Ibid.* Hamilton Warley was a son of Jacob and Sophia Warley. See above note 26. "Mr. Duke" was probably James J. Duke (age 40), a Virginia-born farm manager living near Pendleton in 1860. MS. Census 1860, Pickens Dist., S. C.

cry was that they were in the village. We had Mr. Seimmons'[31] wine destroyed, nine large boxes. It was a pity but had to be done every one said, if not for our own sakes at least for that of the community. We & scarce & [any] one else had not our cloths off for more than an hour or so for three days & nights, & we were all very excited. We had everything burried, but were dreadfully afraid of personal insults. Grandma took it very coolly, & I think improved under the excitement. She is rarely in bed now & gets about the house a good deal. Did *she* think so she would be nearly well I think. Duff Calhoun did good service during the excitement taking five of the eight prisoners captured, & many horses. He went the day before yesterday with some of Gen. Ferguson's[32] men for the Trans Miss. I think he is a brave fellow, & came often to see about us during the excitement. I feel so sorry for these exiles, to high spirited to live in a conquored country for such this is. Mother has just read a proclamation to the effect that hostilities have ceased up to the Chatanoga, & that Johnson has surrendered [April 26] all the troops under his command. I can not comment on this. The cars have been burnt so that we have no communication with the outer world at this *ultima thule.* Aunt Kate has just given me one of her rings. I have longed for one like it all my life, & it is very beautiful. I feel just like a child with a new toy. I think I am getting pretty strong again, perhaps I will get quite well in this climate. We see a great deal of company, & I am getting more contented though often homesick, & longing for friends. I pray God will make us, & me especially truly thankfull *for his many blessings,* & great

mercy. The families we know here are these.[33] Thom. Pickens.—

Fort Hillians.—Rob, Ellison Adger & John Adger.—Judge Frost.—

[31] Probably Thomas Grange Simons, of Charleston. His second wife (married Dec. 8, 1857) was Elizabeth Bonneau Noble (b. Jan. 10, 1837), daughter of Governor Patrick Noble. Floride Calhoun to Anna C. Clemson, Dec. 5, 1857, Clemson Papers; Lewis D. McPherson (comp.), *Calhoun, Hamilton, Baskin and Related Families* (privately published, 1957), pp. 14, 19.

[32] Brigadier General Samuel W. Ferguson, a Charleston native who escorted Jefferson Davis from Charlotte to Washington, Ga. He settled in Mississippi after the war. Gen. Clement Evans (ed.), *Confederate Military History* (12 vols. Atlanta, Ga.: Confederate Publishing Co., 1899), V, 394-95.

[33] See Appendix II for identification of most of these families.

Chs. C. Pinckney.—Dr. Ravenel.—Miss Ford, Mrs. H. E. Ravenel.—
The Van Wycks.—Latta. Mrs. Warley, Holmes, & Bourne.—Mrs.
Gen. Bee.—Mrs. Sadler, Elliot, & Simms.—Mrs. Dickenson, Green,
& Lee.—Rob., Sam, & John Maxwell. Mrs. Lucy Maxwell.—Major
Simpson.—Major Seybourn.—Wm. H. Trescot.—Mrs. Jesse P. Lewis.
—Mrs. Maze.—Mrs. Lewis, Jr.—Mrs. North, Norths, Thurston's.—
Mrs. Lorton, Mrs. Porter.—Rev. Mr. Cornish. Mrs. Tom Sloan.—
John T. Sloan—Ball Sloan &c.—Wm. Gailliard. Elim Sharp. Hayne.—
Mrs. Adams.—Archie Campbell.——Dr. Robinson, Mrs. Moore.—
Andrew Lewis.—A Livingston.—Porcher.——Dr. Cherry.—Mrs. Shu-
brick. & Miss Bert.—Fanny Russell. Mrs. Rag [Wragg]—Mrs. Ton-
neau [Tunno], & Mrs. Hazzard.—Seabrooks, Vallie North.

May 13. Miss Hardee, the Gen's.[34] daughter Anna, was here
yesterday evening, to see aunt Kate. They are passing through to
go to dear only knows where, with the Gen. They were all to come
here to see aunt Kate this morning, but although we got up at a
little after 5, the General only waited long enough to get off his
horse, & say he had not time to see us. I caught a glimpse of him
through the curtain however, & saw a very fine looking officer,
though not handsome. Capt. Simms[35] of the Allabama is with him,
& perhaps we may see him today. It makes my heart ache to see
these poor men flying perhaps for their lives. Gen. Hardee is paroled. Mother got me a piano last Monday from Mr. Groaning's.[36]
one of Hazelton's. 7¼ octaves. The trebble is very sweet, but the
base not very full. It is much handsomer than my Steinvoch, but

[34] Lt. Gen. William J. Hardee (Oct. 12, 1815-Nov. 6, 1873), who had been
in charge of Confederate forces in South Carolina and Georgia during Sherman's march from Atlanta to Savannah and then northward. *DAB*, VIII,
239-40.

[35] Capt. Raphael Semmes (Sept. 27, 1809-Aug. 30, 1877), the famous Confederate naval commander. *DAB*, XVI, 579-82.

[36] Lewis Groaning of Charleston bought property in Pendleton in September, 1863. Anderson deeds, book L-2, pp. 102-03.

not so fine, as an instrument. "A bird in the" &c. I have also a nice carved music stand, & stool, with it. All for $350 gold. Rond keys. My eyes get worse instead of better I fear. Ah well!! There were three funerals this week. Old Mrs. Sadler from Fla. on Tuesday. Mr. Latta on Wednesday, & Mr. Elliot's[37] child on Saturday.

Sunday

May 28th. Last Sunday about a thousand Yankees under Gen. Brown passed through this place. We were in a terrible state of excitement but though they were ca[m]ped near the village all night, & many stayed in it, they did little or no harm to private property. They took all the government meat & corn, & destroyed all public arms but never even took private guns. Thank God not one Yankee put his foot on this place not even a guard although many rode right by the gate, & all passed in full view over the opposite hill. They took almost all the good horses about this country, & much silver, Mr. Trescot's, & Major Simpson's. The latter they visited two or three times, & treated very badly. Of course all we had of value was "put out." Some few negroes went with them. Monday, & Tuesday more passed through but did no harm. They say this is the worst secession hole they have seen, as they were not only treated with contempt but abuse, & swear vengeance against the whole community for they were much bush whacked near here. They were at Fort Hill, & took Johnny's fine horse, & others I believe, but did little or no other damage. Fanny Adams has been staying with me, a day & night. I have given much away to others worse off than myself & fear I shall have to stop. 1 pair shoes, some ribbon, two belts, 6 collars, & 1 pair cuffs, much thread, 1 pair gloves, 1 dress, some undercloths, tatting, &c. &c. &c. &c.

June 11th. The day before yesterday was the 4th aniversary of of Calhoun & father's leaving us, & yesterday for the first time since *early* March, we heard directly from C. He sent us a letter by a Lt. Miles, who took the oath & was returning home. He was well on the 19th of May, when the letter was dated, said he might be here in a week, or perhaps "days might fade away into years," & still

---

[37] James T. Latta (born 1827), a Yale University graduate. He left a widow, Angela Wetherell Latta of New Jersey, and four children. Mrs. Sadler was mother of Catherine Ann Sadler, who first married the Rev. Joseph A. Shanklin. After his death she married the Rev. J. H. Elliott. Simpson, *Old Pendleton District*, pp. 118-19, 168-69; Register, St. Paul's.

find him there. Every one speaks well of him & I think he must have improved much. I do long to see him again. He applied for banish-ment, but did not succeed, poor fellow. I pray he may not be forced to take that degrading oath. I never saw any one improve more than he has in spelling, writing & style, & we hear he reads a great deal. The doctor has at last told us that the ulcer grandma has been so afflicted with has become cancerous, & will in all prob-ability never be cured. She spends most of her time in her room, & her nervous system has so completely given away that she she *screams* & cries for hours every day, but I do not think always from pain by any means. A Lt. Bond was here on his way to Fla. yester-day, a very pleasent man. Mary Berrien spent a day & night with me as also Anna Pickens.[38] We write letters constantly now & send them by private opportunities but get none. They say all property over 20,000, any one owns is to be confiscated.[39] There is no cur-rency here now; nothing passes but coin of which there is none.

Monday

1865

June 26th. Calhoun arrived yesterday, looking very handsome, & well, considering his privations. He was released on the oath of alleigeance on the ninth. It was a bitter pill for him, but all on Johnson's Island took it, as there was no use staying there during the whole of their lives, as they had no longer a country to defend. He passed a day at uncle Elias Baker's, a day & night in Baltimore, & about the same time in Washington, going to see the old place which is covered with soldiers & tents, Mrs. Calvert[40] who has Ella & her children with her, & the Crawford's, Riggs, & Mrs. Stone.

[38] There were several Anna Pickenses, but Floride probably referred to Anna (Nov. 8, 1844-Apr. 13, 1914) who was the daughter of Col. T. J. Pickens. She married Jerry J. Miles. Simpson, *Old Pendleton District*, pp. 192-93; marker in Old Stone Church Cemetery, Pendleton.

[39] A rumor probably arising from President Johnson's amnesty proclamation which excluded from pardon ex-Confederates whose property was valued at $20,000 or more.

[40] Charlotte Augusta Norris Calvert (died Dec. 7, 1876) widow of Charles Benedict Calvert. Their oldest daughter Ella (Mar. 20, 1840-Feb. 17, 1902) married Duncan G. Campbell. See note 37, chap. I. Clemson family letters indicate that Ella was in Pendleton during at least a part of the war. Clemson Papers, *passim*.

He had to walk about 80 miles, between City Point [Virginia] & here, & only brought a valise through. He walked 30 miles in one night which was pretty well for a man who has been in close confinement for 22 months. It was four years the ninth of this month since I saw either him or father, & it has been four months since we have heard from the latter. They say that Kerby Smith[41] has surrendered, that is to say some of his army has, the rest with himself, finding their way to Mexico. Calhoun is very anxious to get to work, & is much more sober than he used to be. He stoops dreadfully but would have a very fine figure if he did not. He is well proportioned, especially from the waist down, for he has a small waist, large well formed hips, & well made legs. He hair is a bright brown, about the color of his eyes, & wavy. I found two white hairs in it, telling of his sufferings. His beard is the same color thick & long. His moustache is lighter, & more delicate. He is much improved by the covering of the lower part of his face which is defective. His teeth are not bad, white, & well shaped though somewhat disfigured by his eye teeth having grown inside, & forcing out the next ones a little. He never cut these till he was nineteen. His voice is musical in speaking, but he does not sing much although he has more ear than I have. He is quite 6 feet 4 in. & will be 24 on the 17th of July. I am so glad to see him again. I do not see that he has changed much in character except that his is graver. He is very profane which I regret & has roughened in his every day manners, although when he choses he is quite elegant, & styleish. His complexion is really beautiful, & his brow. He says that for twelve months, they retaliated upon them in prison, & never gave them half enough to eat, part of the time allowing nothing to be sent to him, or anything but the most meagre half rashions, no candles, nor anything else. He made many attempts to escape but always failed, only half a dozen succeeding in all that time. He says there was no stealing, even the few radishes &c. raised were respected. There were two cases of men killing each other, but more killed by the sentinells. Many died of starvation, confinement, &c. At first they were bowied up by hope but when that faded they sank, & nearly went mad. He says the loss of hope was the most terrible thing,

[41] General Edmund Kirby-Smith (May 16, 1824-Mar. 28, 1893), surrendered the last Confederate military forces on June 2, 1865. DAB, X, 424-26.

down. I also went to a *tea fight* at Dr. Adger's. Young Wade Hampton,[45] my Columbia friend has been to see me. He seems spoiled, & not quite as pleasent as he was. Mother got a letter from her old friend Mrs. Barstowe, who is in California. She writes very affectionately & says she has a wedding present set apart for me. She will probably keep it long. I see a good deal of company here. Sometimes several visits coming together quite fill the room. I have just had a very bad attack with my eyes, & have had my old enemy the diorea untill I had to go to bed for a couple of days. Father is nicer, & more pleasent than I ever saw him. Really affectionate, & amiable. Calhoun I forgot to say brought me a pretty carbuncle ring when he came which he got in quite a singular way. A lady came into the prison bowed, & kissed her hand to him. He sent her a *prisoners ring*, by one of her relations inside. She returned this one with a note signed "the Lady in Brown." He could never learn her name. Father has wonderfully improved in playing on the violin, & really composes some quite good common place tunes. He does look so well, & has given up smoking. He is a dear old fellow.

July 29th. Calhoun remained over a week among the mountains, but killed no dear. Two were killed by the party. Old Maum Kate from Fort Hill ran away, & came to stay with us. She is nursing grandma, & is quite a comfort. They have lost over 70 negroes at Fort Hill in the last year; mostly children, of the whooping cough, & measels, combined. Dr. Rag [Wragg] came & consulted with Drs. Maxwell & Pickens,[46] about grandma. They have decided that she has a cancer, & that it will never get better, but, not being in a

---

[45] Wade Hampton, IV (1840-1879), a Civil War veteran, son of the Confederate general. He died in Mississippi of fever. Manly W. Wellman, *Giant in Gray: a Biography of Wade Hampton of South Carolina* (New York: Charles Scribner's Sons, 1949), pp. 22, 162, 307.

[46] Dr. Thomas J. Pickens, Jr., son of Col. Thomas J. and Keziah Pickens; Dr. William T. Wragg (1804-1885), son of Samuel Wragg (1770-1844) and Mary Ashby I'on Wragg (July 6, 1782-?), married (1) Anne Toomer and (2) Eliza R. Toomer. Mary A. Wragg bought a house and lot in Pendleton on Aug. 23, 1862. Dr. William Wragg was living in Charleston in 1860 and undoubtedly refugeed with his family and his widowed mother in Pendleton. MS. Census 1860, Ward 2, Charleston Dist., S. C.; Anderson deeds, book H-2, p. 169; *SCHGM*, XIX (July, 1918), 121; XXV (Jan., 1924), 14-15; Simpson, *Old Pendleton District*, p. 192.

vital part, it may not kill her for years. She suffers terribly from it, & nervousness combined. She half suspects what it is, & can not bear pain at all. She has to take opiates all the time. It would be a mercy if she could die, & save herself all the misery, she will have to suffer. We are in the midst of a terrible drought, & many say the corn crop is already ruined. The wheat having been also an entire faliure, scarce any one making seed about here, the prospect for winter is terrible. The negroes being freed, almost everyone is turning them away by hundreds to starve, plunder, & do worse. The times ahead a[re] fearful. They have just begun praying in the churches for the Pt. of the United States, & everyone has to take the oath. We are crushed indeed, & humiliated. I have not yet had any letters except two from Mary Latrobe since I have been here. The railroads are fast repairing.

Aug. 10th. I have just received a letter from Lizzie Robinson, & an other from her mother. She is still at the Vinyard, & likely to remain there the winter. Leigh R. is home. Henry, her cousin, dead. Jennie King in in Alexandria, will stay in Md. all winter, the Fair-faxes have settled at Gov. Spraig's⁴⁷ place in the Forrest. Billy Dundas has inherited (he says) half a million, from his uncle & is going to his domains in Scotland. The McCeneys & Woods well. These are the first letters from any but Mary Latrobe since I have been here, & were dated July 12th. I have been quite sick with diarroea again lately, & am not strong yet. My poor eyes so much worse, that I can scarce do a thing. I went to a nice party at the Adam's⁴⁸ last week, & was invited to two more. We see a good deal of company here. Hall Calhoun has opened a store in the village, with all kinds of things in it, at high prices.

Sep 2nd. Gen. Wade Hampton & his wife, (Mary McDuffy⁴⁹ that was) came to see us last Saturday. He is a fine looking man of fifty about with dark brown hair & beard still untinged with grey, & a fine dark blue eye. A very striking dashing look. He said noth-

⁴⁷ William Sprague (Sept. 12, 1830-Sept. 11, 1915), governor of Rhode Island and U. S. Senator, married Kate, daughter of Salmon P. Chase. *DAB*, XVII, 473, 475-76. "The Vinyard" was the Robinson home.

⁴⁸ Mrs. Jasper Adams. See note 10 above.

⁴⁹ Wade Hampton, III, the Confederate cavalry leader and later governor and senator, married (June, 1858) his second wife, Mary Singleton McDuffie. Wellman, *Giant in Gray*, p. 237.

ing kept him in this country *but* a desire to pay his debts. He was staying at Keowee, Hall Calhoun's [home], on his way to his place is Cassier's valley.[50] I have been very sick with sick headaches &c. lately, sometimes in bed for two or three days. *One* week had *four* sick headaches. Dr. Maxwell says the summer was too hot & did not agree with me. Am now a little better. They say the state of things in the low country is terrible. Men, formally wealthy, have litterally not wherewithall to buy bread, & many must starve. Lands which have been abandoned by their owners during the war, are confiscated to be divided by the "freedmen's beaureau" among the negroes. An insurrection is much dreaded. All negroes have now asserted their freedom now. At Ft. Hill all have left but some fifteen hands. Jackson[51] has also quietly & amicably set up as shoemaker, & fidler for himself from here. An oficer of negroes was shot at Walhalla a few days since. Negro garisons are stationed at Anderson, & that place, but none here, though they pay us visits! Got a letter from Miss Olivia Buck to day dated Aug. 3rd. She says among other things that Miss Lane is engaged to Mr. Henry Johnson of Baltimore. I believe this because she told me about him when I was there. He is a Southerner too. I am really glad to hear of it, for Mr. B. is a perfect old tyrant to her. The Riggs are still in Europe. The Woods at their place. Mrs. Harvey in Scotland. Old Dundas in Philla. has left some thirty thousand dollars a piece to Mrs. Everette, Billy, &c. The latter is going to Scottland. All old friends are well. I would so love to go to see them all again. Billy Dundas is going to marry Miss Marron.[52]

Oct 8th. Last Thursday there was a great tournament here. Some fourteen knights rode in various costumes, not at all *knightly* for the most. Two sent their lances to me to trim, & rode for me: Edwin Frost, & Ben. Gaillard.[53] My colors were red, white, & black.

[50] High Hampton Inn, Cashiers, N. C., today stands on the site of Hampton's mountain retreat.

[51] A former slave of Mrs. John C. Calhoun.

[52] Mary Pamela Marron. Letter from Mrs. Florence Dundas Roller, Staunton, Va., Nov. 18, 1959.

[53] Edwin, son of Judge Edward Frost (1801-July 21, 1868) of Charleston. The family refugeed in Pendleton. *SCHGM*, X (Apr., 1909), 109. Judge Frost was president of the Blue Ridge Railroad in 1860. Benjamin S. Gaillard (Nov. 27, 1848-Oct. 13, 1910), was son of W. H. D. and Sallie Sloan Gaillard. Simpson, *Old Pendleton District*, p. 99; Register, St. Paul's.

The Confederate colors, in mourning. The prize was awarded to Ben. Crawford, who crowned Miss Sue Lewis,[54] a mere school girl. The crowning was awkwardly managed. Duff Calhoun was leader of the la[n]ces, as the "Great Mogul," Hall as an I[n]dian, was judged the best rider, he certainly was the best character. Andrew went as a "Highland lad," one of my knights as Billy Bow Legs, the other (Edwin Frost) as the "Red Knight." In the evening there was a fancy dress ball. I went as a Spanish lady with my pink silk skirt trimmed with black lace, a black Spanish body, over a white lace waist, & a black lace shawl over a high comb. I hear every one say I was the best dressed lady in the room. I left early leaving some dozen dancing engagements, because I was worn out, having worked hard at getting up dresses for others, & was sick next day, *of course*. I have received any quantity of letters from my friends lately. From Kate Barton, Lizzie Robinson, Sallie Clemson, Mr. Dunscomb & others. This latter wants to come down to see me, but I wrote telling him he had better not, for he does not seem to have forgotten me. Yet I suppose he will come, I hope not. Indeed I have been very honest with him, & feel sorry he can not forget me. All the family North seems in statu quo. Kate says Clem North is engaged to a nice girl, & Miss Lane has broken her engagement. Meta Sandford has been married some time to a Mr. Glass of Lynchburg. Sallie Clemson seems so well again, & writes in good spirits. I am very glad, for I thought her in a bad way. Lizzie Robinson, & Mary Latrobe urge me to go on & spend the winter with them. I only wish I could, as this country is getting very unsafe. People are constantly called from their houses at night & shot, besides thefts of all kinds & degrees, are of daily occurrence. The country is in a terrible state, & will probably get worse, as the winter proceeds. Some of the refugees are going tomorrow. Mr. & Mrs. Ed. Thurston, & his mother, with Miss Eliza Ford,[55] Mrs. Holms, & others, soon

[54] Sue A. Lewis (1849-1932), daughter of Andrew F. and Susan Sloan Lewis, never married. Simpson, *Old Pendleton District*, p. 168; marker in Old Stone Church Cemetery; Benjamin C. Crawford (Feb. 14, 1846-Jan. 24, 1912), Register, St. Paul's.

[55] Two Thurston households were listed in Charleston in 1860: (1) Robert (age 26) and Maria Thurston (26), two infant children, and Margaret (21) and Eliza Ford (20); (2) E. M. Thurston (age 29), Mrs. E. E. (45), John G. (23), Emily F. (18), and James Thurston (18). Robert was a clerk and E. M. a factor. MS. Census 1860, Wards 2 and 3, Charleston Dist., S. C. The

others are to leave. Gen. Ben Huger[56] is up here, & talks of living at his old place again. Gen. Wade Hampton has his shoulder put out of place which prevented his being at the convention of which he refused to be elected a member, but was. I am ashamed of the action of my state at this.[57] I had rather be kept as a territory than so disgraced. My eyes are better. Grandma about the same. Figs, & haws nice.

Novembre 6th. Aunt Kate talks of going next Tuesday to Abbeville first, & then either to [St.] Augustine, or Canada. I shall really miss her, for she professes to be very fond of me, & is very kind. I grieve very much at the manner of her going, & wish Calhoun had left off making mischief there for once. I have been very busy for over a month, cutting, fitting, planning, & packing for her to go. It is strange no one seems to quarel with me. Grandma is getting worse. She is so nervous, irritable, & cross, that she is almost insuportable at times. I am as well as I ever am again, & my eyes generally better, though for some reason they have been much inflamed of late. Father has bought a horse & carriage. The former for $120 is a strawberry roan, & a very powerful animal, the latter he only gave $48 for. It is a nice little one horse affair, strong, though abused some, & rusty. We had the first killing frost last night, but the oak trees are still pretty green. We have had a delightful fall. Maggie Ford, Mrs. Wm. Ravenel, the two Mrs. Thurston's,[58] & many other refugees have left. All will soon be gone. I shall miss the [Judge] Frosts, especially Lizzie most, as I like them very much. There was a concert here last week, but I would not sing at it. My piano north is sold for what I gave for it.

Dec. 17th. Over a month ago I went to Anna Frosts' wedding. Lizzie Jennings & myself were the only ones among twenty out of

census and diary indicate that Mrs. E. E. was mother of E. M., who apparently married after 1860.

[56] Maj. Gen. Benjamin Huger (1805-1877). *SCHGM*, XLIII (Oct., 1942) 235-36.

[57] This is not clear. Apparently Floride objected to the S. C. Convention's acceptance of President Johnson's conditions for re-admission into the Union.

[58] For Ford and Thurston families see above note 55. Emily Thurston, daughter of Robert and Eliza Emily North Thurston, married Dr. William C. Ravenel (Jan. 11, 1855). Henry E. Ravenel, *Ravenel Records* . . . (Atlanta: Franklin Printing and Publishing Co., 1898), p. 146.

mo[u]rning in the room. She married Pinckney Lownds.[59] Two
weeks ago I went to Lizzie Lee's wedding to Mr. Guillard[60] of
Charleston. There were about 30 there, both places had nice set
suppors. Last Friday there was a sale of farm utensils, produce, &
stock at Fort Hill. Grandma bought two mules, two cows, 500
bushells of corn, 50 of peas, a house of shucks, & much fodder, with
some 12 hogs. All came to $1600 with a year's credit. The boys
seemed very angry at her getting the things, & threatened to "pay
her up" &c. Cousin Ed. Noble has just lost his eldest daughter Bell.
Calhoun is still away at uncle James[61] where he & father both went
the same day there as aunt Kate did. Father returned in two weeks,
& has been very kind & pleasent ever since his return. Calhoun always makes him cross, & makes him disagreeable. Every one expects trouble about Xmas. with the negroes, who expect land.
Matters are pretty quiet now except casual disturbances thefts &
murders. I have heard again from Miss Lane telling me of her
approaching marriage to Mr. Johnson of Balt. & inviting me to
come & see her. Clem North is married to [unfinished].

   Dec. 26th. Yesterday (Monday, Xmas) was a dull, warm, cloudy
day, but towards evening it cleared. I received no gifts except
some mint candy from mother, & a couple of tame squrrells from
the Pickins. I made eight little photograph frames out of pine
burrs, acorns, beechnuts, & beans, two for the Pickens, two for the
Cornishes,[62] two for the Frosts, & two for Ella Lorton.[63] I also made

[59] Thomas Pinckney Lowndes (born Feb. 22, 1839) son of Thomas Pinckney and Margaret Washington Lowndes, married (Nov. 9, 1865) Anne Branford Frost, daughter of Judge Edward Frost. George B. Chase, *Lowndes of
South Carolina* . . . (Boston: A. Williams & Co., 1876), p. 42.

[60] Elizabeth Lee, daughter of Dr. Lawrence and Sarah Dickinson Lee,
married William D. Gaillard. Simpson, *Old Pendleton District,* p. 115.

[61] James Edward Colhoun, whose plantation "Millwood" on the Savannah
River three miles from the present site of Calhoun Falls, S. C., was a brother
of Mrs. John C. Calhoun.

[62] The family of Episcopal minister A. H. (age 46) and Catherine Cornish
(40). Their daughters Kate (18) and Lizzie (16) were friends of Floride.
Simpson, *Old Pendleton District,* p. 146; MS. Census 1860, Anderson Dist.,
S. C.

[63] Ella, daughter of John S. (Feb. 28, 1806-Oct. 16, 1862) and Eliza
Amanda Lorton (Feb. 7, 1812-Feb. 29, 1884). Lorton was a prosperous Pendleton merchant; his only child Ella (age 16 in 1860) became the second

a couple of serpentine braid trimmings, three feather piano dusters, & gave a comb to mother & a cravat to father. I went to church in the morning (which I helped to dress on Saturday) making six ceder, & pine wreaths for it. The evening I spent at Mr. Elliot's, had a pleasent evening, & nice supper, a game of snap draggon, & some pictures of the East to look at & enjoy. I must confess I felt pretty homesick though, thinking of the pleasent merry Xmas times I used to spend with Lizzie Robinson & the Woods. I will never have such happy days again I fear. Calhoun has neither come up as he promised, nor has he written to us. He is still at uncle Jame's I suppose. We had some tableaux last Friday. The Miss Pinckens, Margaret Seybrook, Vallie North, Carro Ravenell, Kate Shanklin,[64] the Frost boys, Gussy Van Wyck, & some other young men acted. I was prime director, costumer, actor, & sugester. They were very beautiful all say. There was scarce any audience, as none were invited but the families of the *actors*. The scenes were the sleeping beauty, telling fortunes, Judith & Hollafernes, the witches in Macbeth, taking the veil, beheading Mary of Scotts, the fair Geraldine, in the magic mirror, the tea party at Chuzzlewits, the old maids' tea party, Mrs. Squeirs giving treakle, the real, & imaginary sheperdess, & the animating of Pigmalion's statue, a pantomine. We had it in the hotel, with stage curtains, & all complete. They say I acted very well, but I took all the ugly scens, housekeeper, gypsy, old maid, witch, abess & maid of honor to Mary. I enjoyed it *hugely*.

---

wife of Gideon Lee, of Carmel, N. Y. (who was married first to Floride Clemson). Simpson, *Old Pendleton District*, pp. 79-80; MS. Census 1860, Anderson Dist., S. C.; markers in Old Stone Church Cemetery.

[64] Margaret, daughter of Archibald H. and Caroline Pinckney Seabrook, refugeed in Pendleton. Later she married Col. Henry Middleton Rutledge (Aug. 5, 1839-June 10, 1921) and of this union was born the author Archibald Rutledge. *SCHGM*, XXXI (Apr., 1930), 99. Valeria ("Vallie") (age 13) daughter of Dr. Edward and Valeria North of Charleston, refugeed in the home of her uncle John Laurens North. MS. Census 1860, Ward 4, Charleston Dist., S. C. Letter from Miss Valeria Chisolm, Charleston, S. C., Oct. 6, 1959. Catherine Ann ("Kate"), daughter of the Rev. Joseph A. and Catherine Ann Sadler Shanklin, Simpson, *Old Pendleton District*, pp. 168-69. Carro Ravenel was probably the refugee daughter Caroline (Dec. 25, 1843-Dec. 21, 1867), of Dr. Edmund (Dec. 8, 1797-July 27, 1870) and Louisa Ford Ravenel (died Dec. 13, 1886). Ravenel, *Ravenel Records*, pp. 144, 158.

IV

Pendleton, South Carolina

1866

Jan. 1st 1866.

Monday Today it is raining steadily, drearily, as it has almost without intermission of two consecutive clear days, for over a month. May this sad weather not bode a sad year to come! I have felt so sad of late, & today, in spite of many things to make me happy, but I dont much like this place, where with the exception of Lizzie Frost, Ella Lorton, & the Pickenses, there are few congenial persons here. My twenty third birth day passed quietly raining in the evening, & dreary nearly all day. Ella Lorton & Miles Pickens spent the evening here & we had an eggnog. Ella sent me some nice flout, & Lizzie Frost a very pretty purple, & white neck ribbon. I spent Saturday evening with Lizzie very pleasently. Thank God thus far we have had no trouble, as was anticipated from the negroes, who had determined to have part of their master's lands at least, but a Yankee Collonel made them some speeches about here, telling them they would not uphold them, & advising them to be peaceable & quiet. Peter who has been the cook here for three or four years is to leave I am sorry to say, as he is a grumpy, but pretty steady, & honest man. The two Miss Adams have returned after a ten days stay in New York. They brought a nice long letter from Mrs. Daub, who seems to long to get back to us; she is still with Mrs. Lee[1] No one knows how I regret having to give up my much hoped for, & anticipated visit to those I love in Md, & other places. I can not get over my feeling of loneliness & homesickness here & I

---

[1] Caroline and Fannie, daughters of the Rev. Jasper Adams. Their elder sister Elizabeth married Archibald C. Campbell, of New York, in 1859. Lisette Daub came to work for the Clemsons as a cook and housekeeper in 1857. She remained in the North when Mrs. Clemson and Floride returned South in 1864. Mrs. Gideon Lee of New York was the mother of Gideon (Jr.) and D. W. Lee. See Clemson Papers, *passim.*

Floride Clemson Lee in her second-day dress

Floride

Calhoun

Thomas Green

Anna Calhoun

THE CLEMSON FAMILY

X

want to see dear Lizzie Robinson especially, for I love her best of all, & I suppose it will be long ere I do so now, as she is probably to leave that place, perhaps for Europe, next spring. My principal pleasure here is in receiving letters from her, Miss Lane, Sallie Clemson, Kate B., Mary Latrobe, & others, all of whom write so affecly to me. Mr. Onderdonk also often writes. He has bought my piano. My pills Dr. Maxwell. Rx Extract Tarax^c. $_3$ ii Bismouth Sub. nit. Ferri Queveuno āā $_3$ i M fit. Pill No 60 1 three times a day.

1866

Monday

Jan. 15th. Last Tuesday Dr. Maxwell came to put a seaton[2] in my neck, for my eyes which have now been partially paralized for over two years. I came to the conclusion that I had tried gentle means long enough. The doctor ran a piece of lavender silk braid through, & it has really been very painful causing a cornel on my shoulder, & being very much inflamed & swolen. I am to keep it on some two months he says, pulling it every day. My maid Marie does it for me. She is really an invaluable servant, & I dont know what I should do without her as she is so devoted to me. Last Saturday evening I invited a few friends to meet Gov. Orr's daughter, Mattie. She is very a[n]xious I should go home with her to spend some time with her, but I dont feel like visiting in her father's family, such men disgrace the State.[3] She is staying at the Van Wycks. Yesterday I went to hear a lecture, to the young delivered by Patric Malaly[4] in the Presbyterian church. It was very good, & he preaches strikingly. Father tells me that if he goes to Europe in the spring as he expects to, he will take me with him. I am delighted of course, for I have never ceased to regret that I did not go with him just before the war, when he wanted me to. I dream, & think of nothing but what I hope to see, do, & hear there.

[2] A seton is an induced ulcer which is supposed to draw the poison out of another area.

[3] Martha, daughter of Governor James L. Orr. Floride apparently objected to Governor Orr's moderate, compromising policies.

[4] F. P. Mullally replaced Dr. John B. Adger in 1865 and continued as Presbyterian minister until 1867. F. D. Jones and W. H. Mills (eds.), *History of the Presbyterian Church in South Carolina Since 1850* (Columbia, S. C.: R. L. Bryan Co., 1926), p. 956.

Tuesday

Jan. 23rd. Cousin Ed. Noble came up two or three days ago partly to take me down to Abbeville with him. I start to day, at twelve o'clock.

March 11th.

Saturday I got back from Abbeville yesterday night at eleven at night, having left Cokesbury at 5½ P. M. I must now chronicle my whole trip, for particulars I refer to my letters to mother, however I went first to Anderson, where I spent the night at Gov. Orr's with Mattie Orr. The next day went to Coakesbury. I found cousin Floride Cunningham's[5] family in a great bustle, as Lou, the youngest daughter about 18 years old was to be married on Friday, two days after. I helped all I could. She was married to Mr. Charles Banks, on Friday morning quite privately, & went off the same day in the cars to Charleston. I liked cousin Floride, the elder, very much, she is a whole souled, kind hearted, fussy woman. Emma Floride, who is some eight months older than I am is a dark, dried up, snaky, little black cat, of a witch, & I cant bear her. Spiteful artificial, &, I think, pretty bad every way. I had to hold myself not to fight her. Lizzie, some two years younger is a little dimpy kitten, pretty, winning, useful, fair, long haired thing. I liked her, & she seemed to take a great fancy to me. Lou was the most lady like, & attractive, has really elegant manners, but not very pretty, auburn style. Bob the oldest son is a little monkey about nineteen, not up to my shoulder, dark, & snaky with a foot, wearing No. 13 misses shoes! Took a fancy to me, of course. Then there is Benjie, walking in his father's tracks, at 16 *good,* & *bad* looking. John 14 stutters,

[5] In 1860 John Cunningham (age 40) was editor of the Charleston *Evening News.* His family included his wife Floride (age 39), and children Emma F. (18), Lizzie P. (17), Louisa B. (15), Robert N. (13), Benjamin (11), John (8), and Clarence (6). MS. Census 1860, Ward 6, Charleston Dist., S. C. In 1860 when Floride planned to visit the Cunninghams in Charleston, her mother sternly warned: "Dont go to a party *with him* [Mr. Cunningham] *alone,* any more than you would with any one else. It is not that I fear or think he would take liberties with you, but he is a *bad man,* & has a *bad reputation.* . . ." Anna C. Clemson to Floride, Jan. 22, 1860, Clemson Papers. Col. Cunningham was from Virginia; his wife was the former Floride Calhoun Noble (Aug. 7, 1819-Aug. 4, 1870), daughter of Governor Patrick Noble. McPherson (comp.), *Calhoun, Hamilton, Baskin and Related Families,* pp. 14, 18.

goodlooking, stooping, but rather promising. Claire about twelve, a very girl in every way. Made a calico skirt for his mother, & plays with dolls, but is right sweet. Mr. Cunningham is the picture of a worn out rouée. Stiff, blind of an eye, bloated, & disgusting. I left these, on Saturday, with Cousin Ed. Noble,[6] & his family. I liked his wife [Mary] very much, she is pretty, stylish, rather proud, but very polite to me. Her eldest son Pat, about sixteen, is a fine, gentlemanly boy. Bell about 15, died in December. Edward about eleven, is very like any well brought up, rather wild boy. Floride, six, is a pretty brunette, & very sweet. Pinckey, three, is a merry little roleypoley, blonde. I spent some two weeks, here, a week with cousin Eugenia Parker, an other with cousin Martha Burt,[7] & ended my trip at cousin Floride Cunningham's again, being nearly 7 weeks away. Cousin Martha has the handsomest garden I ever saw of the prim treeless grassless kind & many of the early hyacynths &c. were out in it on the first of Feb. The house is a nice one, & beautifully kept. I liked cousin Martha, she was very kind to me, & affectionate & handsome, styleish woman, but very deaf, & not healthy, nearly as tall as I am, so is cousin Mary Noble, & Eugenia Parker. The latter has five children, i.e. Tom, an oaf of 17. Mattie a gawk of 16. Willie a rowdy of 12. Helen, a opossam of 10, Teddy, an idiot (almost) of six. Dr. Parker is a silent, uninteresting man. *She* is a simple, good, hardworking, plain woman but also very kind, & affecte. to me. Mr. Burt was not at home. I also met Cousin John A. Calhoun's[8]

[6] In 1860 Edward Noble (age 36), had the following family listed: Martha (Mary) (age 28), Patrick (12), B(ell) (8), Edward (5), and Floride (1). MS. Census 1860, Abbeville Dist., S. C. Mrs. Noble was the former Mary Means Bratton. Pickens, *The Pickens Family*, p. 50.

[7] Eugenia Calhoun, daughter of William (brother of John C.) and Catherine J. de Graffenreid Calhoun, married Dr. Edwin Parker. In 1860 the census listed the family thus: Edwin Parker (age 37), Eugenia C. (34), Thomas (10), Martha C. (9), William C. (5), Ellen L. (3), Edwin (9/12). Martha, sister of Eugenia, married Armistead Burt (Mar. 12, 1827), lawyer and U. S. Congressman. Salley, *The Calhoun Family*, pp. 22-23; *Biog. Dir. Cong.*, p. 924; MS. Census 1860, Abbeville Dist., S. C.

[8] John A. Calhoun (Jan. 8, 1807-Aug. 25, 1874) was son of James, older brother of John C. Calhoun. He married Sarah M. Norwood (May 18, 1814-Dec. 3, 1891). Among their 12 children were Caroline (b. July 9, 1843), Anna Susan (b. May 29, 1849), Williamson Norwood (b. Aug. 28, 1841), Orville Tatum (b. Sept. 6, 1847), and Sarah Martin (b. Jan. 19, 1839), who married Andrew Simonds (Jan. 10, 1860). Salley, *The Calhoun Family*, p. 26.

family. Carry about 20 is an uninteresting girl. Anna about 17 almost as tall as I am, fat as mother, weighing about 200 lbs; but pretty, & honest. Then there are plenty of others I dont know, but I saw Nowwood, & Orville. One of the girls, Mrs. Simons, seems inclined to be fast, but pleasent. They were all very polite to me. Cousin J was very pompus, & polite. I had some twenty parties, little, & big, dinner, & evening. The four largest (set tables with all kinds of good things) were given by Mrs. Wm. H. Parker, Mrs. Dr. Marshal[9] (Fanny Calhoun that was) & Cousins Eugenia Parker, & Martha Burt. The others were by almost every one there, & some in Cokesbury. I had a delightful time altogether, & almost the whole place called upon me, & they say no young lady has caused such a sensation for years. There were plenty of dancing beaux, boys, but only three young gentlemen worth mentioning: Col. Aleck Haskell, a young widdower, with one eye shot out, fits, a little daughter, & a stutter, otherwise agreeable & intelligent. Mr. Charley Pinckney, peculiar interesting, & engaged. & Clark Wardlaw,[10] dull. Lizzie, & Floride Cunningham went about with me, & were a great draw back, as their family has quarrelled with almost all there. I had so much attention shown me, & kindness, that I could not help having a delightful time. I was also very well while there, only having three sick headaches, & getting entirely well of my diahaeroea. The weather was charming also generally too warm for my winter cloth's. They do not seem to have felt the war there, as here, or other places, & there was much fashionable dressing, & style. Calhoun paid a visit home while I was there, I saw him on his way. Grandma looks worse than when I left, but is able to walk a little

[9] Lucia G. (age 26) was the wife of William H. Parker (age 31), attorney-at-law in Abbeville. Frances Josette Calhoun, daughter of Joseph (b. July 22, 1787) and Frances Darricott Calhoun (May 1, 1800-Mar. 21, 1885), married Dr. J. W. Marshall. *Ibid.*, pp. 13-14; MS. Census 1860, Abbeville Dist., S. C.

[10] Alexander Cheves Haskell (Sept. 22, 1839-Apr. 14, 1910) married Rebecca Singleton in 1861. She died the following year. In 1870 he wed Alice Van Yeveren Alexander. They had 10 children. Haskell ran unsuccessfully as a Conservative candidate for governor against Benjamin R. Tillman in 1890. Louise Haskell Daly, *Alexander Cheves Haskell: Portrait of a Man* (Privately published, 1934). See especially pp. 177, 222. Charles Pinckney (1839-1909) was son of the Rev. Charles Cotesworth Pinckney (1812-1898). *SCHGM*, XXXIX (Jan., 1938), 32. Clark Wardlaw was either Joseph C. (age 19), son of Dr. Joseph J. and Mary A. Wardlaw or W. C. (age 22), son of banker Robert H. and Eliza Wardlaw. MS. Census 1860, Abbeville Dist., S. C.

with crutches now, & is a little more patient. Mrs. Ford a perfect musical genious, I met with in Cokesbury, was one of the most interesting women I saw. Lizzie Frost passed down to Charleston, & I just saw her on the cars, while I was in Cokesbury. I found 20 letters wai[t]ing for me at home. One was from Miss Lane, telling me of her marriage to Mr. Henry Elliot Johnston,[11] a banker of Baltimore, where she has to live. She writes for me to come on & see me [her]. She has always kept the name I gave her of "Lady Constance" which I thought suited her. In return she has named me "Fidélité." She was married on the 11th of Jan. I do wish we were to live near Baltimore. Other letters tell me of the marriage of Tom King to Miss Robinson of Va. & Frank Singleton to Gertrude Magoffin. The rebuilding of cousin Richard Washington's place Blakely,[12] aunt Louisa's bad health, & the warm friendship of those I have left behind with their urgent entreaties for a visit. Mr. Alston Hayne's[13] house was burnt down last night, & nearly all destroyed.

May 6th. Hall Calhoun died in Charleston March 27th of dropsy of the chest, & Bright's desease of the kidneys. Teddy[14] did not get down in time to see him. Teddy himself is in such bad health that the doctors have ordered him to go abroad. He left last week for N. Y. from whence he will soon start for Europe. Father left here for Charleston on his way North to day three weeks. We have heard frequently from him now in N. Y. where he says some old friends have treated him very coldly, Mr. Lee for instance. I had to refuse an invitation from Lizzie Frost to visit her in Charleston,

[11] Harriet Lane married Henry Elliot Johnston of Baltimore at "Wheatland," January 11, 1866. They had two sons, both of whom died young. George T. Curtis, *Life of James Buchanan* . . . (2 vols., New York: Harper and Brothers, 1883), II, 632, 656.

[12] Gertrude Magoffin, daughter of Governor Beriah Magoffin of Kentucky, married (Jan. 10, 1865) William Frank Singleton (b. May 5, 1840), a Confederate major. See note 63, chap. I. "Blakely" had been destroyed by fire. Annie C. Washington to Floride Clemson, Feb. 22, 1864, Clemson Papers.

[13] Col. William Alston Hayne, son of U. S. Senator Robert Y. Hayne, married Margaretta Stiles of Philadelphia and resided at "Flat Rock" at Pendleton. His property was valued at $65,000 in 1860. After the fire he moved to California. MS. Census 1860, Anderson Dist., S. C.; *SCHGM*, V (July, 1904), 174; Simpson, *Old Pendleton District*, p. 145.

[14] Edward Boisseau Colhoun (b. Apr., 1841), son of Col. John Ewing and Martha Davis Colhoun. Register, St. Paul's Episcopal Church.

as the letter came so late (being delaid three weeks on the road) that mother feared to let me brave the very great sickliness of the city. That with all my long looked for visits must be put off till Fall. I dislike this place so much, I am all impatience to go. Grandma is scarce able to leave her bed now, & has not for a week wheeled out in her sick chair, but the doctors say there is no imminent danger of death, which perhaps is a sad thing, as she suffers terribly, & can not be kept quiet even by anodynes now. It is very wearing to hear her groans complaints & shrieks almost incessantly night & day, although we know much is only nervousness. She is very unreasonable, & takes three persons to attend to her night & day, & wears them down. We have engaged an experienced nurse Mrs. Burns, & hope she will not drive her away by her exactions. There have been many weddings through the whole country. Here Frank Maxwell married Julia Sloan. Keals Maxwell, Maud Shelton—Susie Campbell, Mr. Rogers.[15] Sam Pickens is engaged to Anna Inghram. I drive a great deal in my little one horse carriage, but am much sick again. I am hairdresser general here. I seem quite a favorite, & am invited almost everywhere. Calhoun still at Millwood.

1866

Sunday

June 3rd. Last evening we received the confirmation of a report Mr. Pinckney heard on the cars near two weeks since, of the death of aunt Kate Calhoun. Fannie Russell[16] writes me that she died of billious dysentery after a very painful three weeks illness, on Friday the forth of May. She had been but two months reunited to her parents at Palatka, on the St. Johns Fla. Her three little boys &

[15] Keels and Frank Maxwell were sons of Samuel and Julia Keels Maxwell and grandsons of Captain John (member of the Secession Convention) and Elizabeth Earle Maxwell. However, Frank Maxwell married Catherine Sloan, not Julia, both daughters of Thomas Majors and Nancy Blassingame Sloan. Julia was still unmarried in 1870. Simpson, *Old Pendleton District*, pp. 104, 175-76; MS. Census 1870, Anderson County, S. C. Susan Earle Campbell, daughter of Archibald and Emily P. Campbell, married George Rodgers, of Charleston (Apr. 4, 1866) and moved to Summerville, S. C. Register, St. Paul's Episcopal Church.

[16] The Rev. Charles Cotesworth Pinckney (1812-1898), grandson of General Thomas Pinckney. *SCHGM*, XXXIX (Jan., 1938), 32. Fanny Russell was a cousin of Kate and in her 23rd year in 1866. Floride Calhoun to Anna C. Clemson, June 14, 1857, Clemson Papers.

Fannie Russell are with her parents. They boys are respectively about eight, ten, & twelve years old now. She was conscious to the last, & knew her state. I trust God will have mercy on her, as I think she was a sincere Xtian [Christian], & tried unceaseingly to do her duty.

June 7th. Received five letters from Father last night, dated from Washington. He is getting our things together, & talks of soon returning. His letters are full of the kindness & sincere warmth of our old friends in asking after us. He mentions having seen the dear Robinsons, Woods, Miss Lane (that was), the Middletons, Dr. Pinckney, Crawfords, Calverts (Mrs. C. in a bad way & Charley to be married in June to Miss McCubbin), Mr. Lowndes,[17] all the diplomats, who have shown him much attention, & offered him a much higher position than he had any right to expect he says, in Mexico, but he refused, & talks much of settleing down here. Oh dear! that is not a pleasent prospect for one might as well be buried alive. Aunt [Elizabeth Clemson] Barton has added to her former kind acts a horrid abusive letter about us, to father, whom she honies [?]. He sent it to us. She says much about mother's falsehood, & tries moreover to set father against aunt North in a very mean way. She is the only one of father's relations I find it difficult to love, & feel kindly to. Kate [Barton] still writes me most affec-[tionate]ly, & Sallie Clemson seems perfectly devoted to me. Father talks of having lost a trunk of clothing. He has sent us his likness but it is a very poor one indeed. He says my friends are crazy to have me with them again, & if I have my way they certainly shall have that pleasure next Fall, but much depends on grandma, whom the doctors fear will not last out the summer, as the hot weather will probably accelerate the already rapid progress of the cancer. She can hardly get out of her room in her rolling chair now. She spends all her time moaning, crying, & shrieking.

June 22nd. Father returned from his two months' visit to the North, the night before last. He looks well. The boxes are on the

[17] Charles Baltimore Calvert married Eleanor Mackubin (June 14, 1866), daughter of Dr. Richard C. and Hester Worthington Mackubin. John B. C. Nicklin, "The Calvert Family," *Maryland Historical Magazine,* XVI (Sept., 1921), 316. Mr. Lowndes and "Dr. Pinckney" were Benjamin O. Lowndes (age 59 in 1870), a Bladensburg farmer in whose home lived William Pinkney (age 60 in 1870), and Elizabeth Pinkney. MS. Census 1870, Prince Georges County, Md.

way. He brought me some 15 peices of music, a white dress &c. &c. mother a plaid, & grandma a dancing negro toy. Mary Latrobe sent me $25 to spend among the destitute, which with Mr. Cocorans $500, & Mrs. Dodge's[18] $50 makes a noble contribution, & gives much relief. Father saw almost all our friends, & brings me many invitations to visit them next fall, which I certainly mean to do if possible. His descreption of the fashions are very amusing, such dreadfully large hoops, with trains, ridiculous little bonnets, & the *befrizzled* bundles of hair as big as the head on behing, or else streaming straight down the back. I have quite broken myself down cuting, trimming, weeding &c. about the place, to make things look nice for father, but I hope in a few days to be as well as I was before & *that* was an uncommon state of salubrity for me! I am drawing from photographs, likenesses of my different friends, & succeed wonderfully they say.

July 8th, 1866. Calhoun came up yesterday from Millwood for a visit. He says he has an interest in a saw mill, "& other irons in the fire," down there. I hope so. He does not look very well. Father exchanged gold pens with me. The one he gave me was sent to him from Europe just before the war. Father got me a half grown fox for a pet. I have dubbed him "*Guy Faux.*" Dr. Maxwell has given me some pills which I began in the midst of a very severe spell of sick headaches about two months' since, & have not had one since, although I had as many as three the week before I began. They also keep off the diorhea. Mr. Dunscombe wrote me an other declaration of his unalterable affection for me, & beggs I will let him come on for me next fall, to be my escort to Md. Poor man. I am really sorry for him. I almost wish such true affection as he bears for me, might not have siezed him, but some one whom I could love in return.

July 22nd. Calhoun's birthday was on the 17th when he was 25 years old. On the evening of that day we went to see a Night Blooming Ceries [Cereus], at Mrs. Cornishe's. It was bell shaped when we left at past ten, but after midnight they say it was opened wide & as large as a plate. It is pearly white with innumerable deli-

[18] Probably Mrs. Mary E. Dodge (age 31) and W. W. Corcoran, of the Bladensburg area. MS. Census 1860, County of Wash., D. C. Corcoran, a prominent investment broker, was occasionally mentioned in the Clemson correspondence. Clemson Papers, *passim.*

cate petals, first nearly white, but when fully open deep orange. The outside of the flower is pink, the stem like a meershaum pipe, growing from the edge of a thick caktus leaf as large as my hand. The odor is heavy & sweet. It is said to bloom but once in seven years, & a blossom lasts but a night. This plant was three years old, grown from a small leaf. Calhoun & father have driven to Dahlonega [Georgia] in the carriage, with the mules, started the 18th to see about our gold mine there. Grandma has taken to her bed at last, & we fear will never be able to get up again, she is so weak, & the desease makes such rapid progress now. She of[t]en wanders in mind, & sleeps but little save by snatches now, in spite of 4½ grs. of morphine she takes nightly. Her appetite heretofor good is failing also, & the odor from the cancerous discharge, is so terribly offensive that even when she is quiet we can hardly stay in the room this hot weather. They tell us she can not out last the summer, & may die very soon if the cancer eats into an artery. Is is too terrible! My health is in some respects much better. My sick headaches have entierly given away before some pills Dr. Maxwell gave me, & while I take them, my diorhea is also well, but the moment I cease, it comes back. I have spasms occasionally still.

July 28th, 1866. Grandmother Calhoun died last Wednesday evening at 6½ o'clock P. M. (July 25th) She had only been in bed a week, & was not alarmingly worse until Monday night. Monday morning Dr. Tom Pickens, & Dr. Maxwell both thought she might linger some weeks, but it is supposed that she had a slight stroke of paralysis on Monday night, & when cousin Tom P. saw her Tuesday morning he gave her up. Her mind wandered a little from the day she took to bed, at times, but she was almost totally insinsible from Tuesday morning with but slight intervals of recognition, until her death. For the last two days she could scarcely articulate at all, & the last intelligeble sentence she said was to me when I tried to make her take some milk punch, (all that she touched after the stroke). They were "Go away child, I dont want any," the morning before she died. She was fearfully emaciated, & changed. Mother says that the cancer had eaten away the lower part of her stomack, & split open her groin, nearly to the bone. I never saw it. It was terribly offensive, & had only become regularly glandular some six months before her death. Was brought on by an abrasion from a kedney affection, which was neglected. It first gave her trouble some two years since. She had not walked since last Fall, but was rolled about in her rolling chair. The funeral took place from the [St. Paul's] Episcopal church at 6 o'clock P. M. Thursday 26th. The church was full, & nearly every one there. There was no sermon. About nine carriages went from this house to the grave, the rest went straight to the church. She was buried between aunt Cornelia, & uncle Willie in the Episcopal church yard here, in aunt Kate Calhoun's lot. I wrote to tell aunt Margaret Calhoun on Tuesday of her state, & she, & Margie[19] spent part of that day, & part next here. I think the second day grandma knew her a little. Margie had not been here for over a year. Cousin Kesiah Pickens spent the two days before, & one next after her death, with us. We sent Mr. Duke down for uncle James Calhoun Tuesday, but we have not hea[r]d from him yet. Father, & Calhoun who started a few days before she died for Dahlonega. Geo. returned only the morning before the funeral. We walked thus: Mother & father— Calhoun & I—aunt Margaret & Johnny—Margie & Andrew—Pat & Jimmie. (Duff is away) I am trying to get some mourning dresses. I shall not go into crepe. The pall bearers were old cousin Thomas Pickens, & Mr. Wm Gaillard,[20] who always attended to her business. He made all the arrangements for the funeral, as father & Calhoun were away when she died. Mrs. Burns staid with grandma & nursed her to the last most devotedly. Poor grandma has passed from so much suffering that we can not but regard it as a blessing. I do not suppose for the past year there has been half an hour at a time of her waking moments this house has not resounded to her groans. I read the praye[r]s for the sick beginning "Oh Lord look down from heaven" & "Hear us Almighty & most merciful father" with "Unto God's merciful protection"—the general confession, & Lords prayer, every morning & night, with her, from the time aunt Kate left. She said Amen to these with me & the praye[r]s for the dying that Mr. Cornish said also to her, the morning of the day before she died, but I scarcely think she comprehended them or

[19] Martha Cornelia Calhoun, William Lowndes Calhoun, Margaret Green Calhoun (wife of the deceased Andrew Pickens Calhoun), and Margie Calhoun (daughter of Margaret and Andrew Calhoun).

[20] William Henry Drayton Gaillard (age 48), railroad agent at Pendleton. He married Sallie T. Sloan, daughter of Benjamin F. and Eliza Earle Sloan. Simpson, *Old Pendleton District*, p. 99; MS. Census 1860, Anderson Dist., S. C.

her state. She never seemed more than to suspect that she had a cancer, & three days before she died told Mrs. Burns she hoped she would recover, but though we never told her, neither did we deceived her, as to her state. Her friends were most attentive in flocking to see her, when they heard of her danger. I trust in God that she has gone to the rest that remaineth for his people, which I believe she most earnestly tried to deserve. She prayed almost without ceasing, during the last few months of her illness & was so low spirited, melancholy, & nervous that she rarely smiled. She cried often. Her appetite lasted wonderfully. She did not care to converse, as she took little or no interest in anything, & was so deaf that it was difficult to talk to her. Her mind however, was as strong, & bright as ever, until the last week or so. I have been quite sick the last few days. Ella Lorton spent night before last, & yesterday with me.

Aug. 7th. Grandmother's will was read yesterday. Sam Pickens & I took copies of it, & the codicil. Besides a few minor legacies as her watch to young Floride Cunningham, some little furniture to aunt Kate, two silver goblets to Margie, & some books, photographs & shells to the other grandchildren, she left this place Mi Casa to aunt [Kate's] boys, to revert to us if they die without issue. Fort Hill, all the rest of her personal property & furniture, silver & jewels to mother first, then to me, then to Calhoun, in case I die without either will, or issue. A fourth part of the Ft. Hill bond & mortgage debt is mine now, & $2000 Calhoun's. The codicil was drawn up last January, the will in 1863. Grandma has done a noble part by me. From present appearences, & at present valuation, I seem to bid fair to be worth $15—or 20000 at mother's death, merely from what grandmother has left, & gave me, besides what I may get from father. Cousin Thos. Pickens Sr., Rev. Wm. [Andrew] H. Cornish, Sam Pickens, father mother & myself were present at the reading of the will by cousin Ed. Noble, who came up for the purpose, & returned in the carriage to day as far as Anderson with Mr. Cornish, & father, to record the will. Calhoun returned to Millwood last Saturday. I have been quite sick. The kitchen chimney caught fire last evening, & alarmed us & the village considirably; it must have burnt above an hour. I may as well here record my jewelry, at least the better part: a diamond breast pin, 1 opal & 108 diamonds, some of which were mother's engagement ring; a fushia flower breast pin, pearls, enamel, & diamond sparks, given me by the queen of Belgium when I was about eight; a pair of ear rings, emeralds, rubies, & garnets heavily chased, given me by the sister of the king consort of Spain (Isabella de Bourbon Infanter of Spain countess Goronsky); also two or three little charms, a toilet stand, wash stand, & woman churning, all from her; a full set of amythysts that belonged to grandma Calhoun, breast pin, two bracelets, ear rings, & small pin; a full set of garnets bought by mother in Europe, big & little breast pin, two bracelets, but the ruby & pearl ear rings to match were my great grandmother Calhoun's; a set of ear rings & breast pin of string seed pearls, my grand mother's; an antique stone cameo, set in heavy gold, bought by father in Europe; a little enameled pin, with heavy pearl drop given me by Mme. Demané de Bieme in Belgeium; a gold two headed snake bracelet given as a wedding present by mother to uncle John's[21] first wife, returned to me; a gold & topaz bracelet, a wedding present from mother to uncle Willie's first wife returned to me; a gold chased bracelet given me by grandma Calhoun; a gold flexable bracelet with hair pansey flowers of all the family, from mother; a gold & Jet breast pin, & bracelet of aunt Cornelia's, a pair of gold link hoop ear rings [aunt Cornelia's]* & gold, enamel, & hair [drawing of a bracelet] this shape, [aunt Cornelia's]*; an oval gold, enamel, & hair (marked Mrs. M Calhoun) which was grandma's; also two oval hair, gold, pearls, & jet; one hair, pearl, & gold crecent; one tiny cameo, one tiny hair & gold; one square hair enamel, & gold, all grandmothe's; one cross of gold with grandfather's hair, cut off in the coffin by, & given to me by Mrs. Ellis of Abbev; a paralelogram shell cameo, the car of the sun, of uncle Willie's first wife; an oval shell cameo of mother's, St. John; an oval malikite given me by Mrs. Ged. [Gideon] Lee with hers, [and granddaughters] Laura, Bella, & Maggie Leupps hair at back; a diamond ring with 8 stones (uncle Willies engagement ring to his first wife) given me by aunt Kate; an oval carbuncle ring given to Calhoun while in prison by an unknown "lady in brown," & given to me; an octagon cornelian seal ring with pansey given to me by Calhoun who got it from Mr. Dunscombe; a heavy chased ring with mother's likeness in it; a small single diamond ring given to

---

[21] John Caldwell Calhoun, Jr. Anzie Adams was his first wife.

* NOTE: indicated by ditto marks in MS.

mother when she was married by cousin Floride Cunningham & worn by mother on the first finger of right hand; a plain gold ring given me by Kate Barton, used with a chain grandma gave me, for a mouchoir ring; one bead agate bracelet; one link agate bracelet; one gold-capped, bead, serpentine bracelet; one pair gold cuff pins; one pair gold sleve buttons [drawing]; some six studs; one gem set cuff pin given to Nina, by aunt Sue Clemson[22]; one mosaic fox head stud of uncle Pats'.[23] A gold watch, & heavy, simple link chain of uncle Pat's bought from his estate, for $100, & given me when I was here just before the war by grandma. Uncle Pat desired I should have my choice of his watches ere he died. One cumpas trinket given me by Mr. Dunscombe. A family hair heart shaped glass locket. A gold fish given me by grandma Calhoun. A hair fish given me by grandma Clemson. A polichinell; locomotive; telle-scope; & bronze, & cornelian seal, two gold enamel & pearl (given by the Infanter to C.) & two diamond studs given him by mother, which Calhoun has given me, but I will only hold in trust for him. A gold chain & pad lock necklace. A hair necklace—mother's hair—a long hair chain—mother's hair. Two light broad hair bracelets, Calhoun found & gave me. Two or three hair bracelets, one with aunt Anzie's hair, & likeness. A hair snake bracelet, aunt Maria's[24] hair. A hair snake breast pin, aunt Cornelia's hair. A pair of hair bell earrings, cousin Annie Clemson's[25] hair—A hair ring, uncle Willie's hair. A gold chased cross, by Miss Greenhow. A miniature locket likeness of Grandma Calhoun's baby sister, with hers, & her parent's hair. A miniature locket likeness of grandma Calhoun's father John Ewing Calhoun with his hair. A miniature medalion likeness of cousin Ed. Boisseau.[26] A horrid mourning breast pin &

[22] Sue Clemson was the wife of William Clemson. Nina was Cornelia (Oct. 30, 1855-Dec. 20, 1858), daughter of Thomas G. and Anna C. Clemson.
[23] Capt. Patrick Calhoun, son of John C. Calhoun, died June 1, 1858, in Pendleton.
[24] Anzie Adams (Feb. 10, 1828-Sept. 15, 1850), first wife of John C. Calhoun, Jr.; and Maria Simkins (d. 1844), the wife of James Edward Colhoun. St. Paul's Register; Salley, The Calhoun Family, pp. 21, 28. Both women died in childbirth. Mrs. John C. Calhoun to Anna C. Clemson, Oct. 1, 1850, Clemson Papers.
[25] Annie Clemson, daughter of John Baker Clemson, married George L. Washington. Forrest Brown to Thomas G. Clemson, Aug. 8, 1885, ibid.
[26] James Edward Boisseau was an investment banker in New York. Thomas G. Clemson to John C. Calhoun, Jan. 8, 1850, Calhoun Papers, Clemson College.

locket Calhoun found. An "I[n] memory of" little pin of grand-mother's. A pair of gold capped, cornelian hair pins, of mother's. A cornelian link bracelet given me. Nina's coral sleavelets. An Amber bead bracelet uncle Johnny gave me. A pair of long gold ear rings, I bought. Uncle Pat's locket daguerotype likeness given by cousin Martha Burt, to whom he gave it, to grandma, then she to me. Betty Burn, engaged to uncle Pat, now Mrs. Porcher Miles,[27] small dagurian locket likeness, taken from uncle P.'s neck when he died, & given to me. One gold sliding pen & pencil of grandma's given me. One gold fitting in pen, & pencil sent father from Europe given me. One small gold pencil (enamelled head) of mothers. One gold & silver filagree, enamelled Chinese fan with $8, of actual metal in it. Bought by father, in a curiosity shop abroad & remark-able for being enamelled on both sides alike. One pair of black glass hoop ear-rings, aunt Barton gave me. One strap & buckle gold watch pin. Two chased common gold breast pins, the least solid looking found, & given me by Mr. Onderdonk. Two agate headed, & one Etruscan gold headed shawl pin. A Topaz cross—a little agate oblong breast pin. A common delicate *quasi* gold pencil. A gold belt buckle. A ring made of the marble from the Capitol at Washington. A gold thimble. A carved ivory breast pin. A pair of jet band bracelets, & cut jet chain & other jet fixings. A crystal Indian-arrow-head, Calhoun found at Millwood. And a great many knick knacks, broken peices, &c. &c. besides my silver. Shawl pins &c.

Aug. 31st. Good old Mrs. North[28] died yesterday, aged 85 years. She was an old friend of grandmother's, before they were married, in the low country, & for the last 59 years she has lived here, they were intimate. Some three months since, she broke her hip bone, & has been confined to her bed ever since, without hope of recovery though the bone knit partially, & she gradually wasted away from the confinement. She is to be buried in the Episcopal grave yard to day, so she & grandmother, will not have been more than a month

[27] Betty Beirne was the daughter of Oliver Beirne, a rich Virginia planter. She married William Porcher Miles (July 4, 1822-May 11, 1889) of Charles-ton. He was a former United States and Confederate Congressman. *DAB*, XII, 616-17.

[28] Eliza Drayton was the wife of John Laurens North (born 1782 in Phila-delphia). Simpson, *Old Pendleton District*, p. 73.

separated, after their long friendship. I never knew any one who was more generally beloved. Pat Noble returned to Abbeville Wednesday, after over a fortnight's visit. He is a pleasant, gentlemanly, studious boy of seventeen, & I enjoyed his visit very much. He read to me, rode, & drove with me, & played chess, & cards. We drove up to Keowee with Anna Pinckney,[29] but the place looks desolate, & deserted since Teddy [Colhoun] is in Europe. We also went to Mrs. Warleys, to look through a telescope Prof. Gibbs had there. It was about five feet long, & magnified 100 times. I saw Saturn & his ring, Jupiter, with his two bands, & four satalites, the moon which was about half, Alpha Lyra, a splended, colored, double star, & an other star in the cross I believe, which six stars, arranged so [drawing], also a pan full of the milky way. Carrie Pinckney, & Anna left the day before yesterday, for good. They are to join the rest of the family at Flat Rock [N. C.], where their father is to be married next week. Carrie herself will be married soon, & her brother Charlie, to Miss Memenger. I shall miss the Pinckneys very much, as I had become quite intimate with Carrie especially, a gentle lovely character. No sooner do I get well acquainted with any one here than they leave. Ella Lorton has been very ill for near 3 weeks now with Neumonia (typhoid) but is better now.

Sunday

Sept. 26th. Cousin Mary Noble with her two sweet little girls Floride & Pickey (or Mary) respectively 7, & 4 years old, spent a week with us, & left last Monday. I enjoyed their visit as it was the first except of a night or two, we have had since we have been here. Lortie C[h]erry[30] died last week of typhoid fever. She was only 15 years old. There has been much sickness about, & some deaths. We hear of much sickness everywher. E[d]win Frost is here, & says there is a vast deal of broken bone fever in Charleston, but

[29] Anna (Annie?) (1847-1895), Caroline (b. 1838), and Charlie (b. 1839) were children of the Rev. Charles Cotesworth Pinckney. Anna did not marry; Caroline married Julian Mitchell; Charlie married Lucy Memminger, daughter of Mary Wilkinson and Christopher G. Memminger, former Confederate secretary of the treasury. MS. Census 1860, Ward 4, Charleston Dist., S. C.; *SCHGM*, XXXIX (Jan., 1938), 32.

[30] Mary Lorton Cherry (b. Apr. 4, 1851), daughter of Dr. William B. and Sarah Lewis Cherry. St. Paul's Register; Simpson, *Old Pendleton District*, pp. 89-90.

no cholera, or yellow fever yet. It seems as if there would surely be a civil war at the North soon. They do not know what it is! I have just finished a set of chemise-linen bands with severl rows of cord stitched in, & linen frills, also a night gown, & some under bodies. I am unusually well. Father has returned from a two week' visit to Millwood.

*Octo 19th '66.** Yesterday week there was a celebration here, for
Friday the Confederate dead within a radius of five miles from this place, gotten up by Miss Sallie Lynch. Some fifty names were collected. Some young lady bore a banner for each of the martyrs draped with black with the name, date, & place of death on one side & an appropriate motto on the other. First, early in the morning, those interested visited the old Stone Church yard, & wreathed the graves there, then we all met at the Baptist church, & formed into a procession so fashion [drawing] in a double pyramid which I did not like. Seppie Sloan[31] marched at the head bearing a banner for the returned soldiers, with a flowery anchor in her hand, & dressed in white, with a long bridal veil. She was followed by a pack of children strewing flowers in the way of the returned soldiers. Then they were graduated up to me, bearing Gen Barnard Bee's banner killed at 1st Manasses, then down to small, & up to Carrie Miller[32] bearing a banner for all the dead, then tapered down again. We marched through the three grave yards; the Baptist, Methodist, & Episcopal, wreathing each soldiers grave as we came to it, with wreaths we wore over our shoulders. Then we mounted Mrs. Van Wyck's porch, & ranged ourselves on either side, (all dressed in half mourning) while Gens. Hampton, & Easly[33] delivered addresses. Father introduced them, & Mr. Mul-

* In the margin opposite the date there is a sketch of the draped memorial banner and standard.

[31] Lucilla Septima Sloan (July 8, 1847-Feb. 4, 1895), daughter of Nancy Blassingame and Thomas Majors Sloan. She married the Rev. G. T. Gresham. Marker in Baptist Cemetery, Pendleton; Simpson, *Old Pendleton District*, pp. 104, 107.

[32] Caroline (Aug. 2, 1847-Dec. 1, 1938), daughter of Caroline Taliaferro and Dr. Henry C. Miller. She married W. W. Simons. St. Paul's Register; Simpson, *Old Pendleton District*, p. 138.

[33] Generals Wade Hampton, III, and William K. Easley. The latter was a brigadier general in the South Carolina militia in 1861. He later became a Confederate cavalry major. A native of Pickens County, Easley married Caroline Sloan of Pendleton. Evans, *Confederate Military History*, V, 558-59.

Floride Isabella Lee, Floride Clemson's only child

Floride Isabella Lee (right) married a distant cousin, Andrew Pickens Calhoun, II, and they had four children. The second, Gideon Lee, lived only six months; pictured below are (left to right) Creighton Lee, Margaret M., and Patrick Calhoun, III.

laly began with prayer. Gen. Hampton is handsome, & soldierly in his appearence. He speaks well enough, & to the point, but is not eloquent. Gen Easly is more finished but less sensible. Gen H. was to have staid with us but through a mistake did not. He apologized to us for not doing so. I did not like the style of the celebration, but had rather do honor to our dead with bad taste, than not at all. I have made all necessary preparations to go north, & will probably start in a week or two. Mother has embroidered me two flanel petticoats, most elaborately. Miss Marie Wardlaw[34] from Abbeville is here & brings me most flattering accounts of the impression I made in her town. A delicious basket of muscadine grapes was sent me by Mr. Wilson, from there the other day. Miss Sallie McBride was united to Wm. Jenkins last week. Helen Lewis will be, to Frank Sloan,[35] next Thursday. I am not so well as I have been all Fall, but am growing very stout, much more so than I ever was before. I weigh 1 [does not complete figure] lbs. I fear I shall soon be too fat, though thus far all compliment me upon its becomeingness. I sing a great deal, & have really improved vastly I know. I have most flattering, & pressing invitations in the letters of my friends, to stay with them, & all want me to spend the *whole winter* at their houses. I do expect to enjoy myself vastly. Father has been in a bad humor ever since he came from Abbeville but I really do not wish to remember why, as it is by no means to his credit. I am so afraied he will not let me go. I know if Calhoun comes he wont. We have not received the decree,[36] & do not know

[34] Probably Mary W. (age 14), daughter of Mary A. and Dr. Joseph J. Wardlaw. MS. Census 1860, Abbeville Dist., S. C.

[35] Sarah Boon, daughter of Mary McClerky and the Rev. Thomas L. McBryde (Feb. 25, 1817-Apr. 15, 1863), married William Gaillard Jenkins (age 20) son of Anna R. and Dr. W. L. Jenkins. MS. Census 1860, Anderson Dist., S. C.; marker in Old Stone Church Cemetery; Simpson, *Old Pendleton District*, pp. 121-22. Ellen (Apr. 2, 1837-Aug. 2, 1916), daughter of Susan Taylor (1807-1879) and Jesse Payne Lewis (1796-1845), became the second wife of Benjamin Franklin Sloan, Jr., a Pendleton merchant. *Ibid.*, pp. 102, 165-67; marker in Old Stone Church Cemetery.

[36] On March 12, 1866, T. G. Clemson (as administrator of the estate of M. Cornelia Calhoun, who died unmarried and intestate in May, 1857) brought an action of foreclosure on the "Fort Hill" property against Margaret Green Calhoun and her heirs. In July, 1866, foreclosure was ordered by the Pickens County court of equity. The defendant appealed; the decree was affirmed by the South Carolina Supreme Court at the April term, 1870. This is the decree Floride refers to. Clemson Papers, *passim.*

115

what our future is. They talk of buying Ft. Hill for an Agricultural College. I hope the State will. I dont want to live there.

See my letters from Md., Va., Penn., & Del. for the next winter & spring till the last Wednesday in July when returned to Pendleton.[37]

Octo. 24th. I will start at twelve o'clock today for the North
Wednesday with Dr. Wragg & his family. I expect to branch off
1866 from these at Cokesbury, where I will stay with the Cunningham's until Miss Pamela Cunningham, & Dr. Norwood[38] start for Washington, which I am informed is to be in a few days. If I am told at the Cokesbury depôt (where I wrote for some of the family to meet me) that this opportunity will fail me, I shall go on to Columbia, & stay with mother's schoolmate Mrs. Harris there until I hear of an escort. I feel very badly at leaving mother & father, but otherwise am delighted at the prospect of so pleasent a winter. I shall go right to the Robinson's first. Calhoun arrived from Millwood on a visit last Sunday night. Father made no objection to my going. I suppose I shall never return to this house, for if I come back here at all, it will be to Ft. Hill. I will not be back till Spring. I feel quite sorry to leave all my kind friends here. I made two new tucked skirts on my machine, & four shirts (flanel) for father lately. Monday I actually made a skirt with five breadths & 7 tucks, & the best part of three shirts! Good bye dear little volume, I shall not take you with me!! There were 12 confirmed here last Sunday by Bishop Davis.[39] Poor old blind man! It was sad to see him. I did not think he preached very well, that is to say, not interestingly. I dont know what makes me hate to leave mother so. I would not do it, but she is never lonely, & I really believe she would be relieved not to have to entertain me. I pray God to bless her, & have her, father, all those I love, & myself in his holy keeping, till we meet again.

[37] This sentence was in the margin of the diary and apparently written much later after Floride returned from the North.

[38] Probably Dr. W. C. Norwood (age 63 in 1870) of Cokesbury. MS. Census 1870, Abbeville County, S. C. Miss Ann Pamela Cunningham (or Cuningham) was one of the founders of the Mount Vernon Ladies Association which collected money for the purchase of Mount Vernon for the Nation. *South Carolina, A Guide to the Palmetto State* (New York: Oxford University Press, 1941), p. 434.

[39] Rt. Rev. Thomas F. Davis, bishop of the Diocese of South Carolina, 1853-1871. Thomas, *The Protestant Episcopal Church*, p. 49.

Floride Clemson's
Northern Trip,
July-October, 1863

Floride Clemson's Northern Trip, July–October 1863

Floride's diary briefly covers her northern trip to Pennsylvania to visit relatives and then the grand tour to Pittsburgh, Cleveland, Niagara Falls, Saratoga, New York City, and back through Pennsylvania to Bladensburg. But her private correspondence with her mother reveals much more.

There are Floride's descriptions of the countryside—mountains, lakes, rivers, farmland, the falls, the cities, the train rides and hotel accommodations, characterizations of her Pennsylvania relatives and traveling companions, her precarious health, and her hidden hopes and anxieties. The letters of both mother and daughter indicate family feuds, and above all, reveal their deep sentimental attachment to the Confederate cause and fear of impending defeat.

We have included Floride's letters in their entirety, with spelling and punctuation unchanged. On the other hand, as Mrs. Clemson's letters contain much household trivia and local gossip of little relevance to Floride's narrative, we have quite liberally edited hers.

*   *   *

Altona. July 29th Wednesday
My Darling Mother,

Every one has gone to take a nap, so I seize this moment of rest, to tell you of my safe arrival here, I was received with great cordiality by cousin Anna, & aunt Hetty, & am very much pleased with them. Cousin Anna is not handsome, but very lady like, & pleasant, so is auntie. This house is one of the hansomest & most elegant I ever saw, the position & grounds beautiful. Cousin Sarah, & Luly, are both here. The former is a brisk, smart little homely woman, & the latter, who is about 11 years old, seems a sweet, bright, pretty little thing. I am sure I shall have a splendid time. Cousin Sylvester I dont much like, he is quiet, & not more than good looking. I saw Carrie McClelland this morning. She is nearly as tall as I am & really beautiful. She was delighted to see me.

Now I will begin my journal. I felt pretty badly at first, at the idea of leaving you, but soon the excitement of traveling woke me from my dumps, & I began to enjoy myself. At Annapolis Junction, I looked out, & who should I see, but Mrs. Rankin, standing on the platform, looking as much like a nut craker, or the nut cracked, as ever. We had

119

to wait an hour & a half in Balt. & started for Philla. at ten. Uncle [Elias] drew my attention from time to time to the crops, which looked splended but spent his trip mostly in the arms of Morpheus. It began to rain after we crossed the Susquehanna (which you do in the cars, without getting out, they are run on the boat) but it was not very hot. We were perfectly covered with cinders, & uncle used one corner of my veil, greatly to his satisfaction. By half past three we reach the city, of brotherly—not love, in the rain, & nearly starved. I went right to aunt North's & found no one but Walter (who has grown to be a tall thin ugly boy of 17 [?]) all the rest being in Atlantic city except Willy & Clem, who had enlisted to drive Lee from the state. They however returned that same evening, after a six weeks experience of a soldier's life. They are both very handsome. Clem has wiskers, & is exceedingly good looking. They were very kind, & made me most welcome. After eating something I got Walter to go down street with me, & bought nearly everything I wanted. I enclose a list, which is pretty exact, I believe, & only left off shopping when the stores closed. The next morning I finished my list, but had no time to get shoes, the night before my feet were too swolen to try them on. I went into almost every millenary store in the city but found only one bonnet that *would do* for 7$ as the season is so bad for such things, & that is a white crape, with red moss roses, which though pretty of the kind, is neither becomeing or suitable they tell me here. The dress is grey alpaca 50 cts. a yard, & very pretty. Everything is much cheaper than with us. I went to the depot then, put my things in the trunk, found uncle, & started at 11½ o'clock.

The cars ran very fast, we soon passed by Kate Barton's station, then through the beautiful Chester valley, which looks like a garden spot, it is so luxuriant, & rich,—neat to excess. Uncle pointed out the crops, (which were very heavy) furnaces, & places, and when we came to the mountains, said "yes very pretty," & nodded! Oh mother I never dreampt of such scenery! From Harrisburg, on the beautiful Susquehanna, we wound around through, & by mountains, & followed the banks of the Juniata from its mouth to this place. Oh I nearly went wild, it was so beautiful. Not the lofty, cloud peircing, barren peaks, I thought of, but bold, rocky, & wooded ridges, some wonderfully regular, some tossing wildly like a stormy sea. The woods, and feilds *so* fresh, and the little green islands in the lovely Juniata spotted with Orrange love weed. It was a splended day to

120

travel, little sun, little rain, few cinders, no dust, & just cool enough. I looked till my eyes were blinded by smoke, then rubbed them, & regretted the time it took to do so. I would not have missed it for the world, and uncle nodded! Harrisburg is beautifully situated among the mountains, & by the river, but is in itself indefferent. I love the magnificent mountains, uncle admires the fine barns, & was very kind. We reached Altona which is quite a nice place before nine, & found auntie waiting for us. This appears to be a large neighborhood, & quite gay. Annie was at a party last night, so I did not see her till this morning. I think I shall like her very much. Indeed I have taken a great fancy to all. I have not heard politics broached, & I think they do not bother their heads about such matters. They all think my trunk preposterous, as I thought they would. Tell Mr. Onderdonk if he never was along this road, it is more than worth his while to do so, & get a seat on the right hand side. Tell Mr. Lee uncle says the Hudson is too far out of the way, oh dear! & is not an inspiering companion; *though kind*, he is lame [?]

I hope you all miss me. If not I wont have anything to do with you when I get home. If you were here, I should be perfectly content, but I feel very badly at leaving you alone. Be sure to write twice a week, & tell me how you are & everything. I am quite well. All our relations are well. Uncle William and aunt Sue are at Claymont [Del.]. Mattie they say still has plenty of beaux. There seems to be a great deal of wealth here. This place, & house are really superb. I am tired now, & will go rest for a little while.—I heard a young lady sing with splended voice to day. Cousin Anna plays. Uncle is very affectionate. Now do take care of yourself, & do not show my letters, I write in such a hurry so that I may rest. They keep very early hours here, in the morning & for meals.

Love to Mrs. D. F, Mrs. Calvert[1] & all.
Your devoted daughter
Floride Clemson

This is frightfully scratched, but I am tired & can not stop to think.

*　　　*　　　*

Before receiving Floride's first letter from Altoona, Anna Maria Calhoun Clemson on July 30 wrote her daughter a lengthy and ram-

[1] Mrs. Lisette Daub, her daughter Wilhemina Floride, and Mrs. Charles Calvert.

121

bling letter telling her the news of the neighborhood and The Home. Henry McCeney was working all day and "sitting up all night to guard their garden &c, which are nightly pillaged in spite of all their efforts." Henry had said that his cousin Eliza's family had lost nearly all their servants. Mrs. Calvert had a letter from Ella & talked of visiting her [in Pendleton, S.C.] "& the means of accomplishing it." Mr. Lee "still continues *charming*, & evinces no intention of returning to his *duties*, in W." Mrs. Clemson reported that the body of a Negro man, dead of foul play about two weeks earlier, had washed down on their back property. Mr. Onderdonk was to leave the next day with his sister for New York. "I have not heard from your grandmother [Mrs. John C. Calhoun] since you left, & am getting anxious." She advised her daughter that "I shall expect quite a journal of all your doings," and added: "enjoy yourself & *be quiet*."

*   *   *

Altona. Aug. 2nd 1863

I have not heard from you yet dearest mother, but I suppose I must wait a little longer in patience, as the mails do not do as they should, & bring the letter in one day. I wrote you a hurried, scratchy letter the day after I got here, and told you in an unsatisfactory, & hasty manner, pretty much all that had happened till then. Now, though I have little of interest to write, I know you want to hear from me, so I will give you the journal of my last four days.

There has been a great deal of visiting to this house, indeed coming nearly all the time, which is pleasant and very filling up, to one's time. There seems to be a great superabundance of young ladies, & very few gentlemen in this country. I have scarcely laid my eyes on one of the other sex, under forty years old. Carrie McClelland lives but a short distance from the enclosure, & comes up every day. Another of my school mates is staying with her now; Lizzie McIlvain. She is a sweet pleasant girl, but not striking.

I have taken the greatest possible fancy to all this family. They are very lovely among themselves. Cousin Annie would please you wonderfully, she is most lady like, and quiet, and seems very affectionate, and simple. Every one loves her. She is twenty seven, but seems, & looks much younger. I should take her to be twenty two. She is not pretty. Aunt Hetty is very sweet. Although she is sixty she would never be guessed over forty five & is very good looking, & not at all fat. I

122

think my dresses might fit her in size. She is also very refined. Lulu is the smartest, & sweetest child I ever saw. She is a little wonder. She sends her love to you; "as she knows me," she says. Her mother is quite intelligent, and very tender hearted, & pure. She is very brisk, and has occasionally a little something Yankee about her, but not much. Dear mother, do you believe it, they have never mentioned politics, & are much more considerate than I ever dreampt of. After all I rather like cousin Sylvester. He is a little cranky but I think he is very honorable, & kind hearted. He seems highly thought of, and is exceedingly quiet.

Uncle has gone East again, & after his return, means to visit Kentucky, where he has invited cousin Anna, & me, to accompany him; of course I do not think of that, or wish to go. I fear much lest our Niagara scheme may fall through, somehow. Oh mother was it not dreadful about Morgan![2] I felt so badly. I could not bear to read the particulars. I have not seen a paper since I came, so dont forget the *summaries*, or I shall be as badly off as Rip Van Winckle, & ask where the country is, on my return home. They keep but two servants here, although they live in such nice style, & are very industrious. I have sent for my shoes to Phila. by the shoemaker here who took my measure. I had to bye a hat (see the above diagram) for $E. It is black, trimmed with velvet, & becomeing. I had nothing to walk in. I went to the Presbyterian church to day, and heard a very dull sermon.

Cousin Sylvester took me up to the ore bank in his buggy yesterday. It is about five miles off & one of the very largest holes I ever saw. The scenery about here is magnificent, & though this house is not more elevated than Mrs. Calvert's, in proportion to the surrounding country, they have a beautiful view of the mountains, & some intervening rolling ground. There are trees at the back of the house, a lovely garden at one side, nice grounds on the other, & terraces & the view in front. The house is one of the finest I ever saw, & very refined. *Our* furniture[3] looks beautiful in their parlor, & they only want pictures to complete it. The family is badly off for horses just now, & there is little chance for rides until the deficiency is supplied. There is talk of several excursions, to the mountains &c. next week I will try to get my new dress done.

[2]General John Hunt Morgan, ill-fated Confederate raider.
[3]The Clemsons had sold some furniture to the Elias Bakers.

They have put out my wash, but will not hear of my paying for it. I received a letter from Kate yesterday. She heard I had passed, & was hurt at my not telling her. I wrote to day, & explained. She is very affecate. Remember me to Mr. Lee & ask if he misses me—or———!!! To Mr. O. also. I hope to see them both. Love to Henry. Take good care of yourself, & write often to your devoted daughter

Floride Clemson.

Have you heard from father? I am pretty well. It was too cool at first, but is very warm today. All join in love to you. Cousin Sarah hopes to meet you, some day, she says. She is very kind to me. I enclose a likeness of cousin Anna taken some time ago, & is not very good. She has an immense head of hair. Love to Lizzie R:[4] Mrs. Daub &c. Mrs Calvert & all.

*   *   *

Upon receiving Floride's first letter August 1, Mrs. Clemson answered the next day, giving her daughter the local news, noting the comings and goings of Messrs. Lee and Onderdonk, and expressing delight in Floride's pleasant visit. She happily informed her daughter that she had earlier sent news "summaries" and a letter from Ella Calvert Campbell giving news of Mr. Clemson and John Calhoun Clemson. "It is quite a relief to find they are both well, after so long a silence, but I am anxious to hear of your grandmother as Mrs. C[alvert]. has had two letters from Ella, since she enclosed one from her [Mrs. Calhoun]. I do hope she is not sick."

Mrs. Clemson also reprimanded Floride about the newly-purchased bonnet: "I charged you, if you did not find one to suit, to have one made, & not *to pick up anything.*" She strongly urged her to write Mrs. Calvert, and lectured her about her conduct: "Dont get excited. This is all the caution I have to give you. If you can only remain *calm*, I have perfect confidence in your behaving just as I would have you, & making a favorable impression. *Do keep hold on yourself.*"

On August 6 Mrs. Clemson again wrote Floride and complained of having received only one letter from the daughter. Word from Mr. Onderdonk in Baltimore was that news by way of steamer from Charleston was suppressed. The heat and stench in Washington was unbearable. Two days earlier, the mother reported, a trip into the city

[4]Elizabeth Robinson

had made her so ill that she had had to go to bed upon returning home. And the evening before, the foul odor from burning animal carcasses had forced them to retreat indoors and close all windows.

Mrs. Clemson had little news "except the excitement of the draft," and some neighboring visitors. As for Mr. Lee, she wrote that "the gallant defender, tho possessed with a silent devil, is still quite pleasant, & makes himself generally useful, & manages me as usual." She reminded Floride that August 21 had been appointed in the South as "a day of fasting & prayer."

*   *   *

(Sunday)
Altoona. Aug. 9th. 1863
My Darling Mother,

I received your letter written on Thursday, yesterday, & was delighted that you were getting on so well. I wrote Mrs. Calvert in the middle of the week, & I must own here little, or nothing of importance to record since, but you must have your letter, whether it merely consists of a few words. You complain of heat; well I must do the same. Although the day only is hot, still I feel it very much, & often wonder if in our own cool home, I could not find a breath of air. This morning I nearly roasted in church & wished myself in some comfortable, free & easy chair, where I should not have to play lady, until I got so fidgetty, & stiff.

I am glad you send me the "Summaries." I can not resist the temptation of reading the papers here sometimes, & they make me feel very gloomy. I have had a fit of the dumps all day, on account of one of these indulgeances this morning. I still have the same forbearence, & kindness to record, for which I am really grateful. My watch is being mended, & I have ordered some shoes from Hipman, through the shoemaker in Altoona. Cousin S. got me a beautiful pair of riding gantlets in Philla., where he spent a day last week.

I wrote to aunt North, Mary C.[5] and Kate Barton. I forgot to tell you that the latter said aunt B. "would be delighted, & would love to see me, with her love!" Strange! Tell Mr. Lee I take regular exercise, & I thank him for taking care of you. I am much obliged for the fencing of my flower beds also. Remember me &c. Govvy[6] seems a fixture. Is

[5]Mary Clemson, daughter of John Baker Clemson
[6]"Govvy" Morris, a frequent visitor to The Home, was apparently a friend of D. W. Lee.

he cleaner? I am so glad of such recent, & good news from *abroad* [South Carolina], but hope grandma is well. It seems strange she does not write, does it not? Again I must tell you how kind every one is. They think me wonderfully straight, & say I carry my hight well. They can not understand my weight. (166 lbs.) My face is a little broken out, but I eat, & sleep *a merveil*. The hours are dreadful, breakfast at seven or a little after, (I am always one of the first down!) dinner at one, or before; a nap soon after, then dress for the evening, supper at six, & to bed after ten. Auntie is an active, neat, clean housekeeper, but the eating is not Mrs. Daub's. I can not get used to so much sweet. Even salad is made sickening with sugar, & ham comes very often. Everything is good of its kind however.

I recorded in the letter to Mrs. C. my two evenings of dissipation. I had to drive the girls in a one horse carriage, & the man had to ride on my old pony. We got along quite nicely, for I trusted to the horse's instinct, & the good road, as I found my eyes useless. The road that passes by here, from Hollidaysburg to Altoona, is made of cinder, & plank, & is excellant, but I find that can be said of no other in this country. It ill behooves me to complain, & I doubt whether they are worse than ours, but of a different style,—very stony, & precipitous, & exceedingly ill made, but not as washed, & boggy as ours. They are so beautiful, & pass over such a romantic country however, that in climbing a bad hill, you only think of the view which will entrance you at the top, & the delight lasts until you reach the bottom. Cousin Sylvester, who I like better every day for his kindness, took me a buggy ride of some fifteen miles, which I enjoyed exceedingly. We just missed a shower which we saw near us, though so very partial, as to look like a grey viel, & so did not feel troubled by the sun. He also took me another, & shorter ride, which was perhaps more beautiful, as he did not confine himself to road, but took me to the top of some mountain-like hills, where the views, were most fine. I am quite prepared to answer questions on ore digging, washing, & burning.

There is a derth of horses, which will not be filled until uncle returns from Kentucky, & which keeps us a good deal at home, but the weather has been so warm that I think buggy riding is perhaps as well. I find it quite pleasant, & a novelty. Pet, as cousin Anna calls the pony, has grown quite round, & fat,—too much so for its slight frame, & is still the tricky little imp, it always was. I have tried riding but once since I came & unless I can get a better horse, & a saddle of more respectable dimensions, & shape, I am quite resigned to staying at home. There are still some trips to the most celibrated spots, in comtemplation, which may come off any day. However, my imagination can picture nothing more beautiful than I have already seen. Anna's cousin Sadie Sterrit, a tall, thin girl of twenty two, is staying here now. I am happy to say she only intends remaining a week or so, for I have taken a dislike to her. She is just a little too sweet, & cat like, & too fond of kissing, &c. Very polite to me however.

You need not think I am not taken care of. I have coughed a little since I came, for you know I had a cold when I left (which soon got well however), & the sound thereof, being not even as hard as usual, did not meet with the approbation of my kind relatives. So here I am, with enough care taken of me, to keep a gross of tender hot-house-plants, through an Arctic winter. In vain I plead that it does not amount to any thing (& it really does not,) the minute I give a hack, there is a general closing of windows, & getting of sugar & water, shawls &c. It is really amusing. Uncle set them on, retailing yours, & Mr. Lee's accounts of my delicacy. Joking apart, they make more fuss than you; & almost roast me with care.

Poor Carrie McClelland, whose mother died of consumption you know, is quite delicate. She spit (or *spat*) some blood last week, but does not cough. Lizzie McIlvain is still with her, & as interesting as ever.

Uncle got back the day before yesterday. He got the papers he says from you. He will go to Kentucky next week, but we have no intention of accompanying him. His movements are too uncertain. He & cousin S. do not sit horses at all. They have not quarell, to my knowledge; but do not get along. Anna is lovely, & quiet, but not very interesting, auntie ditto. Cousin Sarah is by far the most intelligent, & is the only one of the whole set, who has any enthusiasm. I really love her. She seems to have taken a fancy to me, & is very kind. She is very religious, & pure, really one of the best women I ever saw. She is an Episcopalian.

The Clemson's are expected, indeffinately any time. I shall be glad to see Sallie[7] & Mary, who I think are the two that are coming. The sentiments of the family with regard to "Mrs. Marton," & others suits me exactly. I really pitty you for that miserable smell, but hope it will

---

[7]Sallie, a third daughter of John Baker Clemson.

soon pass away. Now I have written you a long letter about nothing, & expect a speedy & punctual answer. My love to Leo[8] & the rest of the family, with oceans to yourself from

Your devoted daughter,
Floride Clemson

Keep well all [and?] tell me everything. The family would send love but are napping & at Sunday school. I shall remember the 21st rest assured. I have been doing no work at all.

*   *   *

On August 9, the same day as Floride's latest letter, Mrs. Clemson wrote of the usual household items: the doings of Mr. Lee and "Govvy" Morris, the heat, anxiety over absence of news from Mrs. Calhoun, the continuing stench from Washington, and the visits of neighbors. She added a bit of gossip picked up in the city from Mrs. Robert Stone to the effect that Lizzie Giles had jilted Washington Baker, a Clemson cousin, for a General Quarles in Mobile. She wrote: "If it is true, she & her mother have both behaved shamefully, & I think your cousin well rid of her. . . . To think of her driving out with him, as his fiancée, while the mother bought her wedding things to marry another man!!!!!"

Mrs. Clemson expressed joy over Floride's pleasant visit and the absence of political discussions, but she warned her to remember "the interest of Northerners cannot be so *vital* as ours in this contest, & that family especially, having no near relative engaged in it, & your uncle's iron being *enormously increased* in value, by it, have no cause for bitterness, indeed the wonder is, that being, as you say, & as I believe, sincere & earnest christians, they or any other good person at the north, could be in favour of a war of invasion, for the avowed purpose of aboltion, & subjugation, against their brethren, & can stand calmly by, & see so much innocent blood shed, to *put down the very principles our common forefathers fought for.*"

On August 13 Mrs. Clemson wrote again, still complaining about the heat and the "bad smells" of Washington almost making her ill. Mr. Lee was still at The Home, she reported, and "like[ly] to be. He talks no more of being ordered off [by whom? to where?], & is not so pleasant as he has been. What a queer man he is, to be sure! I gave him your messages, & he expressed himself *gratified & sent his re-*

---

[8]Floride's dog

spects." She complimented her daughter on her interesting letters and her punctuality at the Bakers. "I hope you make yourself agreeable, & that they like you as much as you do them." After a little lecture to Floride about proper spelling and word usage ("You speak of a 'buggy *ride.*' You *ride* on horseback—You *drive* a carriage of *any kind*"), she ended with the following note: "The news is not bad & I heard the other day all [Confederates] were in good spirits in spite of the late reverses."

On August 16, Mrs. Clemson, increasingly disappointed at not hearing from Floride, wrote that the weather was still hot; some new neighbors had moved in; she had not been to Washington recently; Mrs. Calvert was quite sick and distressed over no news from Ella; Mrs. Clemson likewise was "anxious at not hearing from your grandmother." She enclosed summaries of the war news and a Carlyle article—"the best satire on the war yet." She added: "Does not Charleston hold out valiantly? God bless the old state."

"There is quite (an almost nightly nuisance,) in the shape of an execrable band from Ft. Lincoln, which comes to make night hideous, for several hours, at Yost's & Barney's.[9] No two instruments accord, & they neither play in time or tune, nor any tune worth hearing, so the only effect they produce is setting one's teeth on edge."

Concerning "Govvy," she wrote: "Mr. L. tells me he persuaded 'Govvy' to join his regiment, & as he has not come out today, I suppose he took the advice. I am not sorry, for tho personally I rather liked him & he had become cleaner, I don't wish that kind of cattle too much about the house." Regarding Mr. Lee, she said: "On the whole he makes himself rather agreeable, but 'too much of a *good thing* is worse than none at all.' He gets no letters that I see. Mysterious is it not? *Govvy* told me he [Mr. Lee] wanted to go to Texas, if there was an expedition sent there. I suppose that is what he is waiting for orders."

She closed the letter with a final but serious warning: "Don't be led into going to make visits to *any of the family.* Get off civilly. You have been away so long must go straight home &c &c. I prefer things to remain as they are."

*   *   *

[9]Two nearby places of entertainment.

Altoona. Aug 16th 1863

My dearest Mother,

I have so much to say, that I scarce know where to begin. Last week, we were so constantly on the go; & when at home, so tired, that I had not the time to write to you, but Mr. Onderdonk said he would see you tomorrow, tell you all about me, so you will not miss my letter.

First then, Monday was very quiet; Tuesday we had determined to go up to Cresson, a place about fifteen miles from here, up the Aleghany range, but could not, as the rest of the party were not prepared. So cousin Sylvester took me up to Hollidaysburg, in the buggy, & we had a very pleasant drive. It is not so large a place as Altoona, nor so nice a one, but seems to be thriving. Wednesday, we *all*, with several other persons from the neighborhood, made an early start for Cresson. Cousin S. & one or two other gentlemen, constituted the masculine element; the feminine amounting to some sixteen, or more. Cousin S. with his usual kindness to me, determined to get me a stand on the back platform, so that I might enjoy the view to the greatest extent. We had a couple of engines, & a short train, still the grade was so heavy, that we went slowly. I think I never saw anything grander, or more wild, than the scenery was. We mounted in a most circuitous manner skirting ravines, & making the sharpest possible turns. The idea of being nearly on the top of a high mountain on a railway train! It seemed wonderful. I did enjoy it so. Just before we reached our destination we passed through a tunnel, 200 ft. under ground & well on to a mile long. I did not like that.

Cresson is a summer resort, with no natural attraction, except the mountain air, that I could see. Though so elevated, there is no view, & no fine scenery in the immediate neighborhood, but it is surrounded by deep massive hemlock woods, which are not only magnificent looking, but exceedingly productive of ferns & musketoes. There are some strong *un*medicinal springs, a fine large hotel, some nice cottages, & a promiscuous set of people, besides a ten pin alley, two billiard tables, & a bar room. Also many plank walks. Well after waiting till we were tired for a room to lay off our things in, we were shown one very small one which we sixteen ladies, besides some children, occupied in common with a gentleman & baby, besides other congruous elements I suppose. The gentleman (who was probably tall, as his pants were very long) kept us out of the room while he dressed for dinner, but was not otherwise inconvenient.

We spent the morning most pleasantly rolling ten pins, & walking; besides wondering at the different kinds of people it takes to make a world. At the first amusement, I came out third, after two long games with eight others, most of whom had rolled before. Cousin Sylvester gained the first, & Lizzie McIlvain the last game. I liked it exceedingly at the time, but found my muscles did not, next day. We had right good eating, & a pleasant day. About eight we expect[ed] to start home, but the train was half an hour late. When it came, it was so crowded, that we could not all get seats. I managed to get squeezed next to a woman, whose child occupied the whole of the opposite seat, as a bed. I tried to induce her to pick it up, but she said she was too tired to hold it any longer, so after inquiering if it had no infectuous desease, & seeing that it was clean, I picked it up, & provided two more of the party with seats. The child was very heavy! I left two of my hoops at the plank walk, for incredible as it may seem, my new set [?] is too long. That night we slept without rocking. Next day we rested.

Mr. Onderdonk arrived in the morning, & stayed all day, & evening. We invited him to join a party which had arranged for the next day (Friday) to visit the Wopsenonock mountain, one of the highest about here, & the finest view. Six of us went on horseback, & six in a springless wagon. I was one of the three ladies who rode, Carry, & Anna the others. On account of the scarcity of horses, cousin S. most kindly gave up his (which was lame, & worthless) to Mr. O., & did penance in the conveyance, which cousin Henry McClelland drove. I was on the latter's horse, a huge white beast, which showed much docility of temper in not paying the slightest attention to my whip, & other attempts at urging out of a very hard, & slow walk. My saddle would probably have fitted me at the age of say eight—but I have grown since.

We started about ten o'clock in the hot sun, & thick dust, & I must say I suspected little pleasure from the ride, however after over three hours we reached the crown of the mountain, & as the weather had become a little hazy, & less hot, the road being beautiful, & the company pleasant, I managed to get along passably pleasantly. We had to wait sometime for the waggon, as the roads were well calculated to

131

retard anything like progress, being nothing more nor less than frightful, & nothing but rocks, & holes. After unpacking the lunch, & feeling to see whether there were any bones broken, we seated ourselves in a shady grove right by the Wopsenonock house, a neat tavern, & had a merry, & most refreshing meal. About two o'clock we saddled up, & rode half a mile to the *brink* of the mountain. The brow has been denuded of trees, & you look down near a thousand feet of so abrupt a decent, that a stone can be thrown to the bottom, & a man could roll down, were it not for the bushes. What could be finer than that I can not imagine. It was just dumbfoundering. Though the day was somewhat smoky, we could see over three ranges of mountains, & I believe some 80 miles in one direction. The country looked like a beautiful map. What I had though[t] mountains before, looked like mole hills from there, & Altoona, which was scarce six or seven miles off, seemed just a little place. I do wish you had seen it. It did me good. Most reluctantly, & with many a "longing, lingering look behind," we left it, & after rather a brisker jog back, by an other road, reached home more battered than tired, & with fine food for thought before dark. My horse, who added stumbling, & shying to his phlegmatic temparament, fell with me twice, though he exhibited no symtoms of enough life for the first agrément. However owing to his inertia & my sticking qualities, he recovered without throwing me. Cousin Anna had a sick headache unfortunately, & had to take Lizzie McIlvain's place in the wagon coming home. Mr. O. will probably tell you all about this trip himself.

Yesterday Cousin S. took me all over the machine shops in Altoona, which I enjoyed excessively, as he, & Mr. Brasto [?] (the superintendent) explained everything to me. The works are very extensive, & are for the manufacture of the engines, & other rolling-stock of the road. I saw all possible kinds of working in iron, especially. It was a great treat; & very dirty, & noisy. I would like to go again. I saw them casting in the evening, at uncle's furnace, the liquid iron in [is] beautiful; but rather warm. Uncle started for Kentucky Wednesday, & will probably be back in a week or so, when he will take us to Niagara he says. Cousin S. has to go tomorrow to the East as far as Bauting [?] to sell iron, & will probably be gone a week. I shall miss him much, he has been so good, & kind to me, taking me about, & showing me sights. I really like him now. The Clemson's, uncle, Mary, & Mattie, are coming early this week. I am so disappointed Sallie is not to be one of them. I send you aunt B's letter without comment, what must I say? I know what to *do*. "This world & 'tother country" deciets & straange things! She tells uncle he must "call by for Kate."

The furniture has arrived, & is splended, especially the looking glass, & etagere. I took my dress body & sack to be made yesterday. I have made the skirt myself. I find I will have to send for more. I got my watch fixed for $1.50. Carrie McC. is very delicate, she spit blood last week. —Mr. Latrobe & Mary[10] wrote me nice letters from Bethlehem inviting me to join them, which I would do were it not for the Clemson's. I don't know when I shall get home. I want to see you much, *very much*. I received yours, & Mrs. Calvert's letters last week. Glad you are getting on so well. Remember me to Mr. Lee, & tell him to be in readiness to go with us to Niagara if he can. I cant help getting excited I fear, & being noisy, but they seem to like me, & are certainly *very* kind, & considerate, & affectionate to me. Remember me to Mr. O., Mrs. Calvert, Lizzie, Mrs. D., & F. & all, all, all.

I am your devoted daughter
Floride Clemson

Wednesday
Altoona. Aug. 19th 1863.
Darling Mother,

I have just received your letter of the 16th inst., & Monday one from Mrs. Calvert, & an other one from you. It is such a delight to get your letters, & I look so anxiously for them. Though there is not such an immense variety of news in them, you need not feel that you have nothing to say, for every little trifle sounds like a great deal, when one is away from home. I am really sorry you are suffering so much from the heat. We have had some hot weather, to be sure, but the nights were so cool, that we did not mind it. Though rain is wanted, still there is no appearance of drougth yet.

I hope you received my last letter. It was exceedingly *long*, & *interesting* (I always *was* modest, you know.). Today I have not so much to say. Yesterday afternoon we drove to Hollidaysburg, to spend the evening, & night, at Dr. Lander's. There are three pleasant young ladies in the family. There was a *kind of* a party (wing [?]) and we had a merry dance. One of the daughters of the house sings splendedly. We

---

[10]Benjamin H. Latrobe, Jr., and daughter Mary.

walked over that extensive city, this morning, in search of birth day presents for Luly. I got her the "Arabian Nights." We reached home by one o'clock. Carry went with us, or rather *took* us, as we are scarce of horses yet. The evening before last, we returned some visits, & spend the evening out. On our return we found visitors; among others Mr. Collin, a Sweede who told me much about his country.

Our Niagara trip still holds good. Cousin Sarah, Luly, cousin Anna, Sady Sterritt (her cousin who is still here) & myself, are all going under the shaddow of uncle's wing. My only fear is that his *wing* will not be large enough to cover us all, & I *do* wish we had an other gentleman or two with us. Do tell Mr. Lee to join us, he will be such a pleasant addition & I do not think we will see a thing with uncle, he is so decrepid, & always wants to gallop through night, & day. Then I think a trip will do Mr. Lee *good* &c.&c. We will probably go by Pittsburg, & Cleveland, & get left at our respective homes East, on our way back. Cousin A. is to make a stay in Philla. to attend the wedding of a friend. So Mr. Lee could take me home, without taking uncle so far. Then the party dont want to come down but by the side of the Hudson, or sail on the lake, nor nothing else. I suppose Mr. O. could not go with us, as we will not probably start before ten days, or two weeks. Urge Mr. L., & tell him I wont bother him, *or say a word to him*, if he goes. Wont that do? It will be so agravating, disappointing, vexatious, & stupid to make the trip, & see nothing, but gallop round. Uncle & cousin S. are both away, but will probably return toward the end of this, or the beginning of next week.

I am getting very fat, & well, & have still the same reports to make of kindness & considirateness. I am so happy Charleston still holds out so well. We have not heard from the Clemson's again, but expect them daily. Sallie is not to be one of them, I am sorry to say. —Thank you for correcting my letters & your good opinion of them.

What a fist Emily Wood does write! It dont pay. I some how dont do much of anything but enjoy "dolche for minte." I am sorry Mr. Merrick[11] has left the city. We will have no one we know there soon. Are my gladiolis in bloom, they are nearly over here. They have had no tomatoes yet, is that not late? Remember me to Mr. O, Mrs. C. &

[11]William M. Merrick, a Washington jurist.

all enquiering friends. I will write to Laura I think. Aint aunt B "one of 'em"? All send love to you. I dont because you have all mine.

Yours devotedly,
Floride Clemson

I will write to Mrs. C. soon again.

PRIVATE

Now my darling mother, I want to tell you something I have been thinking for some time, very seriously on religious subjects; for, as I have often told you, I could not be satisfied with what *seems* quite sufficient for you, and many others. Still as you say, one's religion must fit as one's cloths, & every one must have religion and I think I need something more tangible. Since Mary Latrobe was at our house, I have had many conversations with Mr. O.[12] on this subject. Without my knowledge, she spoke to him about me, & as the ice was broken, I saught the topic. He very kindly made many points clear to me, but I was still undecided, when I came here. Cousin Sarah has been kind enough to help me, & I feel now as if I should really like, & feel it my duty, to be, baptized.

I do not pretend to say I am a bit better than I was before, or that I have very *strong* faith, yet I want to believe, & have been convinced of the truth of most of the important points for some time, the rest will come I hope, & pray. I have always felt I needed something of this kind, *perhaps* because I am weak, though this weakness may prove strength, but still it *can* do no harm. Do not think that I have been converted, as they say, "all of a sudden," but ask Mr. Lee & Mr. O. if I have not thought about it for some time. I did not think of making up my mind so soon when I left home, for I was uncertain which I liked best the Episcopal, or Presbyterian church, however on investigation, I find the latter does not suit me, & I had rather join the former. Their faiths are the same nearly.

I wont take any step till I get home if you say so, though I think if Mr. Hall comes here, while I still remain, it can be done quieter. I feel very badly about it, & hope you wont object. I dont expect to get any better right off, but perhaps it may help me to become so. However I have long felt as if I should like to do it, & ought to, & I can not rest

[12]Mary Latrobe and Henry Onderdonk were married December 17, 1868.

135

satisfied without it. Shall I take both, or only one name? Perhaps better both. Now mind, if you had rather, I will wait, but I see no use, for cousin Sarah, who is the only one here to whom I have spoken about it, has used no influence, but just told me what I wanted to know. I do not pretend, to understand many things, but I feel as if it were in the main right & true, & I want to believe.

I spoke to Mr. O. about this matter, which I really feel all important, & whatever I have left unsaid, he may be able to tell you. Write as soon as you get this, & tell me whether it would be better to get uncle Baker to baptize me. Perhaps it would. I do hope & trust I shall be in time, all the better daughter to you for this, & more of a comfort to you, but I know I am weak naturally, & this strength may not make as much change as it should, but it is such a help & comfort to those who earnestly believe & trust. I will say no more, but will wait anxiously for your reply. Indeed mother I do love you so I wish you would think as I do.

Yours devoted daughter
Floride Clemson

(Dont show this)

*   *   *

In her letter of August 20 Mrs. Clemson again expressed pleasure that Floride was enjoying her vacation and that her relatives were so kind. She hoped to be able to welcome them agreeably in The Home.

"As to your aunt's letter [Mrs. Barton], it is simply an impertinence. I see the idea. She would like again to get a foothold, for herself & daughter, in the comfortable quarters she lost by her conduct. *Dont write her.* Answer thro K., that you thank her for her kind invitation, which you 'cannot possibly accept,' &c. &c. Not much—only enough for politeness. Dont go either to your uncle B[aker].'s. When you return home you 'have been so long absent you cannot possibly stop on the road' &c. . . . Be cautious what you say before them. You *don't know where your father is.* Your uncle is very *black*. Old Mr. Latrobe is a nuisance with his letters. When you write Mary put in a kind message for him. Your time can always be too occupied to write such a letter as you would like to send him, &c&c."

As to events around The Home, Mrs. Clemson told of neighborhood visitors, the weather, the flowers, the canary, and that Mr. Lee, "a curious compound," sent his regards but could not join the Niagara excursion. "Dont break your heart!" she significantly added. As usual she had no news from Mrs. Calhoun.

Lastly, Mrs. Clemson discussed at length Floride's queries about baptism. As she believed her daughter needed "a deep & abiding faith," she advised her to be certain that her judgment agreed with her actions. The mother gave her approval of the Episcopal Church, of Mr. Hall to perform the ceremony, and of the use of only the name "Floride." She saw no need for delay.

On August 23 Mrs. Clemson repeated her advice regarding Floride's religion and again warned the daughter not to visit certain relatives. As was her custom she spoke briefly of Mr. Lee, how quiet and uncommunicative he was though still pleasant, and of the other neighbors and doings around The Home. She asked Floride to buy her $5 worth of woolen yarn.

There was not even a rumor from Washington, to which she had not recently been. Pouring out her true Confederate sentiments, she wrote: "Even Charleston affords 'nothing new.' Thank God! That is the best of tidings for *us*. I strictly kept day before yesterday hoping the earnest faith of a whole nation might speak for us. If truth, & justice, can avail, our cause must succeed, but the ordeal is a dreadful one, & my heart aches for my people. I am very anxious about your grandmother. Mrs. C. had a letter from Ella, two days ago, & none from her enclosed—this makes the third, since I have heard, showing she does not write. Something must be wrong, & I imagine everything possible. Perhaps it may be only accidental—I try to hope so. No letters from 'the travellers' [Thomas G. and Calhoun Clemson] either. I cannot but feel this constant suspense."

* * *

Allegany Furnace. Aug. 24th. 1863

Uncle Baker, Mattie, and Mary, arrived here Friday evening. I was very glad to see them, & they seemed to take equal pleasure in meeting me again. I can see no kind of difference in Mary, except that she is a little stouter, & more womanly, she is still quiet, firm, "little Mary," & has just as little to say. She is *not* pretty, but has such a good, sweet face, that she sometimes looks almost so. Mattie looks older, and thiner. She is not at all strong, and has a more *vague*, weak, undecided look, than ever. She *seems* rather more steady than she was, & Mary says she is much more so. I dont think she *takes* here, though every one likes Mary. Uncle Baker is very pleasant, & takes particular pains to be kind to me, almost affectionate. He wears a very long beard (none of the thickest) & does not shave at all, which gives him rather a rabinical appearance in the pulpit.

Mattie in her off hand, foolish, way, is the only one that mentions politics, & even she says nothing unkind, so I must say I think every one wonderfully considirate. I myself have not mentioned politics, & to *their* own kind feelings, & this, I suppose I owe the wonderful considirateness I have met with. Indeed mother, from what I see in my hasty glances in the papers, & hear, I feel very uneasy about our noble city [Charleston]. Would it not be frightful if it fell? I can not bear to think about it. The times are indeed dark. It seems to me as if I should give a good deal to hear, & have a good *Southern talk.* Kate B. from what I hear, seems still to retain her moderate feelings, & they say she will in no way work for the soldiers, according to her promise. Every one speaks so highly of her, & the improvement, & change she has undergone. I thought she was earnest. I really feel a deep respect for one who has struggled so hard to do right, with such temptations as she has had, by nature.

Uncle Elias has not yet returned, but we expect him home to day, or tomorrow. Cousin Sylvester we also expect daily. The Clemsons have gone up to spend to day at Cresson, as they got an excursion ticket, for half price, for that place, & they must get it signed there. It only lasts ten days, so they will have to return on Thursday. Friday morning I went to meet Mr. Latrobe, according to his letter, but was happy not to find him, so I wrote to Mary, & told her of my doing; but made no appology for not writing. I also had my traveling dress tried on, by an Altoona dress maker. It will be done tomorrow. I had the body made plain, with long sleeves, & a point in front, & behing; I had to get cousin S. to send me a couple more yards from Philla. to finish the French sack. It is all trimmed with rows of brai[ds] so wide [*diagram*] half an inch.

I will write to Kate B. today, & make all due excuses. As the Clemson's seem so friendly, I may stop there on my way home, for a day or two, as they press me earnestly to do, & get Kate to meet me there, which will straighten all that matter. I think the breech may as well be healed. Uncle says you are "one of the very finest women he ever knew!" Uncle Will, & aunt Sue are away. The former sent me most affectionate messages by Mary, who says he is devoted to me! "The ways of this world are passed finding out," I think. Cousin Anna B. is not at all well. She has constant, & dreadful sick-headaches, which last longer than mine. I still continue fat, & well. Kate Russel, a second cousin of mine, is now staying with Carry. She is a small dark girl, about nineteen, with a fine (not handsome) face, full of character, & energy. Remember me to Mr. Lee, & Mr. Onderdonk. It seems much more than a month since I left. We will probably leave for Niagara next Monday. We will wear hats, which is customary all over the North. Break up the canarie's nest. She will kill herself setting to no good. Take away the eggs. Love to Lizzie R. Mrs. D. & F. With oceans to yourself I am, (All send love)

Your devoted daughter
Floride

P.S. We will have to hurry through with our trip as cousin Anna will have to be in Philla., at a friend's wedding by the 20th of next month.

Altoona
August 24th.

(Private)

As Mrs. Calvert wrote me that Dr. Hall had given up coming to Altoona, my dear mother, & Mr. Onderdonk wrote me a short note to the same effect, in accordance to my request that he should; I thought one Northerner was as good as an other, and as you said nothing to the contrary, I got uncle Baker to baptize me yesterday. I do not know that I would have spoken to him about it, but he seemed so kind when cousin Sarah did, & so heartily glad of my determination, that I thought it would be better than an entire stranger, as I had to be questioned first. Then Mr. Buck can not feel offended at my not applying to him. Altogether I thought it was better.

When the time came, I must confess I felt very badly, but I thought it was my duty, so I did it. I wanted the cerimony to take place in the evening, but uncle said it was not customary, so I had to go up right after the second lesson in the morning service. It nearly made me sick, & I cried like a baby. The church (St. Luke's) is a very small one, & the congregation still smaller, & as few knew me, I did not mind it so much. Cousin Sarah, & Mary, stood as witnesses. Uncle, & indeed all, were very kind, & I got through pretty well, though I had to go to bed with a headache as soon as I got home. None of the family were there, as there was communion in their church. Auntie advised me to become an Episcopalian, as my family were, & there was no great difference; and then I found I liked that church best after all. I am very glad it is over, & am equally glad to have done it, for it has worried me for a long time. I took but one name, as you said. I was so much obliged to you for your kind letter, & cousin S., & uncle, thought it *beautiful.* Please tell Mr. Onderdonk, as he has been so kind to me, also Mr. Lee, Lizzie, & Mr. Buck. Indeed I dont care who knows it.

Tell Jennie King that Mr. Oliver, the minister, here enquered after her, & sent his love, or something.

I have not taken this step rashly, for I have been thinking about it ever so long, & you know I was always inclined that way. I trust I shall improve more now. I hope you do not mind that Uncle B. performed the cerimony. I think it was more suitable, & I believe he is a good man, though prejudiced. He really gave an excellent sermon in the evening. Do write to me soon again, & tell me how you feel about it. I should be sorry to do anything you would not like. I do not know why it is, but I had rather do anything than make up my own mind. I trust you will find me a better daughter for this.

I do wish we could hear from grandma.—My love to all friends, I am as ever your devoted daughter

Floride Clemson.
P.S. I believe that adult baptism is equal to confirmation. See Prayer book.

*　　　　*　　　　*

Mrs. Clemson's next letter, August 27, complained about the horde of visitors that day, including the tax collector "to whom I paid the sum of $15 very unwillingly." Among her visitors were Mr. Onderdonk and the McCeney family. The latter had recently lost sixteen hands but seemed "to think they must not complain, as others have lost many more." Mr. Lee "is pleasant enough *for him,* & I believe wants to be agreeable." She reported that she had been into Washington to see a number of friends, but the clouds of dust had almost made her sick. "By the way, the bath house has been again broken open, & robbed of the soap, & soap dish, & two towels."

Turning to the war, Mrs. Clemson dismally confided: "I feel, with you, that times are dark with us, but not, I trust, desperate. As to Charleston, I fear more than I hope. Not that I think that the destruction of Ft. Sumter ensures, or *begins even,* the taking of the city,

140

but the position is so without natural defences, such as Vicksburg had, that I fear, *in time*, it must fall. It remains to be seen whether the vandals are willing to pay the price for it. I hope they will get nothing but ashes. I also worry much about your grandmother, father, & brother, but in these dreadful times we must all bear, with patience, the share of suffering which falls our lot."

Finally, she added: "Dont go to your uncles or any where else. *I dont wish it.*"

*   *   *

Thursday 1863
Altoona, Aug. 27th
Darling Mother,

I received your Sunday letter, the day before yesterday, & was glad to see you were still passing your time quietly. I have had the dumps ever since, on account of Charleston, which seems to me, to be in a bad way, by the *headings* in the papers, for I never trust myself to read more. Yesterday I took a good crying spell over the news. They are so kind, & considerate here, that for the last day, or two, they have kept the papers out of my way, & merely say: "nothing official," when I ask for the news, which I suppose portends *nothing good*. I am *so uneasy.*

I received a nice letter from Laura to day, in reply to one I wrote her last week. She never received my last letters, & seems much hurt about Mr. Lee, but I will send you the letter. I also wrote to Kate, merely thanking aunt B. for the invitation, & saying how much I should like to see Kate, and in no way committing myself.

We have put off starting on our trip, until next Wednesday, as Miss Cameron,[13] & some other friends of cousin Anna's, are to come on Monday to stay a day, & night. Uncle got home Tuesday. Cousin Sylvester also returned the same day. Uncle Baker left before either got back, which was fortunate, as he is no favorite with cousin S. at *least.* Mattie, & Mary, were to have gone to day, but the former was quite sick yesterday, so they will start tomorrow. They are both much improved. The one by getting quieter, & the other less so. A favorable exchange.

---

[13]Jennie Cameron was probably Virginia Cameron, youngest daughter of Simon Cameron, Lincoln's first secretary of war.

We have had a terribly cold spell for the last two days & the much-wished-for rain. I found my "gall body," by no means too warm, & had to put on my flanel. I wish I had a skirt with me. To day I am shivering in my traveling dress, which has just come home, & looks quite nicely. I payed $2 for making. I am too unfortunate about my shoes! The ones I had made here, are too broad, & those I sent for to Hipman, an inch too short, so I will have to send them back, & indeed I am put to it for any to wear. It is *too* bad to have such a foot!

Uncle brought *plenty* of horses from Kentucky, & nice ones too, I believe. I have been playing chess a good deal lately, & manage to come out pretty even with my opponents. Mattie [?] & I, have also revived some of our old duetts, to *our* great satisfaction. Yesterday we had quite a house full of company, to spend the day.

Cousin S. told me how sorry aunt North seemed not to see me. I must really stop there on my way back, if I can.—Mrs. Siles' son George, is dead I hear. They say he was engaged to Lizzie W. Mattie heard from cousin Annie[14] last week. All were well. Her youngest child is to be called Louisa, & uncle B. is going to baptize it this fall. They have had a very hard time.—Aunt Hetty is not very well.—We have such a joke on uncle. He was scearched, on suspicion of picking some one's pocket in the cars! We teaze him terribly. I am as well & fat as possible.

I too am most anxious about grandmother. I wish we would hear how she is at *least*. I hope [?] she is not sick. I hope you got some of the late rain. I want to get cousin S. to take me to a coal mine, if I can. Remember me to Mssrs. Lee & Onderdonk; Lizzie, & Mrs. Calvert. Tell the latter I have not had time to write lately, but will try to do so soon. All continue as kindly, & [*illegible*] to me as possible, & send love, in which I most sincerely join.

Your devoted daughter,
Floride.

*   *   *

Mrs. Clemson's letter of August 30 gave a rather full account of the activities of their friends and acquaintances. Mrs. Stone was going to Baltimore for a day or two (Mrs. Clemson declined to accompany her); both Mrs. King and Jennie had suffered serious falls; Mrs.

---

[14]Annie Washington, daughter of Louisa Washington. Their Harewood estate had suffered greatly from the ravages of war.

Calvert was ill; the Robinsons had paid a nice visit; Mrs. Perdicaris had left for Italy; Mrs. Dodge and Mrs. Fone looked better; but the Gallant Defender was "poorly." She had discharged Moses, who wanted a pay raise, and had secured a substitute hand.

Mrs. Stone had reported that a cousin of Lizzie Giles "got a letter from Mrs. Ould (wife of the commissioner on our side, for the exchange of prisoners,) who says, 'you will be surprised to hear Lizzie Giles has discarded the General she came down to marry'!!! What can we believe, for a friend of Mrs. Stones, also, saw the marriage of Miss Giles, & Gen. Quarles announced in a Southern paper. Mrs. Stone still believes she is married."

Continuing, Mrs. Clemson wrote: "Yesterday I went into the city, & saw the usual set, who were all rejoicing over the taking of two gunboats in the Rappahanock & the capturing, by Moseby[15] of forty waggons, & 'from 700 to 1700' soldiers. The Confederates, 800 strong, were over the river day before yesterday, above Georgetown.—From Charleston there is no news at all. I suppose Ft. Sumter is a mass of ruins, but that has been expected for some time. I send you a Federal account of the difficulties yet to be over come, before the city is taken. If only our big iron clads[16] which have, I hope, started from England, can arrive *in time*, it may yet be saved—If not, I hope they will only get ruins, & even those ruins they cannot occupy, before frost, without certain death. Unfortunately, the islands are healthy. I wish, *for their sakes*, they were dismal swamps." Again: "Dont stop at your uncles or cousin Tom's,[17] *I entreat you.*"

*   *   *

Sunday
Altoona. Aug. 30th./63

I take a small sheet again, dear mother, for I have very few events to record since Thursday, when I last wrote. I received your letter, written on that day, this morning, & am *so* glad to think you are well, & getting along comfortably. Must I add all of my selfishness? Well I am not sorry you miss me, for it would not be pleasant to think that I

---

[15]Confederate raider John Singleton Mosby.

[16]The British government intervened and did not permit the "Laird Rams" to leave England.

[17]Tom Clemson, another cousin, apparently living with Aunt Barton and Kate at that time.

wanted to see you so much, & that you did not care to have me home again.

Dear mother, it is so hard these heavy days of trial to our country, to be away from any one who can sympathize with you, & feel as you feel. Although I meet with real sympathy, & kindness, for my anxiety, yet it is very different when one thinks that, how ever kind they are, still they are overjoyed at what makes us miserable. I suppose Charleston is doomed sooner or later to fall, & I feel miserable enough about it, & also about grandma. Oh dear!

The Clemsons left Friday, & I was quite sorry to part from them. I will do as you say, & not go to see them, as I can easily get off. Friday afternoon, I drove Sadie Sterrit to Hollidaysburg, in the buggy, as we had a visit to return & some shopping to do. We started right after dinner, & got home before dark. Our horse was a fat, well kept animal, that the weight of a score of years had made sway-backed & siff, so the whipping, & driving, being too much for one, Sadie did the former, & had the hardest work, by far. We have taken a couple of rides in the new carriage, with uncle's fine horses. Both are most excellent. It is wonderful what good taste the old gentleman has in everything. I had to get some flanel, & make myself a skirt, I was so cold. We had to make a fire today.

We have settled to start Wednesday if nothing happens to prevent. We will go, as I wrote you, & expect to spend near two weeks on the trip, as we mean to take it by easy stages, & slowly; as cousins Anna, & Sarah are not strong. Auntie is still in bed, but as it is only one of her accustomed billious attacks we do not count upon her detainting the party, as she is much better. We will be much crowded for time, as cousin Anna will have to be in Philla before the 17, which is not pleasant.

I saw some of these steel collars & cuffs for ladies, & were they not so expensive (2.50) I would get a set to travel in, they are so nice, & pretty.—We took a pleasant, walk yesterday of about a mile & came home just in time to receive three gentlemen who spent the evening here. One of them played, & sang very well.—I have had such a pleasant visit here, that I shall regret leaving, though I expect to enjoy my trip, & want to see you ever so much.—I went, with cousin Sarah, up to the Sunday school today, where there are 100 scholars all ages, & seizes. Afterwards I took a long walk with cousin Sylvester, to a hill, where there is a glorious view of the surrounding country. On our way we stopped at the family burying ground where cousin Woods[18] lies.

Indeed I do not know where to tell you to direct. We expect to spend next Sunday at Niagara but I do not know at what house. Have a letter waiting at the Leupps [in New York City] anyhow. I shall feel very uneasy at not being able to hear from you. All send love. Give my love to all & respects to Messers. Lee & O. I will try to write as often as possible but dont get uneasy if you dont hear.

I am as ever your devoted daughter,

Floride Clemson

*   *   *

Wednesday.
Altoona. Sep. 2nd/63

You see by the date of this letter my dear mother, that we are still here. Auntie did not get well as soon as we expected, so we put off starting one day, though that is decidedly inconvenient, as we will be still more pushed for time. However it could not be helped, and we confidently expect to get off tomorrow morning at eight o'clock. There is good in all evil for this morning I have been sick with one of my headaches, & though it was not a very bad one, still had I been traveling it might have been worse. Auntie is up and about today but cousins Sarah & Anna, have both very bad sore throats I am sorry to say. I hope there will be no more getting sick once we are started, for we have no time to spare on the road. You must not be surprised at the size of this sheet, as all my larger note paper is done, much to my sorrow. Your Sunday letter came to hand this morning, & as usual was most eagerly read, & reread.

Monday afternoon uncle took us (Sadie, Luly, & I) out a lond 25 mile drive in the new turn out [?]. We started about three o'clock, & did not get back till past eight. We passed through eight different towns & villages, & had one of the loveliest drives, I ever took. At one place there was a canal reservoir, which had all the appearance of a lake as it covered some 400 acres of land. It was surround by mountains, & fine bold scenery & had on its banks a place called Cat Fish, at which we got some sugar crackers, candy & apples. Some of the mountains about here look as if they had the *mange*, as the otherwise thick woods is intersperced with bare patches of slate. The effect is

---

[18]Woods Baker, deceased son of Elias Baker and late husband of Sarah.

very curious. We we got back, we found Miss Jennie Cameron, Miss Mary Willson, & Mr. Blanchard here & they only left this morning. Miss C. is a fine looking, free & easy girl of 25 or so, who put me a little in mind of Miss Laine[19] in figure & style, though not half so lady like & elegant.

By the way, I really have not had time to write to Miss L. I received a sweet letter from Mary C. yesterday. It was by far the pleasantest I ever saw from her. Now mind do not expect my letters *too* hard, for I may not have time to write often. If you get this epistle without a postscript to the contrary, you may know we have started, as I will put it in the post office on our way to the depot.

We went to Hollidaysburg last evening, in the morning took a walk to the mill where I weight 168 lbs. I am very well & fat you see. I am sorry about the Kings. Miss Cameron sings splendedly & we had some fine duetts to gether. Last evening we had a good deal of company to bid us good bye. I really have not time to write any more so must stop with much love to all & hopes that I shall see you soon, & as well as I am. Auntie & all send much love. Remember me to Messrs Lee & O. Love to Mrs. D. & all. I have no time to write to Mrs. C.

Your devoted daughter
Floride Clemson

*   *   *

Pittsburgh
Sep. 3rd. 1863

Here we are my darling mother after a pleasant days travel. We started from Altoona at nine o'clock this morning, & reached this place at a little before two. I am now sitting by the open window which commands a view of the Monogahela River, the suspension bridge, the entrances to several coal mines on the other side, & various manufactories of iron, glass &c. The river is very low, & exposes a bank which is paved with cobble stones in an inclined plane on which the waggons go *into* the stream to the boats which lie as near as they can.

Although we have been here so short a time, we have already *done* the principal of the sights. We have driven through the city, & visited a rolling [?] mill for iron, a glass blowing manufactory, & an iron clad ocean steamer, called the [*illegible*], which is 250 feet long. It

---

[19]Harriet Lane, ex-President Buchanan's niece.

has only the iron shell completed. The glass blowing was most interesting. We saw them making salt sellars, lamp glasses, & pressed tumblers & dishes. The rolling mill was also very interesting. In coming down here we saw the entrances to many coal & iron mines, which seemed to be very extensive. At a small place called Jackson, we saw a good many of both kinds in the side of the mountain, lying in different strata. They manufacture there considerably.

This place is by far the dirtiest I ever saw. Every thing you touch leaves a black spot on your fingers. The mud is black, the houses are black the atmosphere is dark (It has been raining & drizzleing all day) and the smoke hangs in still heavier clouds than the natural ones. There is nothing but dirt, & chimney stacks. However it is very interesting, & I would not have missed it for the world. The ride down here was beautiful, & the scenery, though not as bold as on the other side of the mountains, was fine. The Conamaugh is not near as large or as lovely as the Juniata, but still very beautiful.

We are a nice party of five, & determined to see, & enjoy all we can. Anna is still weak. We are staying at the Monongahela house, & as I started to tell when I said where we were sitting. We have aching feet (Sadie & I) immerced in a tub of cold water & as we did not have our trunks brought to the hotel, but put all strict nesscissaries in our bags, we are comfortably taking our ease in our night gowns, *en guise de robes de chambres*. We will probably stay at the Clifton house on the Canada side of the falls, which I much prefer, for I long to be out of these United States. I am almost afraid to ask for the news, I am so uneasy. Those ironclads (I saw two) make me feel vicious. Tomorrow we start at one, & will reach Cleveland in the evening. On account of our lost day we will not be able to make any stay there but will spend part of Saturday at Buffalo.

Auntie was much better when we left. I was almost sorry to go, I had enjoyed myself *so* much. I hope you will be able to read this. In hopes [*several illegible words*] be as glad to see me as I will you, I am

Yours devotedly
Floride

*   *   *

In her letter of September 3 Floride's mother said the news of the war was "very cheering but one fears to hope too much, disappointment would be so very bitter. We must trust in God's mercy, & the justice of our cause & hope for the best." She had heard of a stampede of 2,000 government horses from a corral "up the country." Rumors were that they had been cut loose to save them from the Confederates.

Anna had just seen a letter to Mrs. Calvert from her daughter Ella [in Pendleton], but there was no mention of Floride's grandmother. She had not heard from her mother, husband, or son. "What could it mean?...It makes me very sad," she wrote.

Anna mentioned visitors, the cold weather, and the impossibility of hiring male servants. D. W. Lee was present and "on the whole amiable." She closed by urging Floride to write. "I am beginning to look forward to seeing you."

*   *   *

1863
Sep. 7th Niagara Falls.
Clifton House, Canada
My Darling Mother,

Here we are at last at the great falls. We arrived safe, & sound, after dark last evening, so we did not see the falls until (I am ashamed to say it) ten o'clock this morning. The rest of the party seemed to be disappointed, not so with me, my highest expectations were *more* than realized. I cannot understand anyone's [*illegible*] disappointment & Niagara in the same day. I must say I was silly enough to cry when they first caught my sight. As you have been here, I suppose you know that from this side, & the porches of this house, you have a "full & particular" view of Goat Island, & both the bodies of water. I never *imagined* any thing so grand. I began to think those powers are rather deficient in me as in point of scenery I have seen so much since I left home, that was far above my highest flights. We have not left the porches of the house yet, as we are a little weary from our journey, but expect to take a walk this evening, & spend the next two days (the limit of our stay) in seeing all the sights, & paying innumerable quarters, I hear are expected at every turn. I do wish you were here to enjoy it with me. However, I will leave this place, with all its English, & its beauties, & take up the thread of my journey.

I wrote you a few hasty lines from Pittsburgh. As we had only our bags along, stuffed with the chief necessaries of life, they had to be written with pencil,[20] & therefore I suppose were almost illegible, but

---

[20]Anna received the penciled note; it is included herein.

148

they at least told you of our safe arrival at that place. The next morning, we breakfasted early, & were in the carriage by eight o'clock, ready to see the [*illegible*] until one, when we started. First we drove though, & around the city in every direction, &, as it was a fine day, it did not look half so dirty, & dismal. However the shading is black enough. The streets are very narrow, & dirty, but it is busy & thriving looking. I was struck by the small proportion of fine houses, which is owing to the fact the Pittsburgh people, mainly live *out* of the city in Alleghany. The suburbs look handsome enough. We drove to the point where the rivers meet, & to the cemetery, which is exceedingly beautiful & well kept. I think it rivals Laurel Hill, in all but its *finest* monuments.

Then uncle took us to another fine rolling mill, where we saw nails, &c., made. After that, we visited a large cannon foundary. We saw dozens of those of every size, & in every stage of completion. The largest weighed 15 tons, & had a 15 inch bore. It made me feel terribly, to see them. Then we went down street & made some purchases. I had to pay $3.00 for a plaid silk scarf, to put around my neck, as it was cold. They are in fashion & very handsome. I wish I had my blancket shawl to wear in changing cars in the evening. My stolle [?] is too thin, for though we have such warm pleasant days, the nights are chilly. The bluffs around Pittsburgh are very high, & beautiful, & fall almost perpendicularly to the smoky city.

At one we left, well laden with peaches, & luncheon. The ride along the river, till we left it in Ohio, is lovely although the water was exceedingly low, & there are no boats on it. After that it was tedious to a degree, until we reached Cleveland, after dark. The country does not seem either very rich, or well cultivated, there ware few streams, few towns of any size, & no striking points in the scenery. It is as flat as a table all the way, & [a] hill twenty feet high would have been a wonder. A dreary monotony of poor corn fields, woodlands, *stumpy*, pastures, & medows, were closed in by worn fences. It was just the same *from* Cleveland. There were two small lakes halfway in central Ohio, & that was all that was pretty. The Monongahala house in P. was good, & the Angier in C. was not extra. We saw very little of the latter place for we started at ten in the morning. We drove around it for nearly two hours however, & thought it very beautiful. The streets are wide, & regularly laid out, & the country flat, with an abrupt slope to the lake, which is for all the world like a quiet ocean, as the eye sees no *other* side. It is a large city (larger than P.) & very busy & clean. The streets are of gravel and sand, for the most part, & perfectly noiseless, not dusty, & very level. They are lined in the outskirts with splended trees, & Euclid st. is magnificent, putting me in mind of Columbia in its gardens, & splended suburban villas surrounded by fine trees, & set back a little from the street. I think we drove through two miles of unbroken fine places. I never saw such a refined looking city. The ladies drove themselves around in buggies a great deal.

From Cleveland to Erie we caught few glimpses of the lake. It was just out of sight the whole way. The day (yesterday) was a fine one, but dusty, & hot (not too hot for me however). The dust was perfectly intollerable, Faces, dresses, & hair, were all of the same color, & the air too thick to breathe. We consoled ourselves with innumerable peaches, & I ate enough of our lunch, for two or three hearty persons. I did not get as dirty as the rest for I, as usual, rode backwards.

Buffalo, which we reached before six, is a large, handsome city. We drove right through it, in an omnibus, & I think it looked more like Baltimore than any other place. I saw either Mr. Lee, or his ghost, in a train that crossed us between B. & here. It was just like him. Now that is pretty much all I have to tell you thus far, except that I took a luxurious bath this morning, & I feel a little done up, & shaky.

We opened our trunks first here. Our present intention is to stay here until Wednesday morning. Go through to Syracuse by evening. Next day to Saratoga, & Saturday to N. Y., where we will stay two or three days, & I will see Laura.[21] Uncle is going to leave us here this evening & spend his time at some springs (St Catharines well) nearby which are good for rhumatism.

I have spent a long time writing, & am crazy to take another look at the falls. They dress very much here, & the place is thoroughly English. I am so glad to be out of the *United* States. The fare is good. Cousin Anna, Sadie, & I are in one room. Luly & her mother in *this*, which we use for a parlor, as it looks on the falls. Take care of your dear self till I get home. Love to all &c.

Your devoted daughter
Floride Clemson

No one, stores nor hacks, keep Sunday here.

---

[21]Laura Leupp.

1863

Niagara, Sep. 9th

We are still here, my darling Mother, but expect to leave tomorrow morning, at half past six o'clock, & I must own I feel sorry to think that I shall so soon see these falls no more. No words have been invented yet strong enough to express my feelings (not thoughts) of them. I can not say that the perpetual sound of rushing waters is pleasant to me, I never liked it, & cousin Anna seemed to feel the same last night, when she could not sleep on account of thinking that they had rushed madly, over that precipice for thousands of years, & never would stop, but go on forever. She said it made her nervous, & so it does me.

I think we have seen all that tourists generally see here. Yesterday we took a carriage, & drove first down to the whirlpool way below the suspension bridge. I will send you a diagram of it. It is perfectly wonderful, as everything about here is, the water in the stream is eleven feet higher in the middle than at the sides, & perfectly mad. The banks rise perfectly perpendicularly on every side to a great height & rather hand [hang] over than slope from the stream. The *whirl* is not much to see. Then we came back to the depôt where we left uncle on his way to St. Catharine wells where he spent the day. After that we were driven to some beautiful views on this side of the falls, & rapids. The others climbed up a lofty latice work pagoda, but owing to my constitutional shortness of breath, I have had to deny myself all hill, & stair climbing, as it breaks me down. I also found that peaches, & traveling had not agreed with me, so I was a little weak, & had to be careful in diet &c. We also visited the museum where we feasted mentally, & occularly on some very good stuffings of birds, & animals, some few horrible wax figures, some interestingly disgusting mummies, & quite a large Egyptian collection, also the usual filling of shells minerals, fossils, mementoes, &c. There are any quantities of Indian stores, full of real, & bogus work; of these I bought a braid box, & some other trifles. We took the usual round of Lundies Lane, & some pretty roads, & last visited the burning spring, which was highly interesting, & bad smelling. The position is beautiful. In short everything is "grand, sublime, & rocky," in the extreme. Yesterday we walked down the river bank, & had a fine view from there.

Today we *did* the American side. Fortunately we had overcast days

151

for both seeings. Yesterday we suffered from the dust a little, & to-day were slightly sprinkled, but this we did not mind, as we did not like the idea of such an other stifleing day's travel as our last. We crossed the Suspension bridge which is really wonderful, & passed through the town of Niagara Falls, but were overtaken by a shower, & had to get out at the Cataract house, which is a very fine one, & also visited some Indian stores right opposite. The town is quite a large, & clean town, not busy, but thriving looking. We then drove over a smaller suspension bridge to Goat Island where we visited all the places of interest, Luna Island, Terrapin tower, saw a mist rainbow, & the Three Sisters. In short we went over, above, below, around, about, among, & I went under the falls! This last acheivement I did much against the wishes of the rest of the party, but I knew it was not dangerous, as it was not, so I took off my hoops, & all above them, & put on a suitable oil cloth dress, & with a mulatto guide went under, from the Canadian side, yesterday. It was most impressing & grand, & I would not have missed it for all the world. The falls shoot about six feet from you, while you stand on a ledge of rock, & look up, & out at them.

This hotel is a perfect den of secessionists, most driven from New Orleans by Butler.[22] The rest are English. There is not much dash [?] but everything, & everybody is genteel, & elegant. Tomorrow we will visit Trenton Falls. Friday to Saratoga, & Saturday to N. Y. where I wrote Laura to be at her sister [aunt] Cornelia's. Dont you think I had better get myself a handsome black rept silk if I can under 30$ for a useful dress. Telegraph to C. Lee[23] if I may. Do you need one? What else shall I get. We leave N. Y. Tuesday. You would be in fashion here. The ladies are all so stout. They wear hats [*illegible*] older and fatter than you! Insane sheppardesses.

Love & respect to all. Your devoted daughter
Floride Clemson

[22]General Benjamin F. Butler, in charge of New Orleans after its surrender in the spring of 1862. Southerners called him "beast" because of his restrictions on local citizens.
[23]Creighton Lee, brother of D. Williamson and Gideon Lee.

Friday
Saratoga. Sep. 12th 1863
My darling mother,

The others have gone out walking, &, as I did not feel well enough to accompany them, I thought I would spend the time in a little chat with you. I am not really sick, but have had the diarrea ever since I left Altoona, more or less badly, & that, with having to be very careful, & sparing in my diet, has made me sick. Indeed I could hardly have chosen a less pleasant traveling companion, for *every* reason. I suppose when I get quietly settled at home again I shall be all the better for it.

We left Niagara, as I told you we would on Wednesday morning, at half past six. I was most sorry to lose sight of that great miracle, & to leave the neighborhood of so many good Southerners. The Clifton was also an excellant unostentatious hotel. The next station to the Suspension bridge having burnt down the night before, doing, some damage to the track, we had to go to a place called Tonawanda, where we waited a weary while, then struck back into the N. Y. Central railroad, at Lockport. Thence through Rochester, which seemed a large thriving place, to Syracuse, which we reached after three o'clock P.M., owing to the delay. By taking this route, you will see by the map, & not the one from Buffalo to Syracuse, we missed all the Lake scenery, & passed through, a fine, but not striking country. I am much disappointed for there seemed no reason for the choice, but where there are so many, unaccountable things are often done. The trip to S. was a very pleasant one, as the rain had laid the dust, & we were pleasantly seated, so on reaching our destination we were quite clean, & fresh. I must confess I often sigh for my warm clothes, & live in my Garibaldi, it is so cold. The leaves are just beginning to turn, still it feels like the next step to winter.

Syracuse is a much larger city than I expected, & a very fine one, situated on a beautiful sheet of water, called Salt Lake. It has the same characteristics as Cleveland which it much resembles, though not as beautiful, in the principal part of the living streets, being built after the suburban style with fine gardens, & great forest trees. It is exceedingly irregularly laid out, & in some parts *puts us in mind* of Venice, with the Erie canal, & its branches which bisect the city.

By the way, we kept along the canal most of the way, until we got to the Mohawk river, near Utica, which we followed to Schenectady.

Selina is a continuation of Syracuse, almost the same city. The evening we took a walk around the latter, & next morning breakfasted at seven, & drove around, & visited the salt works, till ten, when we left. The salt water is drawn from deep wells, or springs, as they call them, & carried in pipes to the factories, where it is boiled in great iron semi-spherical cauldrons (as see diagram)[24] & evaporated. The residue is *common* salt, which is also ground at this place for table use. A great deal is made by solar evaporation, & it is singular to see acres, & acres of sheds, which are slipped over the shallow woden boxes, set upon piles, when the salt is beginning to dry. You see it there in every state from clear water with a slight muddy sediment, to passably clean salt.

We had quite a time when we first got to S. (We were told that the St. Charles was the best hotel, so we went to it, & were shown our rooms. I dont think I ever saw such a dirty place. The rooms looked more like pigs stys than any thing else. We soon saw we could not stay there, & went to the Globe, where we were very nicely accommodated.

Yesterday we had a quite pleasant ride to this place, which we reached about $6^{1}/_{2}$ o'clock, waiting over an hour & a half, at Schenectady, which we saw nothing. We had unfortunately left our guide book, & luncheon basket, full of the most tempting meal; the former we replaced, but the latter we could not, so feasted on crackers. The country we passed through was beautiful, & in parts almost mountainous. We did see mountains, near here, in the distance. I send you the *likeness*[25] of this hotel on the back of this. The place itself is quite a pretty one, but from what I can hear, there is little of interest in the vicinity. The surrounding country is not uncommonly beautiful, as far as I can see. There was a *hop* here last night, which we *looked* at, till eleven. The ladies wear scarcely any hoops "small quakers" are all the fashion, some had none on, still others wore ordinary ones. The hair is worn over rats [?], high in front & hanging down behind thus: in loops or curls, with fancy combs. [Floride made a drawing of the head dress.]

---

[24]Floride's letter included in the margin a crude drawing of the cauldrons.
[25]See "likeness" of Congress Hall in the diary.

I am sorry to say that I shall also miss the steam boat trip down the Hudson. We start in the cars at 7 tomorrow morning. We will keep down the bank of the river, it is true but that is not the same thing; the objection is on account of cousin Wood's death. Anna & Sadie, would not mind it, but it is a hard party to do anything with, & it is all let us go with the others! I am too sorry. I wrote to Laura from Niagara to meet me at her aunt Cornelia's, & I shall stop at the office[26] on Ferry St. to ask for letters. I tore my dress, day before yesterday, my first accident. Will Reach N. Y. at 7½ P. M.

I do wish I could hear from you. I received a letter from Sarah Wharton, & an other from Mary Latrobe forwarded from Altoona. Keep safe till I get home next week, probably Wednesday or Thursday after noon. I will let you know if I can. Respects to Mr. Lee & O. Love to Mrs. D. & all.

Your devoted daughter
Floride Clemson

*   *   *

The same day [September 12] that Floride wrote her mother from Saratoga, Anna wrote her daughter that she had received her two letters from Niagara Falls. Regarding Floride's homecoming, she urged her not to linger in New York and to have her uncle escort her back to Bladensburg. "If there is any doubt of his coming tell him . . . *it is all important I should see him on business.*"[27]

She passed on the news that their neighbor Mr. Samuel Crawford disappeared two days previously. She feared he was in trouble with federal authorities. "I trust he's not in prison,"[28] she added.

She was also sending a message by Creighton Lee, and another by Samuel Van Wyck[29] that she had heard from "*all our folks* & all are well." Anna's letter then included a mysterious reference to a note she had sent to a Miss Welsman by Van Wyck. She asked Floride to visit

[26]She was obviously referring to the office of C. M. Leupp and Company where the Lee brothers held forth.

[27]Anna was anxious to get Uncle Elias to take charge of her property at Bladensburg.

[28]Crawford, a neighbor, was in trouble because a horse with a government mark was discovered in his barnyard. He might also have been suspected of being a Confederate collaborator.

[29]Samuel Van Wyck's wife was the former Margaret Broyles of Pendleton; his mother was the former Lydia Ann Maverick, also of Pendleton.

Miss Welsman and "explain more freely than I could by letter & she be perhaps more willing to answer. Be *cautious* however till *certain* how she feels & say nothing even to the V. W.'s."

*   *   *

Sunday
New York. Sep. 13th. 1863
Darling Mother,

We reached this place about half past three yesterday, after a rather tiresome ride, since seven in the morning. I do not mean that the banks of the Hudson were not even more beautiful than I expected, but it seemed to me that the road was a rough one, probably owing to the sudden bends it makes in following the banks of the river as closely as it does. It was also the noisiest I was ever on, as there was a bank of rocks on one side most of the way, & the bed of the road seems to be stone. We were oftener *in* the river than *by* it, on causeways, piles, & bridges; when we were on land, we passed through many tunnels and cuts, made in the hardest & most solid rock I ever saw. We could not get on the river side of the cars, there was such a rush for it, & as large bodies (like our party) move slowly we do not always get good seats; the the sun being on that side the barbarians put down their shutters closely, so we had not a very good view.

However I managed part of the way to crowd in by a dirty Irish women, & her band boxes, right by the door, which by means of the most praiseworthy industry I managed to keep open, against the will of the conductor, passengers, passersby, & the shaking of the cars. So I saw enough to want to see more, to long for the steam boat, to be lost in admiration, & disappointment. It was by far the finest scenery I ever saw. The Catskill mountains are very grand, & the scenery about West Point, & Newberg, beautiful. I *did* wish so to stop, to see Mr., & Mrs. Brown.

Before we left Saratoga, that is to say, the afternoon, of the day I wrote, cousin Sarah & I took a walk to the springs, & around the town, which is not much, though rather pretty, & neat. Congress Hall is by no means the best hotel, we found out, & we did not see the height of fashion, until in the evening we were lookers on at another hop, at the United States House, for a little while. The Congress, & Columbia water, are perfectly dreadful, & almost made me sick to taste. They were in very fine grounds, & have nice stone *sheds* with collums over them. We also visited the establishment where the water

156

is bottled for transportation. It is quite expensive, & I learned how to wire bottles there. Which accomplishment I shall put into practice when I get home, someday. I suppose it was because I was not well there, but I took no fancy to Saratoga, & would not care to go there again.

We saw Albany on the other side of the river, also Newberg, & West Point, & the place where cousin Woods[30] died. This cast a gloom over the whole party, & put uncle out of humor, so that when we reached here, he could not agree with the hackmen, & made us walk ever so far to Broadway, dirty, & tired as we were. Before we got our trunks, & as soon as I could get my face washed, I looked in the directory, & found that Mr. C. Lee had changed his residence to No. 104 East 30th St., where he has been over a year in a nice brown stone building. Uncle took me there from this hotel (the Metropolitan) & to my great disappointment found *no one* at home. The family[31] were all away, & even Mr. Lee had started that same afternoon to pay them his usual Sunday visit, & will not be back until sometime tomorrow!

Will you believe it mother, I find I made that same abominable mistake Mr. Jackson[32] made, & directed my letter to Laura, telling her of my arrival, to No. 22 Ferry St., & shall probably not get to see her! I know it was silly, but I was so grieved at that, & not hearing from you, as I expected, that I cried the whole afternoon, but I was so tired, it made me weak I suppose, & I could not help it. I want to see L. so very, very, much.

This morning [September 14] we went to church, expecting to hear Dr. Alex. Vinton, who is a splended preacher they say, but he was away, & we only heard a very indifferent minister, in a very ordinary church. It was a good way to walk, & when I got home I was so weary that I laid down on my bed, & never got up till past six, eating no dinner, or supper. I was over wearied, but feel much better now.

Some of the party saw uncle William [Clemson] to day on the street, so I will try to get to see aunt Sue tomorrow, as I suppose she is at Wilmerdings as usual. I did not know they were here. I will have to

[30]Extant family records do not reveal either the time or place of Woods Baker's death.

[31]Laura and other members of her family perhaps resided with her Uncle Creighton.

[32]Jackson was a Bladensburg merchant with whom the Clemsons had business dealings.

buy, some shoes as my feet at [are] nearly bare, & a few other little things also. The others speak of visiting Central Park, & Greenwood also, but how they will find time as we leave Tuesday morning, I do not know. We will leave cousin Sarah & Luly at Princeton, cousin Anna at Philla, & take Sadie as far as Landcaster Penn. Wednesday we expect to leave Philla, probably in the afternoon, the next day, we will spend at Landcaster, when I expect to see aunt Hetty, & Miss Lane, & Friday afternoon you may expect us home in the same train.

It may be that uncle can get through his business earlier in Philla., & if we can start in the morning from there, we will be home on Thursday afternoon, so you had better send both days. We cannot find out the connections, or I could tell for certain when. I want to see you so much, you dont know, & it seems so long since I have heard, then I am tired *with* traveling (not *of* it), so shall be glad to get home to rest.

I have been bothered with my cloths at Niagara, Saratoga, & here. I positively have no dress to wear in the street. I have not seen any but the commonest servant girl in a dress with a figure or bright color. Everything is worn of plain colors, with a frill or two or a trimming near the bottom. Everything I have looks so outré. I had to wear my lawn to church to day, & was ashamed. Black & dark silks plain, or nuteral colors in suits, are the only things worn, also black silk half loose things, like my winter cloak, *long*. The bonnets do not come over the face, & hoops small.

I was unfortunate enough to let my shell comb fall out of my head today, when it broke in two. You know I bought it here, was it not strange? I am so sorry, but it can be mended, as it is *nicely* broken.

Coats tight to the figure are coming in fashion again I see, & hear; low necks have gone out. Almost every one wears these white tucked swiss bodies, or else puffed Talmas are worn instead of jackets, & every thing is trimmed with box plaitings of the same, & braiding in black.

I am going to write to Kate to meet me in Philla. & perhaps she will be able to accompany me as far as Landcaster, if she gets the letter. I do hope I shall see Mr. Lee[33] tomorrow, & hear from you. I never was so grieved as I am at not seeing little Laura.

---

[33]Creighton Lee, not to be confused with D. W. Lee, who was at The Home at that time.

I have no more to say except that I am very fat, do not cough, & no sore throat, & have gotten over what I complained of in my last [diarrhea], but have another trouble, dear! I am only tired out now, & want rest. It is late, & I must stop. I shall be sorry to loose cousin Sarah, I really love her, & she has been very kind to me. My money has flown terribly, & I have very little left, but I can account for nearly all satisfactorily. Hats are much worn even in the city a little turned or rolled up at the sides, & down behind, & in the front, with rather high pyramidal crown, & trimmed with gay, white, or black feathers standing up in front, or lying back over the crown, often gay velvet trimming also. My love to all, & respects to Messers. Lee & O. I am in hopes of soon seeing you well.

Your devoted daughter,
Floride Clemson

P. S. Excuse writing, as gass shines on my paper so that I can scarcely see, & I am tired.

*   *   *

There is only one of Floride's letters extant after 1864. It was written from her home at Carmel, New York, a few months before her death. Much of the letter deals with her daughter Floride Isabella Lee.

Epilogue

FLORIDE CLEMSON left Pendleton on October 24, 1866, the day she wrote the last detailed entry in her diary. She must have rather thoroughly made the rounds of friends and relatives: letters tell of visits in Virginia, Maryland, Pennsylvania, and Delaware. She had planned to return to South Carolina in the spring of 1867, but her visit was protracted to July 31. She did not visit the Lees and the Leupp girls in New York—perhaps because her father had received a cold reception from D. W. Lee when he was there, but probably because Laura, whom she knew best, was spending the winter and spring of 1867 in Spain.

Floride had pneumonia in June, 1868, from which she probably never completely recovered, since she reported that she was suffering from chronic inflammation of the lungs in January, 1869. She recovered sufficiently, however, to be married to Gideon Lee of New York the following July. He was brother of D. W. Lee, the "Gallant Defender" of The Home during the war, in whom Floride had an unrequited romantic interest when she was younger, and a brother-in-law of Charles M. Leupp, through whom the Clemsons and the Lees became acquainted. His nieces, Laura and Isabella Leupp, had visited her at Mi Casa in March and April, 1869.

Gideon Lee was a most unlikely candidate for matrimony. After the Mexican War, in which he served as a lieutenant of a company of scouts known as the "Texas Rangers," he settled for a short time on his extensive holdings in Texas. He returned to New York in broken health, but gradually recovered through outdoor activities and the ministrations of Dr. Mundé's hydropathy. At one time he was so afflicted with inflammation of the brain that motion was completely proscribed. As his health improved, his disposition, reputedly viciously antisocial, also improved. Their marriage took place at St. Paul's Episcopal Church in Pendleton on Aug. 1, 1869, and was witnessed by Floride's parents, her brother Calhoun, and many friends. Like her mother Floride married a man of prominent family many years her senior: Gideon's father had been mayor of New York City and senior member of the largest leather firm in America, and Gideon was almost nineteen years older than Floride. The father image

161

could have been a factor in the choice of a husband by both mother and daughter. Unlike her mother, Floride married a man whose political philosophy was the antithesis of hers.

Floride and Gideon Lee lived at "Leeside," in Carmel, New York, a property which he had purchased from the Anson Hazen estate. To this marriage was born on May 15, 1870, Floride Isabella Lee, Thomas G. Clemson's only grandchild. She was destined not to have the parental care and guidance of her fond mother very long, for on July 23, 1871, Floride Clemson Lee died. She was buried in the Raymond Hill Cemetery in Carmel. On a granite shaft in the Lee plot is etched the record:

> Gideon Lee, March 28, 1824-April 22, 1894
>
> Floride E., his wife, December 29, 1842-July 23, 1871
>
> Ella F. Lorton, his wife, April 5, 1844-January 1, 1921
>
> Isabella Lee Calhoun, daughter of Gideon and Floride Lee, May 15, 1871[1870]–June 4, 1935
>
> Gideon, son of Gideon and Ella F. Lee, April 13, 1878-March 23, 1892
>
> Williamson Whitner, their son, February 20, 1882-October 5, 1918

Thus ended the short but many-sided life of Floride Clemson Lee, protagonist of this biographical sketch. In her last known extant letter written to her mother on February 4, 1871, when Floride was nursing her sick baby back to health she commented in passing that the report of her father's anger at her made her sorry, but that she knew there was nothing she could do to stop it. She wrote, "It is like a cloud way off." Like her father, Thomas Green Clemson, and her grandfather, John C. Calhoun, Floride Clemson Lee was very strong-willed. High-spirited, critical, and perhaps a bit boastful, Floride displayed, however, kindness, noblesse oblige, compassion, loyalty, piety, devotion to her child, and frugality. Her predominant characteristic, however, was strength, apparent in her faults and virtues alike. To label her simply a well bred young woman of high principle and scruple is not enough. When she was a seven-year-old child living in Belgium, she took her grandfather's motto for her own, "The Duties of Life are Greater Than Life Itself"; the dedicated seriousness of this pervaded the rest of her life.

ENVOY

Floride Clemson Lee had been dead only eighteen days when tragedy struck again in the Clemson family. On August 10, 1871, Calhoun, Thomas and Anna Clemson's last surviving child, met with a fatal accident on the Blue Ridge Railroad.

Anna Calhoun Clemson died of a heart attack on September 22, 1875, and Thomas G. Clemson, of pneumonia on April 6, 1888. His granddaughter, Floride Isabella Lee, was his sole surviving descendant.

Fort Hill plantation, the property of John C. Calhoun since 1826, passed to his wife, Floride Calhoun, when he died in 1850. By 1854 the place was falling into disrepair and Mrs. Calhoun decided to sell it to her son, Andrew Pickens Calhoun, who gave his bond and mortgage for $49,000, the full purchase price (of house, land, slaves, and equipment). Andrew failed to pay off the indebtedness before his death on March 16, 1865, and a foreclosure bill was filed against his estate on March 12, 1866, by Mrs. Calhoun and Thomas G. Clemson (as administrator for Cornelia Calhoun, her daughter who had died in 1857). Foreclosure was ordered, the judgment was appealed, and the original order was affirmed. During this period of litigation Mrs. Calhoun died, leaving a three-fourths interest in the Fort Hill bond and mortgage to Mrs. Clemson and the remaining one-fourth to Floride Clemson or her heirs. When Fort Hill was sold at auction January 21, 1872, Clemson bought it with Andrew's bond and mortgage. The property was not legally partitioned until November, 1873, when Thomas G. Clemson as trustee for Mrs. Clemson received 814 acres (on which the house was situated) and Gideon and Floride Isabella Lee, heirs of Floride Clemson Lee, 288 acres.

When Anna died in 1875, Thomas G. Clemson inherited her share of Fort Hill. Before her death she and her husband had often considered leaving the property to found an agricultural college in the destitute Southland. In deference to his wife's wishes and because of his interest in scientific agriculture, Clemson, who had no immediate heirs, bequeathed the bulk of his estate to found Clemson Agricultural College at Fort Hill (appraised at $106,179 after his death in 1888). The bequest was contested by Floride Isabella Lee through her father and guardian, Gideon Lee, on the grounds that Clemson did not hold valid title to the property. Lee lost the case and in December, 1889, the State of South Carolina accepted the bequest according to the provisions of Clemson's will, which further provided that if his granddaughter, Floride Isabella Lee, contested any part of it, she would lose the $15,000 legacy bequeathed her in the will. Executor R. W. Simpson, however, was authorized by the legislature to pay the inheritance to Isabella. Later she sold her share of Fort Hill property to Clemson College for $10,000, and the original Calhoun holdings were reunited. Today Clemson University stands on John C. Calhoun's Fort Hill because of the will of Thomas G. Clemson.

APPENDIX I

Final Entries in Floride Clemson's Diary[1]

Retrospect.

John Caldwell Calhoun was born March 18th. 1782. Died March 31st. 1850 at 7 o'cock A. M. at Washington city, D. C.

Floride Calhoun his wife was born in Charleston S. C. Feb. 15th. 1792. Died at Pendleton.

John Caldwell Calhoun, & Floride Calhoun were married Jan 8th. 1811.

Elizabeth Baker was born March 30th. 1774. Died Ap. 17th. 1857 at Philadelphia, Penn.

Thos. Green Clemson, Jr. was born in Philadelphia Penn. July 1st. 1807.

Anna M. Calhoun was born in Abbeville Dist. S. C. Feb. 13th. 1817.

Thomas G. Clemson & Anna M. Calhoun were married at Fort Hill the residence of her father in Pickens Dist. S. C. Nov 13th. 1838.

Their eldest daughter was born at Ft. Hill Aug. 13th. 1839. Lived 3 weeks.

John Calhoun Clemson was born at Ft. Hill July 17th. 1841.

Floride Elizabeth Clemson was born at Ft. Hill Dec. 29th. 1842.

Cornelia Clemson was born at The Home near Bladensburg Prince George[s] Co. Md. Oct. 3rd. 1855 at 20 minutes past one o'clock A. M.

Died 20th. of Dec. 3½ o'clock P. M. 1858.—Thos. G. Clemson states as a strange coinsidence that some few days previous to the commencement of this daughter's illness, when she was in the bloom of perfect health, he awoke much excited in the night, & his wife asked him what was the trouble. He answered that he had just seen his mother distinctly, & his little daughter (whom she had never seen) was sitting on her right shoulder. Signed T. G. C. dated Dec. 22nd. 1858.

[1] It is not known when Floride entered these remaining passages in her diary. The diary indicates that the last entry was in January or February, 1869.

165

A Rebel Came Home

Copied from Anna C. Clemson's manuscript.

"Mr. Clemson was appointed Superintendent of Agriculture.

Mr. Clemson went on official business to Europe in July 1860 staid away till the 31st. of Octo. 1860.

Calhoun went to my uncle James Ed. Calhoun's in Abbeville Dist. S. C. Oct. 29th./60.

"Cronological Summary of the married life of Thos. G. Clemson & his wife Anna C. Calhoun.

"Passed the winter of 1838 between the city of Philadelphia & that of Washington. The Spring of 1839 at Harewood Jefferson Co. Va. the residence of Mrs. Louisa Washington his sister, & the summer & fall of the same year at Fort Hill. The winter of 1839 & part of 1840 at Millwood, the residence of James Ed. Calhoun in Abbeville Dist. S. C. Returned to Ft. Hill & staid there till Nov. 1841 when Mr. Clemson went with his brother-in-law Patrick Calhoun to Havana in the Isd. of Cuba where Mrs. Clemson joined him with their son John C. Clemson then six months old. In the month of Feb. 1842. Returned to Ft. Hill in May 1842. Passed the summer of that year at Mr. J. C. Calhoun's gold mine on the Chestatee river near Dahlonega, in Geo. Returned to Ft. Hill, & remained there till Feb. 1843. Went then to the plantation called the Canebrake in Edgefield Dist. S. C. where they remained till July 1844., when Mr. Clemson was appointed Chargée d'Affairs to the court of Belgium. Sailed from N. Y. city, with his wife & two children in the sailing packet Argo, Capt. Anthony, for Havre in France Aug. 8th. 1844 & arrived at Havre 13th. Sep. Went to Paris from thence to Brussels, where they arrived Octo. 4th 1844. Remained in Brussels till the fall of 1848. Octo 4th. 1848 sailed from Antwerp in the sailing packet Roscoe Capt. Riker for N. Y. Encountered a hurricane on the Banks of New Foundland & were in great danger for twelve hours. Arrived at N. Y. city Nov. 5th. 1848. Remained in America till the spring of 1849 passing the winter at their plantation the Canebrake, & the spring at Washington. Left N. Y. in the sailing packet Northumberland Capt. Griswold for London May 24th. 1849. Arrived in London June 26th. 1849. Arrived at Brussels July 9th. 1849. Mr. Clemson was recalled in Dec. 1850, & left Brussells with his family Ap. 9th. 1851. Sailed from Liverpool Ap. 16th. in the Steam Ship (screw) City of Glasgow Capt. Campbell, for

Philadelphia where they arrived (a[fter] a stormy passage, & having struck the first night out from Liverpool on the rocks in Blackwater Bay off of the Tuscoe Light House on the coast of Ireland) on the 5th. of May 1851. Passed the summer at Fort Hill, the Winter & fall at Philadelphia. The winter 1851-52 was passed at Trenton N. J. Ap. 1852 went to Glen Cove Hempstead Harbor on the Northern coast of L. I. May 1st. of the same year went to live on the Isd. Dosoris belonging to Henry M. Weston 3 miles from Glen Cove. Dec. 4th. 1852 left Dosoris & came to the Relay House 7 miles from Balt. on the Washington R. R. where we remained till Aug 1st. 1853 then left for Bladensburg Prince George Co. Md. Mr. Clemson having bought the place a mile from the village May of the same year. Moved to the place, Tuesday Aug. 9th. 1853.

The first volume of Floride Clemson's diary will suply most of the rest of the family chronicle from this time to her return to Pendleton in July 1867. From that time there is little worth telling. Calhoun went to the north on business during the months of of June & July 1868 & was in Wash., Altoona, N. Y. & Balt. I had pneumonia in June 1868. Laura & Bella Leupp spent the months of March & April of 1868 in Pendleton with us. I took a Sunday school class during Lent of 1868. Mr. Benj. H. Latrobe to whom I had sent my poetry to see if I could make some money for the poor by publishing in periodicals had it printed in a volume of 72 pages, Dec. 1868. Unfortunately a bad selection. 513 copies.[2] The whole edition & many more were engaged by my friends before it was out. Clear profits $ [blank]. Rode about with Lizzie Cornish to get some of the poor into our Sunday School. By giving them decent suits out of this money got near 30 together before the end of Jan. 1869. I put Albertine & Marion Hapenelt to school to Sue Dickenson[3] at 1 dollar per month Jan. 1st 1869. I had taught the former

[2] [Lee, Mrs. Floride (Clemson)] d. 1871. *Poet skies and other experiments in versification,* by C. de Flori [*pseud.*] Baltimore, J. W. Woods, printer, 1868 6, [9]—72 p. 2 pl. 19½ X 11½ cm. Library of Congress PS2236. L27 28-2219

[3] Marion (age 4) and Albertine (2) were daughters of Emily (age 31) and B. G. Happoldt (32), a Charleston gunsmith in 1860. In 1870 Emily Happoldt and family of five children were living in Pendleton township. MS. Census 1860, Ward 3, Charleston Dist., S. C.; MS. Census 1870, Anderson County, S. C. Susan Dickinson (age 24 in 1870) was the daughter of Rachel Miles and Francis W. Dickinson, a Charleston lawyer. *Ibid.;* Simpson, *Old Pendleton District,* pp. 114-15.

for some time. I suffered with chronic inflamation of the lungs from my attack of pneumonia in June 1868 till now Jan. 1869. Unable to walk from shortness of breath sometimes better sometimes worse. Am not strong though very stout to what I have been.

[At this point, page 121 of the manuscript, Floride pasted two prescriptions.]

Dr. Wm. Fahnestock & his wife came to look after a place to settle, & stayed with us from [blank] 1868 to [blank] 1869.

Mary Latrobe & Mr. Henry Onderdonk were married Dec. 17/68.

Kate Latrobe[4] to Cornelius Weston in the spring of 1867.

During the last week of Jan. 1869 Gov. Pickens,[5] & Mrs. Grange Simmons both died.

[4] Kate, daughter of B. H. Latrobe, Jr.
[5] Francis W. Pickens (Apr. 7, 1805-Jan. 25, 1869), Civil War governor of South Carolina. *Biog. Dir. Cong.*, p. 1679. Mrs. Grange Simons was the former Elizabeth Bonneau Noble.

APPENDIX II

People mentioned in the Diary as "the families we know here" [Pendleton, S. C., 1865]

Col. Thomas J. Pickens (Simpson, *Old Pendleton District*, p. 192).

Robert, Joseph Ellison, and John B. Adger, D.D. (Simpson, pp. 123-24).

Judge Edward Frost (*Cyclopedia of Eminent and Representative Men of the Carolinas. . . .* 2 vols., Madison, Wisc.: Brant & Fuller, 1892, I, 143-44).

Rev. Charles C. Pinckney (*SCHGM*, XXXIX (Jan. 1938), 32).

Dr. William C. Ravenel (Ravenel, *Ravenel Records*, p. 146).

Margaret or Eliza Ford, wartime refugees (MS. Census 1860, Ward 3, Charleston Dist., S. C.).

Selina Eliza Porcher Ravenel, widow of Henry Edmund Ravenel (Ravenel, pp. 65, 145, 147).

William Van Wyck, a New York-born lawyer who married Lydia Ann Maverick (Simpson, pp. 109, 173).

James T. Latta (Simpson, pp. 118-19).

Sophia Fraser Warley, widow of Jacob Warley, and daughters Mrs. Elizabeth Bourne and Mrs. Anna Holmes (Simpson, pp. 201-02; Register, St. Paul's Episcopal Church).

Sophia Elizabeth Bee, widow of General Barnard Bee (*DAB*, II, 124-25; Register, St. Paul's).

Rev. John H. Elliott married Catherine Sadler Shanklin, widow of Rev. Joseph A. Shanklin. Mrs. Sadler, of Florida, lived with them. Simms (unidentified) was probably a Symmes, a well-known Pendleton name. (Simpson, pp. 168-69).

Rachel Miles Dickinson, wife (widow?) of Francis W. Dickinson, and daughters Mrs. Rachel Green and Mrs. Lawrence Lee (Simpson, pp. 114-15).

Samuel and John H. Maxwell, M.D., sons of Capt. John Maxwell, a member of the Secession Convention. Another son, Robert, M.D., died on June 24, 1859, leaving a widow, Lucy Sloan Maxwell, and eight children. (Simpson, pp. 175-76; marker in Baptist Cemetery,

Pendleton; MS. Census 1860, Anderson Dist., S. C.). Rob. Maxwell was son of Robert A. Maxwell, a wealthy Pendleton farmer (*Ibid.*).

Major R. F. Simpson, a member of the Secession Convention and father of Richard W. Simpson (Simpson, pp. 5-8).

Major George Seaborn (Simpson, p. 150; Register, St. Paul's).

William H. Trescot, the diplomat (*DAB*, XVIII, 639-40).

Susan Taylor Lewis, widow of Jesse Payne Lewis, who died on October 12, 1845 (Simpson, pp. 165-67; markers in Old Stone Church Cemetery, Pendleton).

Miriam Earle Mays, who bought property in Pendleton in 1841, was listed as the only person in her household in the 1860 census. (MS. Census 1860, Anderson Dist., S. C.; Anderson deeds, book E-2, p. 733). She was the daughter of Major Sam Earle and wife (widow?) of James Butler Mays (Simpson, p. 147).

Mrs. Lewis, Jr. (unidentified).

Eliza Drayton North, widow of John Laurens North; Norths (unidentified); Thurstons were the Charleston refugee families of Robert Thurston or E. M. Thurston, or both. (Simpson, p. 73; MS. Census 1860, Wards 2 and 3, Charleston Dist., S. C.).

Eliza Kilpatrick Lorton, widow of John S. Lorton, who died on Oct. 16, 1862 (Simpson, pp. 79-80; marker in Old Stone Church Cemetery); Mrs. Porter (unidentified).

Andrew H. Cornish, Protestant Episcopal clergyman (Simpson, p. 146; MS. Census 1860, Anderson Dist., S. C.).

Nancy Blassingame Sloan, widow of Thomas M. Sloan, who died on Sept. 8, 1849; John T. Sloan; John B. E. ("Ball") Sloan (Simpson, pp. 94-99; MS. Census 1860, Anderson Dist., S. C.; markers in Baptist Cemetery, Pendleton).

William Henry Drayton Gaillard, Pendleton railroad agent (MS. Census 1860, Anderson Dist., S. C.). Elam Sharpe married Frances Hayne, daughter of Gov. Robert Y. Hayne. (Simpson, p. 145; MS. Census 1860, Cheohee P. O., Pickens Dist., S. C.

William Alston Hayne, son of Robert Y. Hayne (Simpson, p. 145; *SCHGM*, V (July, 1904), 174).

Placidia Mayrant Adams, widow of Rev. Jasper Adams, who died on Oct. 25, 1841, and mother of Anzie, who married Dr. John C. Calhoun, Jr. (*SCHGM*, XXVII (Jan., 1926), 87; Simpson, pp. 145-46).

Archibald Campbell, of New York, married for his second wife Elizabeth Adams, daughter of Rev. Jasper Adams. (Simpson, pp. 145-46; *SCHGM*, XXVII (Jan., 1926), 87; Register, St. Paul's).

Dr. William Robinson; his daughter Elizabeth, widow of Major John V. Moore, who was killed in the Civil War (Simpson, pp. 85-86).

Andrew F. Lewis (Simpson, pp. 165-67; marker in Old Stone Church Cemetery).

A. Livingston (unidentified).

Richard S. Porcher (Register, St. Paul's; MS. Census 1860, Pickens C. H., Pickens Dist., S. C.).

William B. Cherry, dentist (Simpson, pp. 89-90; MS. Census 1860, Snow Creek P. O., Pickens Dist., S. C.).

Elizabeth C. Shubrick, who was the widow of Edward Shubrick, a naval officer in 1860 (MS. Census 1860, 1870, Anderson Dist., S. C.); probably Kitty Burt, sister of Congressman Armistead Burt, Jr. (Simpson, pp. 76-77).

Fanny Russell, cousin of Kate Putnam Calhoun (Floride Calhoun to Anna C. Clemson, June 14, 1857, Clemson Papers); Mary I'on Wragg, widow of Samuel Wragg, who died in 1844, bought property in Pendleton in August, 1862. (*SCHGM*, XIX (July, 1918), 121; Anderson deeds, book H-2, p. 169).

"Mrs. Tonneau," widow of Dr. John C. Tunno, who died on May 22, 1859 (Register, St. Paul's); Mrs. Hazzard (unidentified).

The Archibald Hamilton Seabrook family refugeed in Pendleton during the Civil War (*SCHGM*, XVII (Apr., 1916), 70; letter from Archibald Rutledge, McClellanville, S. C., July 29, 1959); Valeria North, daughter of Dr. Edward North of Charleston, refugeed in Pendleton. (Letter from Miss Valeria L. Chisolm, Charleston, S. C., Oct. 15, 1959).

APPENDIX III

Anna C. Clemson's panegyric on her daughter Nina.[1]

Oh Nina oh my angel where are you? Why are you taken? When shall I see you again. Never—never. When we lose a friend of mature years we look forward to meeting them in another world with unmixed delight, for let our separation be long or short we resume our intercourse as we should on this earth after a long absence but when a mother loses her child it is lost forever. She may here after meet its pure spirit & enjoy a happiness of which we can here have no conception in so doing but her *child* she never meets again. That sweet dependence on the mother is lost, that feeling that no one can supply our place is gone, *it has learned to do without us & looking at it from here* every change in the sweet relation of mother & daughter must make their meeting hereafter a disappointment to a mother's heart.

What should we do without the memory of the loved & lost! When with others life drags on in its dull round but when alone the closed doors of my heart open & the dwellers in those silent chambers come out & surround me once more. Then my Nina plays around me or climbs my knees & puts her arms around me with loving words. Then my father holds out to me his hand with his sweet smile & glorious eyes & say[s] "my daughter" as I so often saw him in life. My sister sits & looks at me with loving eyes—poor Pat with his kind manners & noble heart is once more there & John & Willie live once more in the recollections of childhood. Farther back in the vista of years I see Maria & enjoy once more her friendship & I am once more young & happy & the many friends "I've seen around me fall leaves in wintry weather" once more make life a long dream of happiness. So live I in the past but a footstep approaches & they all flee before it, the heart closes, & life is once more sad and gloomy.

[1] From the unpublished album of Anna C. Clemson. Clemson Papers.

APPENDIX IV

Record of a vision Anna C. Clemson had of her father,
John C. Calhoun, ten years after his death.[1]

I lay in bed, but not it seemed to me asleep, though my eyes
were shut, when suddenly, but with an evident intention to avoid
alarming, or surprising me, my father stood beside me. I come, my
daughter, said he, to speak with you, & I do so now, that your mind
is more independent of your body, than when you are awake, that
I may spare you the shock, always felt, when matter comes in con-
tact with disembodied spirit. You are right, my daughter, not to
give way to the delusions of spiritualism—I do not say there are
devils, *for evil is not created,* but from want of knowledge, comes
error. I cannot explain to you many things—human language has
no words for what the human mind cannot conceive—of the great
mysteries *on this side.* Continue to strive to know, & do the right,
& to elevate by every means your soul, & when you come on this
side all will be clear. Tell Mr. Clemson he must do this also, or
those he loves will be as invisible to him on this side as they are
now—for the universe is vast, & *like dwells with like.*

Tell him he has not fulfilled the trust I had in him, when I gave
him my daughter.

And now I go, my daughter, but before I leave you, it is permitted
you to see all those you love on this side. Then I saw them all, each
with the most familiar & loved expression. Their eyes were more
living than in life, & as I encountered the glances of each, they
seemed to emit as it were, an unspoken language soul spoke to soul.
Tho' perfectly *life like,* they seemed less *flesh like.* The soul seemed
to pierce its outward covering. It seemed to me there was less of
form than countenance.

March 1860

[1] From the unpublished album of Anna C. Clemson. Clemson Papers.

173

APPENDIX V

A Catalogue of Letters from Floride Clemson in the Clemson College Archives

Thomas G. Clemson, Claymont, [Md.]	September 2, 1856
Anna C. Clemson, Altoona, [Pa.]	July 29, 1863
Anna C. Clemson, Altoona, [Pa.]	August 2, 1863
Anna C. Clemson, Altoona, [Pa.]	August 9, 1863
Anna C. Clemson, Altoona, [Pa.]	August 16, 1863
Anna C. Clemson, Altoona, [Pa.]	August 19, 1863
Anna C. Clemson, Alleghany Furnace [Altoona, Pa.]	August 24, 1863
Anna C. Clemson, Altoona, [Pa.]	August 24, [1863]
Anna C. Clemson, Altoona, [Pa.]	August 27, 1863
Anna C. Clemson, Altoona, [Pa.]	August 30, 1863
Anna C. Clemson, Altoona, [Pa.]	September 2, 1863
Anna C. Clemson, Pittsburgh, [Pa.]	September 3, 1863
Anna C. Clemson, Clifton House, Niagara Falls, Canada	September 7, 1863
Anna C. Clemson [Clifton House,] Niagara [Falls, Canada]	September 9, 1863
Anna C. Clemson, Saratoga, [N. Y.]	September 12, 1863
Anna C. Clemson, Congress Hall Hotel, Saratoga, N. Y.	[September 12, 1863]*
Anna C. Clemson, New York, [N. Y.]	September 13, 1863
Anna C. Clemson, Baltimore, [Md.]	January 26, [1864]
Anna C. Clemson, Baltimore, [Md.]	February 2, 1864
Anna C. Clemson, Leeside [Carmel, N. Y.]	February 4, 1871

* fragmentary

INDEX

Abbeville, S.C., 100, 102, 113, 115
Adams, Anzie, *see* Calhoun, Anzie Adams
Adams, Caroline, 98
Adams, Elizabeth, *see* Campbell, Elizabeth Adams
Adams, Frances ("Fanny"), 74, 87, 98
Adams, the Rev., Jasper, D.D., 74, 98, 170, 171
Adams, Placidia Mayrant (Mrs. Jasper Adams), 74, 86, 92, 170
Adger, Ellison; *see* Adger, Joseph Ellison
Adger, the Rev. John B., D.D., 77, 78, 85, 91, 99, 169
Adger, Joseph Ellison, 85, 169
Adger, Robert, 85, 169
Agricultural Bureau, 18
"Alabama" (Confederate raider), 29, 56, 86
Alexander, Alice Van Yeveren; *see* Haskell, Alice Van Yeveren Alexander
Altoona, Pa., 37, 38, 51, 119, 121, 125, 130, 132, 133, 139, 141, 143, 145
Anderson, S.C., 84, 93, 100
Andy ("little Andy," son of slave Nelly), 7, 18, 68
Angier House, Cleveland, 149
Atlanta, Ga., 67
Augusta, a Clemson servant, 9, 10

Babcock, Mrs. Sarah H. Harwood, 46
Baker, Anna, 38, 40, 119, 121, 122, 123, 126, 127, 131, 132, 134, 139, 141, 144, 145, 147, 150, 151, 155, 158
Baker, Elias, 16, 35, 37, 38, 48, 51, 52, 61, 68, 88, 120, 121, 123, 126, 127, 132, 134, 138, 140, 141, 142, 145, 149, 150, 155, 157, 158
Baker, Mrs. Elias; *see* Baker, Hettie
Baker, Elizabeth; *see* Clemson, Elizabeth Baker
Baker, Hettie ("Auntie"), 38, 61, 119, 122, 126, 139, 142, 144, 145, 147, 158
Baker, Luly, 38, 40, 119, 123, 134, 145, 150, 158
Baker, Sarah (Mrs. Woods Baker), 38, 40, 119, 127, 134, 135, 144, 145, 150, 156

Baker, Sylvester, 38, 40, 119, 123, 125, 126, 130, 131, 132, 134, 138, 140, 141, 142, 144
Baker, Washington, 34, 35, 128
Baker, Woods (deceased), 38, 145, 155, 157
Baltimore, Md., 27, 28, 34, 35, 36, 40, 56, 120, 142
Banks, Charles, 39, 100
Banks, Mrs. Charles; *see* Banks, Louisa B. Cunningham, and Banks, Zeruah Van Wyck
Banks, Louisa B. Cunningham, 100
Banks, Gen. Nathaniel P., 52
Banks, Zeruah Van Wyck, 39, 73
Barnard, John J., 45
Barnard, Kate Hope Keech (Mrs. John J. Barnard), 45
Barton, Mrs. Elizabeth Clemson ("Aunt Barton"), 8, 9, 10, 12, 14, 19, 21, 38, 40, 60, 105, 125, 133, 135, 136, 141, 143
Barton, Graff, 62
Barton, Miss Hetty, 62
Barton, Kate C., 8, 19, 40, 60, 61, 94, 99, 105, 111, 120, 124, 125, 133, 136, 138, 141, 143, 158
Basil (a Clemson slave), 4
Bee, General Barnard, 114, 169
Bee, Sophia Elizabeth (Mrs. Barnard Bee), 86, 169
Beirne, Betty; *see* Miles, Betty Beirne
Beirne, Oliver, 112
Beltsville, Md., 30, 35, 51, 53, 56, 57, 71
Berrien, Mary, 88
Berry, Eliza (Mrs. William Berry), 47
Berry, Jerry, 47
Berry, William, 47
Bladensburg, Md., 7, 9, 12, 15, 18, 21, 36, 42, 56, 155, 165, 167
Blair, Francis Preston, 52, 56, 57
"Blakely," 103
Blassingame, Nancy; *see* Sloan, Nancy Blassingame
Boisseau, James Edward, 111
Blondell, Baron (diplomat), 17
Bourne, C. J., 42
Bourne, Elizabeth Warley (Mrs. C. J. Bourne), 42, 86, 169
Bowie, Eliza Coombs; *see* McCeney, Eliza Coombs Bowie

Bowie, Johny, 47
Bradford, Gov. Andrew W., 56, 57
Bragg, Gen. Braxton, 28, 37, 46
Bretto, Bernard and Richard, 32
Bright, Sen. Jesse David, 27
Brown, Gen., 87
Brown, John's raid, 17
Brown, Lt. E. H., 73
Brown Metropolitan Hotel,
    Washington, 32
Broyles, Margaret; see Van Wyck,
    Margaret C. Broyles
Brussels, Belgium, 4, 6, 166
Buchanan, President James, 4, 11, 19,
    20, 40, 60, 63, 64, 93
Buck, Olivia, 93
Buffalo, N.Y., 39, 150
Burks, Emily, 50
Burks, Nina, 50, 51
Burns, Mrs. (nurse), 104, 108
Burt, Armistead, Jr., 101, 171
Burt, Kitty, 86, 171
Burt, Martha Calhoun (Mrs.
    Armistead Burt, Jr.), 101, 102
Butler, Gen. Benjamin F., 68, 152

Calhoun, Andrew Pickens, 2, 3, 7, 16,
    77, 78, 79, 163
Calhoun, Mrs. Andrew Pickens; see
    Calhoun, Margaret Green
Calhoun, Andrew P., Jr., 77, 79, 94,
    108
Calhoun, Anna Maria; see Clemson,
    Anna Maria Calhoun
Calhoun, Anna Susan, 101-102
Calhoun, Anzie Adams (the first Mrs.
    John C. Calhoun, Jr.), 111, 170
Calhoun, Caroline ("Carrie"), 101-102
Calhoun, Catherine; see Noble, Mrs.
    Catherine Calhoun
Calhoun, Catherine J. de Graffenreid
    (Mrs. William Calhoun), 101
Calhoun, Cornelia; see Calhoun,
    Martha Cornelia
Calhoun, Duff Green, 77, 78, 79, 80,
    82, 84, 85, 94, 108
Calhoun, Eugenia; see Parker,
    Eugenia Calhoun
Calhoun, Floride Bonneau Colhoun
    (Mrs. John C. Calhoun, "Grandma"
    in Floride's diary), 1, 5, 7, 8, 9, 11,
    13, 14, 15, 16, 17, 18, 20, 21, 22,
    23, 30, 35, 36, 50, 55, 71, 74, 76,
    77, 80, 85, 88, 91-92, 95, 96, 102,
    104, 105, 107, 108, 109, 122, 124,
    126, 128, 137, 140, 141, 148, 165
Calhoun, Floride Isabella Lee (Mrs.

Andrew Pickens Calhoun, II), 159,
    162, 164
Calhoun, Frances Darricott (Mrs.
    Joseph Calhoun), 102
Calhoun, Frances Josette; see
    Marshall, Frances Josette Calhoun
Calhoun, Hall; see Colhoun, Henry
    Davis
Calhoun, James (brother of John C.
    Calhoun), 101
Calhoun, James E. ("Jimmie," son of
    Andrew Pickens Calhoun), 77, 78,
    80, 108
Calhoun, James Edward, 19
Calhoun, James Edward of Millwood;
    see Colhoun, James Edward
Calhoun, John A., 101, 102
Calhoun, John Caldwell, 1, 2, 3, 4, 5,
    6, 42, 80, 101, 162, 163, 165, 172,
    173
Calhoun, John C., Jr., 6, 8, 11, 170,
    173
Calhoun, Mrs. John C., Jr.; see
    Calhoun, Anzie Adams, and
    Calhoun, Kate Kirby Putnam
Calhoun, Joseph, 102
Calhoun, Mrs. Joseph; see Calhoun,
    Frances Darricott
Calhoun, Kate Kirby Putnam (Mrs.
    John C. Calhoun, Jr., and Mrs.
    William Lowndes Calhoun), 11, 13,
    14, 71, 76, 78, 80, 85, 86, 90, 95,
    96, 104, 108, 109, 171
Calhoun, Lula, see Calhoun, Mary
    Lucretia
Calhoun, Margaret ("Margie"), 77,
    79, 80, 83, 108, 109
Calhoun, Margaret Cloud (the first
    Mrs. William Lowndes Calhoun), 8
Calhoun, Margaret Green (Mrs.
    Andrew Pickens Calhoun), 16, 77,
    79, 80, 108, 115
Calhoun, Martha; see Burt, Martha
    Calhoun
Calhoun, Martha Cornelia, 7, 8, 11,
    108, 115, 163, 172
Calhoun, Mary Lucretia ("Lula"), 79,
    80, 90
Calhoun, Orville Tatum, 101-102
Calhoun, Patrick ("Pat"), 13, 14, 77,
    79, 111, 166
Calhoun, Putnam, 71
Calhoun, Sarah M. Norwood (Mrs.
    John A. Calhoun), 101
Calhoun, Sarah Martin; see Simonds,
    Sarah Martin Calhoun
Calhoun, William, 101

Calhoun, Mrs. William; *see* Calhoun, Catherine J. de Graffenreid
Calhoun, William Lowndes, 8, 11, 13, 14, 71, 108, 172
Calhoun, Mrs. William Lowndes; *see* Calhoun, Margaret Cloud, and Calhoun, Kate Kirby Putnam
Calhoun, William Lowndes, Jr., 13
Calhoun, Williamson Norwood, 101-102
Calvert, Charles Baltimore ("Charlie"), 35, 47, 105
Calvert, Mrs. Charles Baltimore; *see* Calvert, Eleanor Mackubin
Calvert, Charles Benedict, 35, 44, 51, 88
Calvert, Charlotte Augusta Norris (Mrs. Charles Benedict Calvert), 35, 44, 45, 51, 88, 122, 123, 124, 125, 126, 129, 133, 137, 139, 143, 148
Calvert, Eleanor Mackubin (Mrs. Charles Baltimore Calvert), 105
Calvert, Ella; *see* Campbell, Ella Calvert
Calvert, Eugene Stier, 35
Calvert family, 105
Calvert, George Henry, 35, 44, 47
Calvert, William Norris, 35
Cameron, Jennie, 38, 141, 146
Campbell, Archibald, 56, 104, 171
Campbell, Mrs. Archibald; *see* Campbell, Emily P., and Campbell, Elizabeth Adams
Campbell, Duncan G., 88
Campbell, Elizabeth Adams (the second Mrs. Archibald Campbell), 98, 171
Campbell, Ella Calvert (Mrs. Duncan G. Campbell), 35, 88, 122, 124, 129, 137, 148
Campbell, Emily (the first Mrs. Archibald Campbell), 104
Campbell, Susan Earle; *see* Rodgers, Susan Earle Campbell
"Canebrake" plantation, 2, 3, 5, 6, 166
Cape Hatteras, N.C., 28
Carmel, N.Y., 159, 162
Carusi's Hall, Washington, 31
Cashier's Valley, N.C., 93
Cass, Sec. Lewis, 11, 42
Castle Pinckney, Charleston, S.C., 22, 32
Chain Bridge, near Washington, 56
Chambersburg, Pa., 58
Chancellorsville, Va., 52
Charleston, S.C., 13, 29, 37, 42, 44, 52, 74, 76, 81, 129, 134, 137, 138, 140, 141, 143, 144
Charleston Hotel, 13
Charlotte, N.C., 73
Chase, Salmon P., 92
Chattanooga, Tenn., 85
Cherry, Mary Lorton, 113
Cherry, Sarah Lewis (Mrs. William B. Cherry), 113
Cherry, Dr. William B., 86, 113, 171
Chew, the Rev. John H., 45
Chew, Sophia (Mrs. John H. Chew), 45
Claiborne, Charlotte Virginia; *see* Latrobe, Charlotte Virginia Claiborne
Claiborne, Gen. Ferdinand L., 27
Claymont, Del., 8, 10, 55, 61, 121
Clemson, Anna Maria Calhoun (Mrs. Thomas Green Clemson, Jr., "Mother" in Floride's diary), 1, 2, 3, 4, 5, 6, 8, 9, 10, 11, 12, 13, 14, 16, 17, 18, 20, 21, 22, 23, 31, 32, 40, 41, 42, 44, 45, 47, 48, 51, 53, 64, 67, 75, 77, 90, 109, 115, 119, 121, 122, 124, 125, 128, 129, 130, 133, 136, 137, 140, 141, 144, 146, 147, 148, 151, 153, 156, 163, 165, 166, 172, 173
Clemson, Baker; *see* Clemson, the Rev. John Baker
Clemson, Calhoun; *see* Clemson, John Calhoun
Clemson, Catharine; *see* North, Catharine Clemson
Clemson College (now Clemson University), 82, 116, 163, 164
Clemson, Cornelia ("Nina"), 8, 14-15, 90, 111, 165, 172
Clemson, Elizabeth Baker (Mrs. Thomas Green Clemson, Sr., ("Grandmother" Clemson), 11, 35, 62, 90, 165
Clemson, Floride: Activities, *acting*, 97, *church*, 44, 46, 77-78, 97, 135-36, 137, 139, 140, 157, *drawing*, 47, 106, 154, *riding*, 16, 30, 37, 46, 47, 55, 56, 83, 90, 123, 126, 130, 131, 144, 145, *music*, 12, 14, 16-17, 31, 46, 48, 49, 56, 78, 142, 146, *shooting*, 50, *swimming*, 60, *writing*, 9, 129, 167; Advice to, 8, 9, 10, 11, 12, 13, 14, 15, 16, 124, 128, 129, 136-37, 141, 143; Beaux, 47, 54, 55, 60, 67, 91, 93-94, 102, 106; Birth, 1, 165; Description, 5, 16, 20, 47, 49, 126; Daughter,

162-64; Death, 159, 162, 166-67; Education, 4, 5, 8, 11, 12; Health, 7, 13, 14, 16-17, 28, 29, 30, 31, 35, 37, 40, 41, 42, 47, 48, 49, 50, 51, 61, 65, 66, 67, 71, 78, 80, 87, 92, 93, 99, 104, 107, 119, 127, 139, 145, 146, 153, 157, 159, 161, 167, 168; Homes, 2, 3, 4, 7, 48, 51, 53, 71, 161, 162; Possessions, 46- 47, 66, 68, 85, 86-87, 94, 109-112, 114, 116, 120, 125, 133, 142, 149, 158; Marriage, 161; Travels and Visits, 4, 6, 7, 15, 16, 19, 21, 22, 27, 28, 32, 35, 37-40, 41, 48-49, 50, 52, 53, 54, 55, 59-63, 64, 71-74, 100-103, 119-59, 161

Clemson, the Rev. John Baker, 8, 10, 13, 15, 19, 38, 55, 60, 61, 62, 111, 127, 132, 136, 137, 138, 139, 140, 141, 143, 144

Clemson, Mrs. John Baker; see Clemson, Pheby

Clemson, John Calhoun ("Calhoun"), 1, 5, 7, 8, 9, 10, 12, 17, 21, 22, 29, 30, 32, 34, 36, 37, 41, 42, 43, 44, 46, 47, 49, 51, 67, 74, 75, 78, 79, 80, 82, 87, 88, 89, 90, 91, 95, 96, 97, 102, 104, 106, 107, 108, 109, 115, 116, 124, 137, 141, 161, 163, 165, 166, 167

Clemson, Louisa; see Washington, Louisa Clemson

Clemson, Mary, 38, 60, 61, 125, 127, 132, 137-38, 139, 141, 146

Clemson, Mattie, 15, 38, 40, 61, 62, 121, 132, 137-38, 141, 142

Clemson, Nina; see Clemson, Cornelia

Clemson, Pheby (Mrs. John Baker Clemson), 61

Clemson, Sallie or Sally, 60, 61, 94, 99, 105, 127, 132, 134

Clemson, Sue (Mrs. William Clemson), 40, 111, 121, 138, 157

Clemson, Mrs. Thomas Green, Sr.; see Clemson, Elizabeth Baker

Clemson, Thomas Green ("Father" in the diary), 1, 2, 3, 4, 5, 6, 7, 8, 9, 10, 12, 13, 15, 16, 17, 18, 19, 20, 21, 29, 32, 34, 46, 49, 55, 73, 79, 82, 87, 89, 90, 91, 96, 99, 103, 105, 106, 107, 108, 109, 114, 115, 124, 136, 137, 141, 161, 162, 163, 165, 166, 167, 173

Clemson, Mrs. Thomas Green; see Clemson, Anna Maria Calhoun

Clemson, Tom, 40, 61, 143

Clemson, William, 13, 18, 40, 121, 138, 157

Clemson, Mrs. William; see Clemson, Sue

Cleveland, Ohio, 38-39, 149-50, 153

Clifton House, Niagara Falls, Canada, 39, 147, 148, 153

Cockerille, Dr. J. J., 31

Cockerille, Dr. Samuel T., 31

Cokesbury, S.C., 100, 102, 103, 116

Colhoun, Edward Boisseau ("Teddy"), 103, 113

Colhoun, Henry Davis ("Hall"), 82, 92, 93, 103

Colhoun, James Edward ("great Uncle James"), 2, 8, 22, 96, 108, 111, 166

Colhoun, Mrs. James Edward; see Colhoun, Maria Simkins

Colhoun, Col. John Ewing, 82, 103, 111

Colhoun, Mrs. John Ewing; see Colhoun, Martha Davis

Colhoun, Maria Simkins (Mrs. James Edward Colhoun), 111, 172

Colhoun, Martha Davis (Mrs. John Ewing Colhoun), 82, 103

Columbia, S.C., 73, 75, 76, 77, 150

Confederate forces, 56-58, 143, 148

Confederate memorial service, 114

Confederate money and prices, 55, 72, 74, 75, 80, 81, 82

Confederate Nitre and Mining Bureau, 34, 41

Congress Hall, Saratoga, N.Y., 156

Contee, Mrs. Ann L., 54, 71

Contee, Charles, 54

Contee, Elizabeth, 54

Cook, Dr. Septimus, 68, 71

Corcoran, W. S., 106

Cornish, the Rev. Andrew H., 86, 96, 109, 170

Cornish, Catherine (Mrs. Andrew H. Cornish), 96, 106

Cornish, Lizzie, 96, 167

Cornish, Kate, 96

Cornish, the Rev. William; see Cornish, the Rev. Andrew H.

Crallé, Richard K., 6

Crawford, Benjamin C., 94

Crawford, Samuel C., 36, 47, 48, 88, 105, 155

Crawford, Mrs. Samuel C., 45, 88, 105

Cresson, Pa., 130, 138

Cuningham; see Cunningham

Cunningham, Ann Pamela, 116

Cunningham, Benjamin ("Benjie"), 100
Cunningham, Clarence ("Claire"), 100, 101
Cunningham, Emma Floride ("Floride"), 100, 102, 109
Cunningham, Floride Calhoun Noble (Mrs. John Cunningham), 100, 101, 111
Cunningham, John, 100, 101
Cunningham, Mrs. John; see Cunningham, Floride Calhoun Noble
Cunningham, John, Jr., 100
Cunningham, Lizzie P., 100, 102
Cunningham, Louisa B.; see Banks, Louisa B. Cunningham
Cunningham, Robert N. ("Bob"), 100
Curley, Miss (sister of Mrs. J. C. Fairfax), 53

Dahlonega, Ga.; see gold mine
Dare, Dr., 31, 48
Dare, Mrs., 45
Darricott, Frances; see Calhoun, Frances Darricott
Daub, Lisette (Clemson servant), 21, 22, 45, 68, 98, 121, 126
Daub, Mr. (husband of Lisette Daub), 22
Daub, Wilhelmina Floride ("Mina"), 45, 121
Davis, Pres. Jefferson, 81, 84, 85
Davis, Martha; see Colhoun, Martha Davis
Davis, Bishop Thomas F., 116
de Graffenreid, Catherine J.; see Calhoun, Catherine J. de Graffenreid
del Prado, Eufraria Lisboa (Mme. Mariano del Prado), 31
del Prado, Mariano, 31
Dickinson, Francis W., 167, 169
Dickinson, Rachel Miles (Mrs. Francis W. Dickinson), 86, 167, 169
Dickinson, Rachel; see Green, Rachel Dickinson
Dickinson, Sarah; see Lee, Sarah Dickinson
Dickinson, Susan, 167
Dodge, Mrs. Mary E., 106, 143
Dosoris Island, N.Y., 167
Dougherty, Caroline T. Hickey (Mrs. William Dougherty), 34, 63
Dougherty, William, 34
draft riot, N.Y. City, 37

Drayton, Eliza; see North, Eliza Drayton
Duke, James J., 84, 108
Dundas, Mary Pamela Marron (Mrs. William O. Dundas), 37
Dundas, Mary Y. (Mrs. William H. Dundas), 37
Dundas, William H., 20, 37, 43
Dundas, Mrs. William H.; see Dundas, Mary Y.
Dundas, William O. ("Billy"), 16, 20, 37, 43, 93
Dundas, Mrs. William O.; see Dundas, Mary Pamela Marron
Dunscomb, G. H. ("A Southern Friend"), 17, 18, 47, 48, 50, 51, 58, 60, 66, 67, 72, 76, 79, 82, 94, 106

Earle, Elizabeth; see Maxwell, Elizabeth Earle
Earle, Miriam; see Mays, Miriam Earle
Earle, Maj. Sam, 170
Earle, Sarah Anne; see Seaborn, Sarah Anne Earle
Early, Gen. Jubal A., 56, 57
Easley, Caroline Sloan (Mrs. William K. Easley), 114
Easley, Gen. William K., 114, 115
Edward VII, 19-20
Egg Harbor Bay, N.J., 59
Elliot; see Elliott
Elliott, Catherine Sadler Shanklin (Mrs. John H. Elliott), 86, 87, 169
Elliott, the Rev. John H., 76, 78, 87, 97, 169
Emack, A. G., 57
Emack, Capt. George, 57
Enterprise, Fla., 17
Evans, Lt. Col. D. M., 72
Eversfield, Dr. John T., 47, 48, 53, 54, 56, 58, 60, 63, 65, 66

Fahnestock, Dr. William, 168
Fairfax, Dr. John C., 30
Fairfax, Mrs. John C., 53, 55
Fairfax family, 71, 92
Ferguson, Gen. Samuel W., 85
Flat Rock, N.C., 113
"Flat Rock" in Pendleton, 103
"Florida" (Confederate warship), 68, 73
Ford, Eliza, 86, 94, 169
Ford, Louisa; see Ravenel, Louisa Ford

Ford, Margaret ("Maggie"), 86, 94, 95, 169
"Fort Hill" plantation, 1, 2, 3, 6, 7, 16, 77, 83, 90, 93, 96, 109, 115, 116, 163, 164, 167
Ft. Lincoln, Md., 129
Ft. Massachusetts, Md., 56
Ft. Ripley, S.C., 29, 30
Ft. Sumter, S.C., 21, 29, 140, 143
Ft. Slocum, Md., 56
Ft. Totten, Md., 57
Fortress Monroe, Va., 72
Franklin, Tom, 59
Fraser, Sophia; see Warley, Sophia Fraser
Frederick, Md., 55, 59
Fredericksburg, Va., 52
Free, Mrs. (Grandma Clemson's sister), 62
Frost, Anne Branford ("Anna"); see Lowndes, Anna Frost
Frost, Judge Edward, 85, 93, 95, 96, 167
Frost, Edwin, 93, 94, 96, 97
Frost, Lizzie, 95, 96, 98, 103

Gaillard, Benjamin S., 93
Gaillard, Elizabeth Lee (Mrs. William D. Gaillard), 96
Gaillard, Sallie T. Sloan (Mrs. William Henry Drayton Gaillard), 93, 108
Gaillard, William D., 96
Gaillard, Mrs. William D.; see Gaillard, Elizabeth Lee
Gaillard, William Henry Drayton, 86, 93, 108, 170
Gaillard, Mrs. William Henry Drayton; see Gaillard, Sallie T. Sloan
Galveston, Texas, 29
Geddings, Dr. Eli, 13
George Washington medal, 19
Gettysburg, Battle of, 36
Gibbs, Dr. James G. (dentist), 31
Gibbs, Prof. (of Pendleton), 113
Giger, Hannah, 40
Giles, Lizzie; see Quarles, Mrs. Lizzie Giles
Giles, Mrs., 34
Gill, Dr. Theodore Nicholas, 55
Girard Hotel, Philadelphia, 40
Gittings, Mrs. John S., 28
Glass, Mrs. Meta Sandford, 94
Glen Cove, Long Island, N.Y., 167
Globe Hotel, Syracuse, N.Y., 154

gold mine, Dahlonega, Ga., 2, 107, 166
Goldsborough, Richard ("Dick"), 44, 54
Goldsborough, Robert, 79
Goldsborough, William, 44, 54
Gottschalk, Louis Moreau, 32
Gould, Jay, 15
Gourdin, Henry, 12, 20, 84
Grant, Gen. U. S., 34, 36, 46, 55, 59, 67, 68, 81, 83
"Great Eastern" (steamship), 19, 29
Green, Duff, 77
Green, Margaret; see Calhoun, Margaret Green
Green, Mrs. Rachel Dickinson, 86
Greenville, S.C., 81
Gresham, the Rev. G. T., 114
Gresham, Lucilla Septima Sloan (Mrs. G. T. Gresham), 114
Groaning, Lewis, 86

Hagerstown, Md., 30, 55
Hall, Dr., 29, 135, 137, 139
Hall, S. D. ("Davy"), 44, 54
Hampton, Gen. Wade, III, 92, 93, 95, 114, 115
Hampton, Mary Singleton McDuffie (Mrs. Wade Hampton, III), 92
Hampton, Wade, IV, 91
Happolt (Hapenelt), Albertine, 167
Happolt, B. G., 167
Happolt, Emily (Mrs. B. G. Happolt), 167
Happolt, Marion, 167
Hardee, Anna, 86
Hardee, Gen. William J., 86
"Harewood," Jefferson County, (West) Va., 8, 17, 142, 166
Harpers Ferry, (West) Va., 58
"Harriet Lane" (revenue cutter), 29
Harris, Sallie, 73
Harris, Mrs. Sarah Jeter, 73, 116
Harrisburg, Pa., 36, 40, 121
Harvey, Charles, 30, 43
Harvey, Emma Yost (Mrs. Charles Harvey), 30, 93
Harwood, H. H. (Capt., USN), 46
Harwood, Sallie; see Babcock, Sarah A. Harwood
Haskell, Col. Alexander Cheves, 102
Haskell, Mrs. Alexander Cheves; See Haskell, Alice Van Yeveren Alexander, and Haskell, Rebecca Singleton
Haskell, Alice Van Yeveren Alexander

180

(the second Mrs. Alexander Cheves Haskell), 102
Haskell, Rebecca Singleton (the first Mrs. Alexander Cheves Haskell), 102
Havana, Cuba, 166
Hawkes, the Rev. Francis L., D.D., 49
Hayne, Frances; see Sharpe, Frances Hayne
Hayne, Margaretta Stiles (Mrs. William Alston Hayne), 86
Hayne, Sen. Robert Y., 103, 170
Hayne, Col. William Alston, 103, 170
Hayne, Mrs. William Alston; see Hayne, Margaretta Stiles
Hays, Dr. Isaac, 61, 62
Hazzard, Fisher, 60
Hazzard, Lizzie Clemson (Mrs. Fisher Hazzard), 60, 86
Herbert, Edward, 53
Herbert, Mr. and Mrs. Edward, 54, 55, 60, 71
Hickey, Caroline T. ("Carrie"); see Dougherty, Caroline T. Hickey
Hickey, Cecilia A. (Mrs. William Hickey), 34, 52
Hickey, William, 34
Hickman, Ann S.; see Stephens, N.C.
High Hampton Inn, 93
Hill, Gen. D. H., 73
Hollidaysburg, Pa., 130, 133, 144, 146
Holmes, Anna Warley (Mrs. John H. Holmes), 84, 86, 94, 169
Holmes, John H., 84
Hood, Gen. John B., 67
Huger, Gen. Benjamin, 95
Humphreys, Robert, 4, 5
Hunter, Gen. David, 57, 59
Hyatt, Frances (Mrs. Christopher Hyatt), 45
Hyattsville, Md., 40, 57

Ikleberger ("Ickleberger"), Kitty Baker, 40, 62
Ingham, Sally, 48, 49
Inghram, Anna, 104
I'on, Mary Ashby; see Wragg, Mary Ashby I'on

Jackson ("Fort Hill" slave), 93
Jackson, President Andrew, 52
Jackson, Gen. Thomas J. ("Stonewall"), 33
Jefferson County, (West) Va., 28, 55
Jenkens, Lizzie, 54
Jenkens, the Misses, 54

Jenkins, Anna R. (Mrs. W. L. Jenkins), 115
Jenkins, Sarah Boon McBryde (Mrs. William Gaillard Jenkins), 115
Jenkins, William Gaillard, 115
Jenkins, Dr. W. L., 115
Jenkins, Mrs. W. L.; see Jenkins, Anna R.
Jennings, Lizzie, 93
Jeter, Sarah; see Harris, Sarah Jeter
Johns, Dr. Montgomery, 54
Johns, Mrs. Montgomery, 54
Johnson, Pres. Andrew, 83
Johnson, Gen. Bradley T., 56, 57, 58
Johnson, Gen.; see Johnston, Gen. Joseph E.
Johnson, Henry Elliot; see Johnston, Henry Elliot
Johnson's Island, Ohio, 41, 43, 47, 49, 51, 90
Johnston, Harriet Lane (Mrs. Henry Elliot Johnston), 103; see also Lane, Harriet
Johnston, Henry Elliot, 93, 96, 103
Johnston, Gen. Joseph E., 73, 81, 85
Jones' Rifles, 84
Jones, W. R., 84

Kate, "Old Maum" (ex-slave at "Fort Hill"), 91
"Kearsarge" (warship), 56
Keech, Alexander, 45
Keech, Kate Hope; see Barnard, Kate Hope Keech
Keech, Rose Keech (Mrs. William S. Keech), 45
Keels, Julia; see Maxwell, Julia Keels
Kenner, Duncan mission, 75
Kenrick, Most Rev. Francis Patrick, Archbishop of Baltimore, 37
Kenuff; see Knauff
"Keowee" plantation, 93, 113
Kilpatrick, Eliza; see Lorton, Eliza Kilpatrick
King, Dr. Benjamin, 44, 53, 65, 71
King, Mrs. Benjamin, 53, 65, 71, 142
King, T. M. ("Tom"), 44, 103
King, Virginia ("Jennie"), 44, 55, 66, 92, 142
Kirby-Smith, Gen. Edmund, 89
Knauff (Kenuff), William James, 84

"Laird Rams" (iron clads), 143
Lancaster, Pa., 11, 40, 62, 63, 158
Lane, Harriet, 19, 20, 40, 55, 60, 62, 63, 68, 93, 94, 96, 99, 103, 105,

146, 158; *see also* Johnston, Harriet
Lane
Latrobe, Benjamin H., 27
Latrobe, Benjamin H., Jr., 34, 167
Latrobe, Benjamin H., Jr., family, 28,
63
Latrobe, Charlotte Virginia Claiborne
(Mrs. John H. B. Latrobe), 27, 49
Latrobe, John H. B., 27, 133, 136, 138
Latrobe, John H. B., family, 22, 27
Latrobe, Kate, 168
Latrobe, Mary Elizabeth, 34, 35, 40,
48, 51, 66, 72, 82, 92, 94, 99, 106,
133, 135, 138, 155, 168
Latrobe, Nora; *see* Vinton, Maria
Eleanor Latrobe
Latrobe, Osmun, 27
Latta, Agnes Wetherell (Mrs. James T.
Latta), 87
Latta, James T., 86, 87, 169
Laurel, Md., 40
Lee, D. Williamson ("The Gallant
Defender"), 20, 21, 28, 29, 30, 31,
32, 36, 37, 40, 41, 43, 47, 60, 64,
66, 67, 71, 79, 98, 103, 122, 124,
125, 127, 128-29, 133, 134, 135,
136, 137, 139, 140, 141, 143, 148,
150, 152, 157, 158, 161
Lee, Elizabeth; *see* Gaillard, Elizabeth
Lee ("Lizzie")
Lee, Floride Isabella; *see* Calhoun,
Floride Isabella Lee
Lee, Gideon, 28, 29, 97, 98, 152, 161,
162, 163
Lee, Gideon, Sr., 28
Lee, Mrs. Gideon, Sr., 98
Lee, Gideon, III, 162
Lee, Dr. Lawrence, 96
Lee, Mrs. Lawrence; *see* Lee, Sarah
Dickinson
Lee, Gen. Robert E., 37, 46, 67, 81,
83, 120
Lee, Sarah Dickinson (Mrs. Lawrence
Lee), 86, 96
Lee, W. Creighton, 28, 67, 152, 155,
157, 158
Lee, Williamson Whitner, 162
"Leeside," Carmel, N.Y., 162
Leo (Floride's dog), 68
Leopold, King of Belgium, 11
Letcher, Gov. John, 57
Leupp, Charles M., 14, 15, 16, 18, 20,
33, 161
Leupp, C. M. Company, 12, 20
Leupp family, 19, 145
Leupp, Isabella ("Bella"), 161, 167

Leupp, Laura S. (later Mrs. Frank
Marbury), 18, 33, 39, 67, 135, 141,
150, 152, 155, 157, 158, 161, 167
Lewis, Andrew F., 86, 94, 171
Lewis, Mrs. Andrew F.; *see* Lewis,
Susan Sloan
Lewis, Jesse Payne, 115, 170
Lewis, Mrs. Jesse Payne; *see* Lewis,
Susan Taylor
Lewis, Sarah; *see* Cherry, Sarah Lewis
Lewis, Sue A., 94
Lewis, Susan Sloan (Mrs. Andrew F.
Lewis), 94
Lewis, Susan Taylor (Mrs. Jesse Payne
Lewis), 86, 115, 171
Lincoln, President Abraham, 20, 21,
32, 43, 56, 68, 83
Lisboa, Mme. Isabel (Mrs. Miguel M.
Lisboa), 31
Lisboa, Miguel M., 31
Lititz, Pa., 62
Livingston, A., 86
Long Beach, N.J., 59
Longstreet, Gen. James, 27
Lookout Mountain, Tenn., 46
Lorton, Eliza Amanda Kilpatrick
(Mrs. John S. Lorton), 86, 96, 170
Lorton, Ella F. (the second Mrs.
Gideon Lee), 96-97, 98, 109, 113,
162
Lorton, John S., 96, 170
Lorton, Mrs. John S.; *see* Lorton,
Eliza Amanda Kilpatrick
Lowndes, Anna Frost (Mrs. Thomas
Pinckney Lowndes), 95-96
Lowndes, Benjamin O., 105
Lowndes, Margaret Washington (Mrs.
Thomas Pinckney Lowndes, Sr.), 96
Lowndes, Thomas Pinckney, 96
Lowndes, Mrs. Thomas Pinckney; *see*
Lowndes, Anna Frost
Lowndes, Thomas Pinckney, Sr., 96
Lowndes, Mrs. Thomas Pinckney, Sr.;
see Lowndes, Margaret Washington
Lynch, Sallie, 114

Mackubin, Eleanor; *see* Calvert,
Eleanor Mackubin
Mackubin, Hester Worthington (Mrs.
Richard C. Mackubin), 104
Mackubin, Dr. Richard C., 105
Magoffin, Anna Nelson Shelby (Mrs.
Beriah Magoffin), 45
Magoffin, Gov. Beriah, 45, 103
Magoffin, Gertrude; *see* Singleton,
Gertrude Magoffin

Magruder, Dr. Archibald, 32
Magruder family, 52
Magruder ("McGruder"), Gen. John Bankhead, 29
Maguire, Nannie; *see* Merrick, Nannie Maguire
Mahone, Gen. William, 66
Marbury, Frank, 39
Marbury, Mrs. Frank; *see* Leupp, Laura S.
Marie (Floride's maid), 99
Marietta, Ga., 58
Markoe, Francis, 72
Markoe, Mary (Mrs. Francis Markoe), 72
Marron, Mary Pamela; *see* Dundas, Mary Pamela Marron
Marshall, Frances Josette Calhoun (Mrs. J. W. Marshall, "Fanny"), 102
Marshall, Dr. J. W., 102
Mary (Calhoun servant), 80
Maryland Agricultural College, 7, 30, 44, 53, 54
Maryland, University of; *see* Maryland Agricultural College
Maverick, Lydia Ann; *see* Van Wyck, Lydia Ann Maverick
Maxwell, Catherine Sloan (Mrs. Frank Maxwell), 104
Maxwell, Elizabeth Earle (Mrs. John Maxwell), 78, 90, 104
Maxwell, Frank, 104
Maxwell, Capt. John, 78, 90, 104, 169
Maxwell, Mrs. John; *see* Maxwell, Elizabeth Earle
Maxwell, Dr. John H., 78, 86, 91, 93, 106, 107, 169
Maxwell, Julia Keels (Mrs. Samuel Maxwell), 104
Maxwell, Keels, 104
Maxwell, Mrs. Keels; *see* Maxwell, Maud Shelton
Maxwell, Lucy Sloan (Mrs. Robert Maxwell), 86, 170
Maxwell, Maud Shelton (Mrs. Keels Maxwell), 104
Maxwell, Robt., 86, 170
Maxwell, Dr. Robert, 169
Maxwell, Robert A., 170
Maxwell, Samuel, 86, 90, 104, 169
Maxwell, Mrs. Samuel; *see* Maxwell, Julia Keels
May, Hon. Henry, 28
Maynard, Dr. Edward, 31, 44
Mayrant, Placidia; *see* Adams, Placidia Mayrant

Mays, James Butler, 170
Mays, Miriam Earle (Mrs. James Butler Mays), 170
McBride; *see* McBryde
McBryde, Mary McClerky (Mrs. Thomas L. McBryde), 115
McBryde, Sarah Boon; *see* Jenkins, Sarah Boon McBryde
McBryde, the Rev. Thomas L., 84, 115
McBryde, Mrs. Thomas L.; *see* McBryde, Mary McClerky
McCeney, Eliza Coombs Bowie (Mrs. Edgar McCeney), 30, 33
McCeney, George, 30
McCeney, Harriet Patterson (Mrs. George McCeney), 30, 50
McCeney, Henry Cole, 30, 47, 53, 71, 122, 124
McCeney family, 140
McClellan, Gen. George, 22, 64
McClelland, Carrie, 38, 119, 122, 127, 131, 133
McClelland, Henry, 131
McClerky, Mary; *see* McBryde, Mary McClerky
McDuffie, Mary Singleton; *see* Hampton, Mary Singleton McDuffie
McIlvain, Lizzie; *see* McIlwain, Lizzie
McIlwain, Lizzie, 38, 122, 127, 131, 132
McKnew, Capt. Morris, 58
Meade, Gen. George C., 46
Memminger, Christopher G., 113
Memminger, Mrs. Christopher G.; *see* Memminger, Mary Wilkinson
Memminger, Lucy; *see* Pinckney, Lucy Memminger
Memminger, Mary Wilkinson (Mrs. Christopher G. Memminger), 113
Merrick, Dick, 49
Merrick, Nannie Maguire (Mrs. Dick Merrick), 49
Merrick, Judge William Matthew, 35, 49, 134
Merrick, Mrs. William Matthew, 72
Metropolitan Hotel, New York City, 39, 157
"Mi Casa," Pendleton, S.C., 13, 14, 15, 16, 30, 34, 109
Middleton, E. J., 42
Middleton, Mrs. E. J.; *see* Middleton, Ellen R.
Middleton, E. J., Jr., 42
Middleton, Ellen R. (Mrs. E. J. Middleton), 42, 52
Middleton, E. J. family, 51, 54, 105

Middleton, Mary V. ("Jennie"), 42, 67
Miles, Anna Pickens (Mrs. Jerry J. Miles), 88
Miles, Berry Beirne (Mrs. William Porcher Miles), 112
Miles, Jerry J., 88
Miles, Mrs. Jerry J.; see Miles, Anna Pickens
Miles, Keziah A.; see Pickens, Keziah A. Miles
Miles, Rachel; see Dickinson, Rachel Miles
Miles, William Porcher, 112
Miles, Mrs. William Porcher; see Miles, Betty Beirne
Miller, Caroline ("Carrie"); see Simons, Caroline Miller
Miller, Caroline Taliaferro (Mrs. Henry C. Miller), 114
Miller, Henry C., 114
"Millwood" plantation, 8, 96, 104, 109, 114
Mimi (Clemson servant), 5, 6, 8, 9
Missionary Ridge, Tenn., 46
Mitchell, Caroline Pinckney (Mrs. Julian Mitchell), 113
Mitchell, Julian, 113
Mobley, John, 4
"Monitor," (U.S. warship), 28
Monongahela House, Pittsburgh, 147, 148
Moore, Elizabeth Robinson (Mrs. John V. Moore), 86, 171
Moore, Maj. John V., 171
Morgan, Gen. John Hunt, 42, 46, 123
Morris, "Govvy," 35, 125, 128, 129
Mosby, Gen. John Singleton, 65, 143
Mount Vernon Ladies Society, 116
Mullaly, the Rev. F. Patrick, 114-15
Mundé, Dr. Charles, 9, 161
Murfreesboro, Tenn., 28
Murfree's Station, Va., 72
Murphys Depot; see Murfree's Station

Nelly (a Calhoun slave), 7
Newman, C.M., 54
Newport, R.I., 14
New York City, 4, 14, 19, 20, 37, 39, 155, 156-58
Niagara Falls, 39, 148, 151-53
Noble, Bell, 96, 101
Noble, Mrs. Catherine Calhoun, 80
Noble, Edward, 80, 96, 100, 101, 109
Noble, Mrs. Edward; see Noble, Mary Means Bratton
Noble, Edward, Jr., 101

Noble, Elizabeth Bonneau; see Simons, Elizabeth Bonneau Noble
Noble, Elizabeth Bonneau Pickens (Mrs. Patrick Noble), 80
Noble, Floride, 101, 113
Noble, Floride Calhoun; see Cunningham, Floride Calhoun Noble
Noble, Martha; see Noble, Mary Means Bratton
Noble, Mary Means Bratton (Mrs. Edward Noble), 101, 113
Noble, Gov. Patrick, 80, 100
Noble, Mrs. Patrick; see Noble, Elizabeth Bonneau Pickens
Noble, Patrick ("Pat"), 101, 113
Noble, Pinckey (or Mary), 101, 113
Norfolk, Va., 68, 72
Norris, Charlotte Augusta; see Calvert, Charlotte Augusta Norris
North, Bessie, 40, 60
North, Catharine Clemson (Mrs. George W. North, "Aunt North"), 8, 37, 40, 59, 60, 61, 105, 120, 125, 142
North, Clarence ("Clarrie"), 40, 60, 61
North, Clem, 38, 60, 94, 96, 120
North, Dr. Edward, 97, 171
North, Mrs. Edward; see North, Valeria
North, Eliza Drayton (Mrs. John Laurens North), 112, 170
North, Eliza Emily; see Thurston, Eliza Emily North
North, George, 59, 60
North, George W., 37, 40
North, Mrs. George W.; see North, Catharine Clemson
North, Herbert, 40, 60, 61
North, John Laurens, 97, 112, 170
North, Valeria ("Vallie"), 86, 97
North, Valeria (Mrs. Edward North), 97, 171
North, Walter, 37, 40, 60, 61, 120
North, Willie, 38, 40, 61, 120
Norths (of Pendleton), 86
"North Star" (steamer), 66
Northhampton, Mass., 9, 10
Norwood, Dr. W. C., 116
Norwood, Sarah M.; see Calhoun, Sarah M. Norwood
Nott, Su, 46

Onderdonk, Henry, 30, 38, 47, 50, 51, 53, 54, 55, 58, 60, 66, 67, 99, 121,

122, 124, 130, 131, 132, 134, 135, 136, 139, 140, 168
Orr, Gov. James L., 74, 99, 100
Orr, Martha ("Mattie"), 99, 100
Owens, Richard, 54

Palatka, Fla., 104
Parker, Dr. Edwin, 101
Parker, Mrs. Edwin; see Parker, Eugenia Calhoun
Parker, Edwin, Jr. ("Teddie"), 101
Parker, Ellen L. ("Helen"), 101
Parker, Eugenia Calhoun (Mrs. Edwin Parker), 101, 102
Parker, Hetty, 63
Parker, Lucia G. (Mrs. William H. Parker), 102
Parker, Martha C. ("Mattie"), 101
Parker, Thomas ("Tom"), 101
Parker, William C. ("Willie"), 101
Parker, William H., 102
Parker, Mrs. William H.; see Parker, Lucia G.
Pendleton, S.C., 7, 8, 11, 13, 14, 15, 16, 18, 21, 30, 42, 148, 161, 165, 169-71
Peter (the cook at "Mi Casa"), 98
Petersburg, Va., 59, 68
Philadelphia, Pa., 4, 5, 6, 7, 9, 12, 37, 59, 60, 120, 125, 134, 139, 158, 165, 167
Pickens, Anna; see Miles, Anna Pickens
Pickens, Gov. Francis, 4, 6, 168
Pickens, John Miles, 82, 98
Pickens, Keziah A. Miles (Mrs. Thomas J. Pickens), 82, 91, 108
Pickens, the Misses, 96, 97, 98
Pickens, Col. Samuel B., 82, 104, 109
Pickens, Col. Thomas J., 82, 84, 85, 88, 90, 91, 108, 109, 169
Pickens, Mrs. Thomas J.; see Pickens, Keziah A. Miles
Pickens, Dr. Thomas J., Jr., 91, 107
Pinckney, Anna, 113
Pinckney, Caroline ("Carrie"); see Mitchell, Caroline Pinckney
Pinckney, Caroline; see Seabrook, Caroline Pinckney
Pinckney, Charles ("Charlie"), 102, 113
Pinckney, Mrs. Charles; see Pinckney, Lucy Memminger
Pinckney, the Rev. Charles Cotesworth, 86, 102, 104, 113, 169
Pinckney, Lucy Memminger (Mrs. Charlie Pinckney), 113
Pinckney, Gen. Thomas, 104

Pinkney, Elizabeth (Mrs. William Pinkney), 45, 105
Pinkney, Bishop William, 45, 105
Pittsburgh, Pa., 38, 146, 148-49
Pittsburgh industry, 146-47, 149
Polk, President James K., 4
Porcher, Richard S., 86, 171
Porcher, Selina Eliza; see Ravenel, Selina Eliza Porcher
Port Hudson, La., 34, 36, 37
Price, Gen. Sterling, 68
Prince of Wales; see Edward VII
"Princeton" (U.S. warship), 3
Putnam, Judge Benjamin, 13
Putnam, Kate Kirby; see Calhoun, Kate Kirby Putnam

Quarles, General, 35, 128, 143
Quarles, Mrs. Lizzie Giles, 34, 35, 128, 143

Ravenel, Caroline ("Carro"), 97
Ravenel, Dr. Edmund, 97
Ravenel, Mrs. Edmund; see Ravenel, Louisa Ford
Ravenel, Emily Thurston (Mrs. William C. Ravenel), 95
Ravenel, Henry Edmund, 169
Ravenel, Mrs. Henry Edmund; see Ravenel, Selina Eliza Porcher
Ravenel, Louisa Ford (Mrs. Edmund Ravenel), 97
Ravenel, Selina Eliza Porcher (Mrs. Henry Edmund Ravenel), 86, 169
Ravenel, Dr. William C., 86, 95, 169
Ravenel, Mrs. William C.; see Ravenel, Emily Thurston
Reis, Leopold, 7, 8
Reives; see Rives, John C.
Relay House, Md., 167
"Retribution" (privateer), 29
Richmond, Va., 34, 67, 81
Riggs, Alice, 49, 71
Riggs, Cecilia, 49, 71
Riggs family, 50, 88, 93
Riggs, George W., 49
Riggs, Mrs. George W.; see Riggs, Janet
Riggs, Katherine ("Kate"), 49, 71
Riggs, Janet (Mrs. George W. Riggs), 49
Ritchie, Margaret; see Stone, Margaret Ritchie
Ritchie, Thomas, 32
Rives, John C., 51-52
Roberts, L., 54
Robinson, Cary, 33, 66

Robinson, Conway, 33, 66
Robinson, Mrs. Conway; *see* Robinson, Mary
Robinson, Conway family, 65, 66, 67, 71, 105, 116, 143
Robinson, Elizabeth ("Lizzie"), 33, 43, 46, 47, 51, 52, 53, 54, 65, 71, 80, 92, 94, 99, 124
Robinson, Elizabeth of Pendleton; *see* Moore, Elizabeth Robinson
Robinson, Henry, 92
Robinson, Leigh, 33, 92
Robinson, Mary (Mrs. Conway Robinson), 33, 53
Robinson, Dr. William, 86, 171
Robinson, William ("Willie"), 33, 44
Rock Creek Church; *see* St. Paul's
Rockville, Md., 36, 58
Rodgers, George, 104
Rodgers, Mrs. George; *see* Rodgers, Susan Earle Campbell
Rodgers, Susan Earle Campbell (Mrs. George Rodgers), 104
Rosanna (Clemson servant), 21
Rosecrans, Gen. William S., 28
Ross, Lizzie, 42
Ross, Mary, 66
Roswell, Ga., 58
Russell family of Lancaster, Pa., 40, 62
Russell, Fanny, 86, 104, 105, 171
Russell, Kate, 38, 62, 104, 139
Russell, Margery, 62
Rutledge, Archibald, 97
Rutledge, Col. Henry Middleton, 97
Rutledge, Margaret Seabrook (Mrs. Henry Middleton Rutledge), 97

Sadler, Catherine Ann; *see* Shanklin, Catherine Ann Sadler
St. Aloysius Catholic Church, 37
St. Augustine, Fla., 13, 14
St. Charles Hotel, Syracuse, 154
St. James School, Hagerstown, Md., 30
St. Paul's Episcopal Church, Pendleton, 161
St. Paul's Episcopal Church, Rock Creek, 37, 66, 78
Sanders, Mrs. Caroline C., 30, 53, 54, 56, 65, 71
Sandford, Meta; *see* Glass, Meta Sandford
Sandusky, Ohio, 41, 43, 44, 48, 51; *see also* Johnson's Island
Saratoga Springs, N.Y., 39, 156-59

Sauer, Babette, 9, 10, 12, 17
Savannah, Ga., 74, 75, 81
Schenck, Dr. Noah H., 49
Schenectady, N.Y., 154
Scott, Gen. Winfield, 21
Seaborn, Major George, 84, 86, 170
Seaborn, Sarah Ann Earle (Mrs. George Seaborn), 84
Seabrook, Archibald Hamilton and family, 86, 97, 171
Seabrook, Caroline Pinckney (Mrs. Archibald H. Seabrook), 97
Seabrook, Margaret; *see* Rutledge, Margaret Seabrook
Secessionists, 152
Selina, N.Y., 154
Semmes (Simms), Capt. Raphael, 86
Seward, Sec. William H., 83
Seybourn, Major; *see* Seaborn
Seymour, Mr. (English diplomat), 37, 47, 52, 53, 55, 58, 60, 67, 71
Shanklin, Catherine Ann ("Kate"), 97
Shanklin, Catherine Ann Sadler (Mrs. Joseph A. Shanklin); *see also* Elliot, Catherine Ann Sadler Shanklin), 97, 169
Shanklin, the Rev. Joseph A., 87, 97, 169
Sharpe, Elam, 86, 170
Sharpe, Frances Hayne (Mrs. Elam Sharpe), 170
Shelby, Anna Nelson; *see* Magoffin, Anna Nelson Shelby
Shelton, Maud; *see* Maxwell, Maud Shelton
Shepley, Gen. George Foster, 68, 72
Sherman, Gen. William T., 58, 67, 75, 76
Shreveport, La., 46, 49, 52
Shubrick, Edward, 171
Shubrick, Elizabeth C. (Mrs. Edward Shubrick), 171
Simkins, Maria; *see* Colhoun, Maria Simkins
Simms, Captain; *see* Semmes, Capt. Raphael
Simms, John, 57
Simonds, Andrew, 101
Simonds, Sarah Martin Calhoun (Mrs. Andrew Simonds), 101, 102
Simons, Caroline Miller (Mrs. W. W. Simons), 114
Simons, Elizabeth Bonneau Noble (Mrs. Thomas Grange Simons), 85, 168
Simons, Thomas Grange, 85

186

Simons, W.W., 114
Simons, Mrs. W.W.; *see* Simons,
  Caroline Miller
Simpson, Maj. Richard F., 82, 84, 86,
  87, 170
Simpson, Richard W., 82, 164, 170
Singleton, Gertrude Magoffin (Mrs.
  William Frank Singleton), 45
Singleton, John W., 42
Singleton, Rebecca; *see* Haskell,
  Rebecca Singleton
Singleton, William Frank, 103
Singleton, Mrs. William Frank; *see*
  Singleton, Gertrude Magoffin
Sloan, Ball; *see* Sloan, John B. E.
Sloan, Benjamin Franklin, 108
Sloan, Mrs. Benjamin Franklin; *see*
  Sloan, Eliza Earle
Sloan, Benjamin Franklin, Jr.
  ("Frank"), 115
Sloan, Mrs. Benjamin Franklin, Jr.;
  see Sloan, Ellen Lewis
Sloan, Caroline; *see* Easley, Caroline
  Sloan
Sloan, Catherine; see Maxwell,
  Catherine Sloan
Sloan, Eliza Earle (Mrs. Benjamin
  Franklin Sloan), 108
Sloan, Ellen Lewis (Mrs. Benjamin
  Franklin Sloan, Jr., "Helen"), 115
Sloan, John B. E. ("Ball"), 86, 170
Sloan, John T., 86, 170
Sloan, Julia, 104
Sloan, Nancy Blassingame (Mrs.
  Thomas M. Sloan), 86, 104, 114,
  170
Sloan, Sallie T.; *see* Gaillard, Sallie T.
  Sloan
Sloan, Seppie; *see* Gresham, Lucilla
  Septima Sloan
Sloan, Susan; *see* Lewis, Susan Sloan
Sloan, Thomas Majors, 104, 114, 170
Sloan, Mrs. Thomas Majors; *see* Sloan,
  Nancy Blassingame
Smith, Jennie, 49
Smithsonian Institution, 55
Southgate, Bishop, 66
Sprague, Kate Chase (Mrs. William
  Sprague), 92
Sprague, Gov. William, 92
Squan Beach, N.J., 55
Stanton, Sec. Edwin, 43, 44, 68
Stephens, N. C. (trustee for Ann S.
  Hickman), 48
Sterrit, Sadie, 38, 40, 127, 134, 144,
  145, 150, 155, 158

Stiles, Margaretta; *see* Hayne,
  Margaretta Stiles
Stone, Margaret Ritchie (Mrs. Robert
  King Stone), 32, 34, 71, 88, 128,
  142, 143
Stone, Dr. Robert King, 32, 50
Stoneman, Gen. George, 83
Stoneman's Raiders, 84
Stonestreet, the Rev. Charles, 37
Stuart, Gen. J. E. B., 55
Syracuse, N.Y., 39, 153-54

Taliaferro, Caroline; *see* Miller,
  Caroline Taliaferro
Taylor, Susan; *see* Lewis, Susan Taylor
Taylor, Tazewell, 68
Taylor, Pres. Zachary, 5, 6
Terry, Gen. H. D., 51
Thackery, William Makepeace, 48
"The Home," 7, 8, 12, 14, 15, 17, 18,
  21, 22, 53, 122, 128, 136, 137, 158,
  161, 165
Thomas, Zarvona, 49
Thompson, Sec. Jacob, 17, 18
Thurston, Mrs. E. E., 94-95
Thurston, Mr. and Mrs. Ed., 94
Thurston, Eliza Emily North (Mrs.
  Robert Thurston), 95
Thurston, E. M., 94-95, 170
Thurston, Emily; *see* Ravenel, Emily
  Thurston
Thurston, Emily F., 94
Thurston family, 86
Thurston, James, 94
Thurston, John G., 94
Thurston, Maria, 94
Thurston, Robert, 94, 95, 170
Thurston, Mrs. Robert; *see* Thurston,
  Eliza Emily North
Tillman, Benjamin R., 102
Tonneau; *see* Tunno
Toomer, Anne; *see* Wragg, Anne
  Toomer
Toomer, Eliza R.; *see* Wragg, Eliza R.
  Toomer
Towers, Edward, 53
Trenton, N.J., 167
Trescot, William H., 74, 86, 87, 170
Tunno, Dr. John C., 171
Tunno, Mrs. John C., 86, 171
Turner, George, 17
Turpin, W. T. P., 54

United States House, Saratoga, 156
Upshur, Judge Abel, 3

187

Vallandigham (Vallandingham), Sen.
Clement L., 64
Vallenhoff, George, 48-49, 54
Van Dorn, Gen. Earl, 33
Van Wyck, Augustus ("Gussy"), 16,
73, 74, 97
Van Wyck, Benjamin ("Bennie"), 73,
74
Van Wyck family, 16, 86, 99, 114, 156
Van Wyck, Lydia ("Lilly"), 73, 74
Van Wyck, Lydia Ann Maverick (Mrs.
William Van Wyck), 39, 73, 169
Van Wyck, Margaret C. Broyles (Mrs.
Samuel M. Van Wyck), 73
Van Wyck, Robert, 73
Van Wyck, Dr. Samuel M., 73, 155
Van Wyck, Mrs. Samuel; see Van
Wyck, Margaret C. Broyles
Van Wyck, William, 39, 73, 74, 169
Van Wyck, Mrs. William; see Van
Wyck, Lydia Ann Maverick
Van Wyck, William, Jr., 16
Van Wyck, Zeruah; see Banks, Zeruah
Van Wyck
Vicksburg, Miss., 34, 36, 37
Vinton, Dr. Alex, 157
Vivier, Mlle. Louise, 32

"Wachusett" (U.S. sloop of war), 68
Walhalla, S.C., 93
Walker, Elizabeth ("Lizzie"), 45, 47,
50, 65
Walker, Mrs. Mary, 45
Wardlaw, Clark, 102
Wardlaw, Eliza (Mrs. Robert H.
Wardlaw), 102
Wardlaw, Joseph C., 102
Wardlaw, Dr. Joseph J., 102, 115
Wardlaw, Mary A. (Mrs. Joseph J.
Wardlaw), 102, 115
Wardlaw, Mary W. ("Marie"), 115
Wardlaw, Robert H., 102
Wardlaw, Mrs. Robert H.; see
Wardlaw, Eliza
Wardlaw, W. C., 102
Warley, Anna; see Holmes, Anna
Warley
Warley, Elizabeth; see Bourne,
Elizabeth Warley
Warley, Hamilton ("Ham"), 84
Warley, Jacob, 42, 84, 169
Warley, Sophia Fraser (Mrs. Jacob
Warley), 42, 84, 86, 113, 169
Washington, Anna Clemson (Mrs.
George L. Washington), 55, 111, 142
Washington, Augustine, 65

Washington, Christine and son
"Johny," 65, 66
Washington, Dick, 17
Washington, D.C., 4, 5, 7, 14, 33, 49,
56, 124, 125, 128, 129, 137, 165,
166
Washington, George L., 18, 55, 111
Washington, Mrs. George L.; see
Washington, Anna Clemson
Washington, Lewis, 27
Washington, Louisa Clemson (Mrs.
Samuel Washington), 17, 18, 19, 27,
65, 66, 103, 142, 166
Washington, Lucy, 65
Washington, Margaret; see Lowndes,
Margaret Washington
Washington, Mary, 49
Washington, Richard, 103
Washington, Mrs. Samuel; see
Washington, Louisa Clemson
Weldon, N.C., 72, 73
Weston, Cornelius, 168
Weston, Henry M., 167
Wetherell, Angela; see Latta, Angela
Wetherell
Wharton, Elizabeth ("Lizzie"), 35, 48
Wharton family, 48
Wharton, Dr. G. O., 35
Wharton, Sarah, 35, 48, 54, 155
Wharton, William, 35
"Wheatland" (Home of Pres.
Buchanan), 40, 64, 103
Wheeler, Gen. Joseph, 83
White, Mr. (Anna Clemson's hired
man), 67
Wigfall, Gen. Louis T., 73
Wigfall, Louise, 73
Wilkinson, Mary; see Memminger,
Mary Wilkinson
Willson, Mary, 146
Wiltberger, Charles H., 50
Wiltberger, Mrs. Charles H.; see
Wiltberger, Verlinda M.
Wiltberger, Edith, 50, 66
Wiltberger, Emma, 50, 66
Wiltberger, John B., 50
Wiltberger, Mary E. (Mrs. John B.
Wiltberger), 50
Wiltberger, Verlinda M. (Mrs. Charles
H. Wiltberger), 50
Winchester, Va., 58
Wood, Mrs. Elizabeth D., 50, 54
Wood, Emily, 54, 71, 134
Wood family, 46, 66, 67, 93, 105
Wood, Gertrude, 54
Wood, Jefferson, 54

Wood, Virginia ("Jennie"), 54, 68
Wopsenonock Mt., Pa., 131, 132
Worthington, Hester; *see* Mackubin,
Hester Worthington
Wragg, Anne Toomer (the first Mrs.
William T. Wragg), 91
Wragg, Eliza R. Toomer (the second
Mrs. William T. Wragg), 91
Wragg, Mary Ashby I'on (Mrs. Samuel
Wragg), 86, 91, 171

Wragg, Samuel, 94, 171
Wragg, Dr. William T., 91, 116
Wragg, Mrs. William T.; *see* Wragg,
Anne Toomer, and Wragg, Eliza R.
Toomer

Yost, Benedict, 30
Yost, Elizabeth (Mrs. Benedict Yost),
30
Yost, Emma; *see* Harvey, Emma Yost